"Games are serious business. Watch anyone play a digital game and you soon realize that games are varied, draw on knowledge and skill, and are deeply motivating. Filled with gaming stories across varied contexts, *Serious Play* humanizes game play in consequential ways. Beavis, Dezuanni, and O'Mara offer readers a much-needed collection for contemplating how we see, feel, and live through games and the tremendous potential they have for remaking literacy research and practice."

—**Jennifer Rowsell,** *Professor and Canada Research Chair in Multiliteracies in the Department of Teacher Education at Brock University, Canada*

"Drawing on data from the project of the same name, *Serious* Play provides fascinating insights into the opportunities and challenges of using digital games in the classroom. Scholarly and accessible, this is an important and authoritative volume that speaks to the concerns of the wider educational community. Driven by the hard work of teacher participants, *Serious Play* is important reading for all who are concerned with developing a relevant, contemporary curriculum."

—**Guy Merchant,** *Professor of Literacy in Education in the Sheffield Institute of Education at Sheffield Hallam University, UK*

"This is a refreshing, in-depth look at game-based learning that puts teachers and students at the center of the field of study, while making seamless connections to theories of learning, gaming, consumption, and identity. The book moves well beyond questions about efficacy of games in relation to learning and addresses deeper questions about pedagogy and student identities that are highly relevant to educators and researchers today."

—**Rebekah Willett,** *Associate Professor of Library and Information Studies at the University of Wisconsin-Madison, USA*

SERIOUS PLAY

Serious Play is a comprehensive account of the possibilities and challenges of teaching and learning with digital games in primary and secondary schools. Based on an original research project, the book explores digital games' capacity to engage and challenge, present complex representations and experiences, foster collaborative and deep learning and enable curricula that connect with young people today. These exciting approaches illuminate the role of context in gameplay as well as the links between digital culture, gameplay and identity in learners' lives, and are applicable to research and practice at the leading edge of curriculum and literacy development.

Catherine Beavis is Professor of Education in the Faculty of Education and the Arts at Deakin University, Australia, and program leader for the Curriculum, Assessment, Pedagogy and Digital Learning program in REDI – Research for Educational Impact: Deakin University's Strategic Research Centre in Education.

Michael Dezuanni is Associate Professor in the Creative Industries Faculty at Queensland University of Technology, Australia.

Joanne O'Mara is Associate Professor of Education in the Faculty of Arts and Education at Deakin University, Australia.

DIGITAL GAMES AND LEARNING
Series Editors Sara de Freitas and Paul Maharg

Online Gaming and Playful Organization
by Harald Warmelink

Aesthetics and Design for Game-based Learning
by Michele D. Dickey

SERIOUS PLAY

Literacy, Learning and Digital Games

Edited by Catherine Beavis,
Michael Dezuanni and Joanne O'Mara

Routledge
Taylor & Francis Group

NEW YORK AND LONDON

First published 2017
by Routledge
711 Third Avenue, New York, NY 10017

and by Routledge
2 Park Square, Milton Park, Abingdon, Oxon, OX14 4RN

Routledge is an imprint of the Taylor & Francis Group, an informa business

Library of Congress Cataloging-in-Publication Data
Names: Beavis, Catherine, editor. | Dezuanni, Michael, editor. | O'Mara, Joanne, editor.
Title: Serious play : literacy, learning, and digital games / edited by Catherine Beavis, Michael Dezuanni, and Joanne O'Mara.
Description: New York : Routledge, [2017] | Includes bibliographical references.
Identifiers: LCCN 2016043205| ISBN 9781138689404 (hbk) | ISBN 9781138689411 (pbk.) | ISBN 9781315537658 (ebook)
Subjects: LCSH: Video games in education. | Educational games. | Computers and literacy.
Classification: LCC LB1028.75 .L57 2017 | DDC 794.8--dc23
LC record available at https://lccn.loc.gov/2016043205

ISBN: 978-1-138-68940-4 (hbk)
ISBN: 978-1-138-68941-1 (pbk)
ISBN: 978-1-315-53765-8 (ebk)

Typeset in Bembo
by Saxon Graphics Ltd, Derby

CONTENTS

CONTRIBUTORS

Catherine Beavis is Professor of Education in the Faculty of Arts and Education at Deakin University, Australia.

Michael Dezuanni is Associate Professor in the Creative Industries Faculty at Queensland University of Technology, Australia.

Sandy Muspratt is an Adjunct Senior Research Fellow in the Griffith Institute for Educational Research at Griffith University, Australia.

Joanne O'Mara is Associate Professor of Education in the Faculty of Arts and Education at Deakin University, Australia.

Sarah Prestridge is Senior Lecturer in the School of Education and Professional Studies, Griffith University, Australia.

Kynan Robinson is a PhD student in the Faculty of Arts and Education at Deakin University, Australia.

Leonie Rowan is Associate Professor in the School of Education and Professional Studies at Griffith University, Australia.

Roberta Thompson is a Research Fellow in the School of Education and Professional Studies at Griffith University, Australia.

Jason Zagami is Coordinator for Community Partnerships and Lecturer in Computer Education in the School of Education and Professional Studies at Griffith University, Australia.

PREFACE

Digital games are part of most young people's cultural experience of living and learning in post-industrial societies in the 2010s. Even young people who do not fit the typical 'gamer' profile are likely to have at least some experience of digital games as they interact with smart phones and tablet devices as part of their overall digital culture experience. Games consoles like Nintendo's Wii system, Microsoft's Xbox and Sony's PlayStation have become convergence devices that also provide users with access to a host of other entertainment, including music, television and film. Games content is amongst the most popular on YouTube, and games and game-like apps are amongst the biggest sellers on Apple's App Store and the Google Play Store. Digital games, then, have moved to the centre of many young people's entertainment experiences, whether they are occasional or avid gamers.

Learning with and about digital games generally occurs outside formal schooling as young people learn to play games with their friends and with online resources like forums, Wikis and video-sharing sites. The organisation of 'learning' resources and experiences by peer networks, games communities and commercial entities potentially become part of the overall ecologies, and associated literacies, of digital gameplay. In the meantime, there exists a well-established history of the use of digital games in formal education. As with other forms of popular culture, educators have seen the potential to leverage digital games' ability to engage young people in curriculum-aligned learning. Digital games are seen by educators to have the capacity to engage and challenge players, to present complex representations and experiences, to foster collaborative learning and to promote deep learning that effectively connects with the dispositions and orientations of young people today.

In this book, we argue that for schools to fully benefit from digital games in the classroom, it is necessary both to recognise the influence of context on how games are understood and played and to understand the ways in which gameplay is linked to issues of identity, performance and sense of self. This means recognising differences between how players approach games in and out of school. It means moving from seeing games as simply a way to promote the smarter transmission of information to exploring how games might promote deep learning in the discipline areas, teach critical reflective competence with new literacies and promote imagination and creativity, through production, analysis and use. *Serious Play* argues that educators must have an awareness of the role of context in gameplay and of the links between digital culture, gameplay and identity in young people's lives.

This book has been developed as a key outcome of the research project 'Serious Play: Using digital games in school to promote literacy and learning in the twenty first century'. The book is unique because it provides an account of classroom practice across time, which allowed the research team to observe how teachers' and students' approaches to using games in the classroom changed and evolved in different locations. The book draws on data from multiple schools and age groups within a singular project, providing generally unavailable insights into the specifics of situated practice and learning with digital games. Few studies have brought such socio-material perspectives on literacy, learning and identity to bear on how students and teachers approach learning through games in school. In addition, the book reflects the genuinely cross-disciplinary approach of our research as indicated in the authorship of the chapters across the sections of the book. We (Catherine, Michael and Joanne) have acted as editors, but the study has been a true team effort and it reflects the strengths of our different disciplinary backgrounds as we have striven to gain a better understanding of the role digital games play in the classroom. Our research team colleagues – Leonie, Sarah and Jason – have made essential contributions to the project and the development of this book, providing key insights into the overall picture of the use of digital games in education.

Our research would not have been possible without the support of a range of people and organisations. Serious Play was funded by the Australian Research Council in partnership with Griffith University, Deakin University, the Queensland University of Technology, Nanyang Technical University in Singapore, the Department of Education and Early Childhood Development (Victoria) and one government secondary college and several independent schools in Queensland. We are indebted to Roberta Thompson, who provided research assistance throughout the project, in addition to being one of the project's researchers. We thank Yam San Chee, our Partner Investigator in the project; and Sandy Muspratt who assisted with the design, development and analysis of two surveys we conducted for the project. Research Assistant Christy McGillivray completed essential aspects of the research in the Victorian schools, for which we are grateful. We thank Colleen Stieler-Hunt of the University of the Sunshine Coast, who assisted with key aspects of the project in one of our Queensland schools, Research Assistant Geraldine Townend, and Sophie Bigum who provided artwork for Chapter 13. Thanks go to graphic designer Joy Reynolds who designed the Games as Text and Games as Action Model, discussed in Chapter 9, and the project website. Thanks also go to Michael Kavanagh whose attention to detail during the editing process provided us with confidence as we brought this book together. We would also like to thank Filip Laurent, who developed the video accounts of key aspects of the project, available on the project website: www.seriousplayproject.org. A number of the images in this book are taken from these videos, and we acknowledge Filip for this contribution also.

It goes without saying that we are deeply indebted to the many teachers[1] who became our co-investigators in this project, including Kynan Robinson who co-wrote Chapter 8. Without them, the research would not have been possible. The professionalism of these teaching colleagues and their willingness to invest their valuable time was an inspiration, and a reminder of the essential role that teachers play in designing meaningful learning experiences for students. Of course, we would also like to thank the hundreds of students[2] who took part in various aspects of our project, and whose insights into the use of digital games in the classroom were revealing and provocative.

Finally, we would like to thank our families and loved ones for their patience and support as we undertook the research and spent long hours writing this book.

Notes

1. Unless otherwise specified, the names used for teachers discussed or quoted in this book are pseudonyms.
2. The names used for students discussed or quoted in this book are pseudonyms.

DIGITAL GAMES AND LEARNING

Series Introduction

Sara de Freitas and Paul Maharg

While clearly the use of games for supporting education is not new, the use of digital games is comparatively recent. With the emergence of web-based services, increased broadband and the growth of online communities, the use of digital games presents us with a unique set of engaging tools and techniques, based upon game mechanics such as competition, narrative, missions and quests.

Increasingly, games are being seen not as a technology but as a cultural form with its own genres, be they casual games played by everyone, serious games played to learn and engage, or gamification whereby game elements are used to reach new audiences. Games offer us new toolsets that can be used effectively in activities as wide-ranging as therapy, awareness-raising or marketing as well as more conventional curricula. The versatility of digital games to be applied to any problem or challenge has gained for games a new cultural status that they did not have previously. Digital educational games seek to inform, educate and motivate learners and to extend the range of our ability to learn in classrooms by making the world our classroom, and by putting social interaction rather than curriculum objectives at the centre of the learner's experience.

Game science is evolving too, and game mechanics are just beginning to transform education and how it is produced and how learning is assessed, with real potential for providing just-in-time learning and supporting hard-to-reach learner groups. However, the growth and spread of digital games in educational contexts is still relatively in its infancy, and the best methods for developing, assessing and deploying these approaches are also in their earliest stages of advancement. This book series thus aims, primarily, to bring existing game theory and practices together to support the ongoing development of game science as a sub-disciplinary and cross-disciplinary academic body of evidence, as a methodology of investigation, and as a set of tools and approaches, methods and frameworks for learning.

While game science has the power to transcend normal silos of disciplines, the academic communities in different disciplines and in different continents have had too few opportunities to work as an interdiscipline, in part because the field is so new and research has been taking place in such diverse disciplinary, sectoral and international contexts. This book series therefore specifically aims to build bridges between diverse research, teaching, policy and learner communities and is inspired by the next generation of young researchers currently completing their early studies in the field. Towards this end, the series brings together leading theorists, thinkers and practitioners into a community of practice around the key themes and issues of digital games and learning. These theorists come from areas as diverse as health and well-being, business and innovation, education, computer science and engineering, to name but a few. Their perspectives include views from professional practice as well as from theoretical perspectives.

It is important not to underestimate the scale of the work ahead in this new field, but it is also important to recognise the power of these new tools beyond our current understanding of what they can do or will do in the future. Games will always be a central part of early-stage learning, but now the capability of games to save lives, to inform citizens and to contribute positive outcomes socially are just beginning to be understood. We have always understood the power of games to entertain: this series shows us scientifically how the power of play can be harnessed for more profound purposes, more altruistic reasons in new forms of sustainable and scalable education. *Digital Games and Learning* will explore the lineaments of the new learning, and will reveal how and in what contexts that learning will take shape.

Professor Sara de Freitas, Coventry University, Coventry, UK
Professor Paul Maharg, The Australian National University,
Canberra, Australia
June 2013

1

SERIOUS PLAY

Literacy, Learning and Digital Games

Catherine Beavis

Introduction

Young people's social and cultural experiences are increasingly digital. Their everyday lives are characterised by digital play and online interaction, and their futures will involve work with digital texts, regardless of the career paths they follow. Digital games played on handheld devices, gaming consoles and computers have become a central part of young people's daily lives for play, entertainment and social interaction. Increasingly, digital games are also being used in education, and the potential for digital games to transform learning has been the focus of increasing interest and research. Digital games, it is argued, have the capacity to engage and challenge players; present complex representations and experiences; foster collaborative learning; promote deep understanding; and enable curriculum and learning that effectively connect with the dispositions and orientations of young people today (Gee 2007; Davidson 2008; Whitton 2014).

Despite the acknowledgement of the potential of digital games for education and learning, it is less clear how games might be put to work effectively in schools, and what learning with games might look like in a range of educational contexts. In part, this lack of clarity results from the different, often conflicting, paradigms and underlying assumptions concerned with digital games, gameplay and learning; in part, from the lack of detailed, long-term studies of games-based learning over a range of contexts that recognise the diversity and granularity of students' and teachers' experience and dispositions towards games and gameplay. Not all students are games players. Not all teachers are keen advocates for the use of games, or experienced with using games to enhance learning in the classroom. While there are numerous studies of the use of games in individual classrooms, by teachers who are expert and experienced, there is little research that explores the use of games by a wider cohort of teachers and students: how this might happen, how it is experienced, what issues arise, and what learning, and of what kinds, might be achieved. Research is needed which shows 'what happens when …'. This book presents case studies from specific classrooms undertaken across a range of schools, year levels and subject areas; and, through a range of lenses, looks across the experiences of teachers, students and schools over a period of three years, in a picture of developing complexity.

How to work with digital games is part of a wider set of concerns facing teachers, students and schools in the twenty-first century. The ways in which schools and teachers might work proactively in supporting students to become critical, capable and creative users of online forms; how they might make use of the powerful qualities and affordances offered by digital games to support learning; and how teaching, learning and curriculum are challenged, extended and changed by so doing, are all vexed but highly important questions for education and for educators. So too is the need for students' familiarity with digital culture and digital literacies to be recognised and built upon in school, so that schooling overtly addresses and utilises the affordances of technology and the online world, building bridges between students' experience in and out of school, while also more closely linking with twenty-first century forms of knowledge and representation, technologies, sensibilities and ecologies. How to recognise and work with digital games to achieve such ends, effectively and appropriately, and the implications of this for pedagogy, curriculum, relationships, skills and resources, were some of the central issues that teachers wrestled with in the project reported on in this book, in their work in classrooms with their students; in discussions with each other and with members of the project team, with the teachers and administrators at their schools, and with parents; and in planning and aligning their games-based work with centrally mandated curriculum and assessment policies and requirements.

Serious Play,[1] the project on which this book is based, set out to explore the diverse experiences and expectations of students and teachers in everyday schools, the ways they worked with games, the challenges entailed in doing so, and what the use of games was able to achieve. In presenting the work of Serious Play, this book brings together the fields of digital culture and new literacies, games-based learning and games studies, embedded within sociocultural perspectives that see learning as situated and purposeful, and literacy and literacy practices deeply intertwined with, and constitutive of, relationships, meaning making and identity. It similarly calls on media studies theory and research concerned with the production, analysis and consumption of media culture, and the role of digital culture in young people's lives.

FIGURE 1.1 Year 8 Studies of Society and Environment students and *Statecraft X*.
Source: News Corp.

The chapter begins with a consideration of the issues for education in the context of the shape and locatedness of contemporary learning lives. Core issues here include recognition of the pervasiveness and importance of the internet and the online world; the need to understand more about digital culture, and the nature of young people's engagement with it; and an awareness and understanding of the qualities and affordances of specific digital technologies and forms. From there, the discussion turns to participatory culture, and then specifically to digital games – games 'in the wild' – that is, out of school, and what they have to teach us about learning and literacy (Gee 2007). Games-based learning and the use of games in schools are introduced, together with a brief overview of the current state of research. The chapter then turns to the Serious Play project itself, and describes its aims, structure, organisation and activities. The ways in which teachers, students and researchers worked together and independently across the three years are outlined, as is the project design. The final part of the chapter outlines the structure of the book; discusses the five themes into which it is organised; and concludes with observations about three notable developments across the course of the project: the emergence of *Minecraft* (Mojang 2011) and its subsequent development; the rapid expansion of the use of tablets in schools; and the concept of 'curation' as a way to understand and make visible the nature of young people's ownership and (re)creation of digital artefacts and culture.

Learning Lives, Schooling and Digital Games: Learning in the Twenty-First Century

In their book *Identity, Community and Learning Lives in the Digital Age*, Erstad and Sefton-Green (2013) used the phrase 'learning lives' to signal that learning needs to be situated intricately and intimately in a matrix of "transactions": experiences, life trajectories, voluntary and involuntary learning contexts, affective frames and social groupings that make up experience across our "lifeworlds", with associated attention to issues of identity and subjectivity, and 'how we construct learner identities and narratives about what we know and do' (p. 1).

The phrase also conjures the rhetorics and expectations associated with the view that learning is lifelong, and that learning should prepare one for life. Both aspects of 'learning lives' are of central relevance to the ways in which digital culture, particularly digital games, is understood, taken up and worked with to enhance learning in schools.

While the view that all students are 'digital natives' has long been problematised, it is nonetheless the case that for most children and teens living in places like Australia, Europe, the United States and the UK, the internet has been in existence for all of their lives, and, as the figures below suggest, is a significant part, for many, of the ways in which they interact, communicate and play. Playing digital games, for many teenagers and children, is part of a larger online ecology, encompassing engagement with an assemblage of online media forms, platforms and technologies, including games themselves of multiple kinds, virtual worlds, virtual realities, chat sites, forums, fan fiction sites, apps and all manner of social media. The Pew Research Center study, *Teens, Social Media and Technology Overview 2015* (Lenhart 2015) found that 92 per cent of teens in the United States aged 13 to 17 were going online daily, over half (56 per cent) several times a day. This engagement was facilitated particularly by access to mobile devices, mainly phones, with 88 per cent having access to a mobile phone. Seventy-one per cent of teens played videogames in the same period – 59 per cent of girls and 84 per cent of boys – playing on a computer, game console or mobile phone (Lenhart 2015). In Australia, the 2014 Australian Communications and Media Authority report *Aussie Teens Online* (Raco 2014) found that 82 per cent of teens aged 14 to 17 years rated the internet as 'very important' or 'extremely important' in their lives, with 'entertainment' (90 per cent) topping activities undertaken online. The *Digital Australia 2016* report (Brand and Todhunter 2015) found that videogame players in the Australian population included 77 per cent of children and young adults under the age of 18. The pattern is a familiar one elsewhere. A survey commissioned by the UK Internet Advertising Bureau, for example, released in 2014, found that 99 per cent of children and teenagers aged 8 to 17 in that country had played digital games in the previous six months (Stuart 2014).

Increasing usage of the internet is not all benign, however. By 2014, the ongoing *EU Kids Online* project, encompassing 25 European countries, found that as

> children go on the internet more and more, and younger and younger, we can see that they are encountering many more opportunities, and they are developing skills, as they use the internet, but they are also encountering more of the risks.
>
> *(Livingstone 2014, n. p.)*

The challenge Livingstone and her colleagues were repeatedly presented with by parents and educators responding to interviews and surveys was how to support those children in these interactions without exposing them to harm and risk. For many parents and educators, the answer seemed to be to simply reduce exposure. However, as Livingstone noted:

> The struggle is that as we restrict children we also prevent them from gaining those learning opportunities which give them the chance to develop resilience and build skills, and also get many of the opportunities that the internet can offer. ... Parents and educators are getting so worried that children are not gaining many of the opportunities that they could, and that the internet is so brilliant at providing, in terms of learning, participation, creativity and expression.
>
> *(Livingstone 2014, n. p.)*

Rather than managing risk through avoidance, approaches that teach critical media literacy, and work proactively with media texts, technologies and literacies, are better placed to help students build resilience and informed and proactive participation. Such approaches enable the flow of perspectives, experiences and ideas to cross boundaries between in- and out-of-school engagements with the online world, strengthen students' capacities to critically evaluate what they encounter online, and support them in becoming savvy, capable and discerning creators and consumers of digital culture (Buckingham 2016).

A related response to the significance of digital media in young people's lives, and the potential for engagement and learning offered by digital texts and new media, focuses on the ways in which students' experience with digital media may be shaping their expectations or orientations towards learning, and the ways in which work in school might reflect and respond to these. Young people's experience with the online world, it is argued, promotes particular dispositions or orientations towards learning – new literacy practices and new habits of mind (Lankshear and Knobel 2006; Merchant 2009) such that their out-of-school experience and expectations flow into the ways in which they approach learning in schools.

Considerable research has been undertaken into the qualities and characteristics of online spaces and technologies together with the ways in which young people create, communicate, learn and engage. Such forms and spaces include digital games (Gee 2007; Marsh 2010), social media (boyd 2008; Davies 2013), blogs and/or other forms, as sites for engagement with what Jenkins *et al.* characterised as 'participatory culture':

> A culture with relatively low barriers to artistic expression and civic engagement, strong support for creating and sharing one's creations, and some type of informal mentorship whereby experienced participants pass along knowledge to novices. In a participatory culture members also believe their contributions matter, and feel some degree of social connection with each other (at the least, members care about others' opinions of what they have created).
>
> *(Jenkins et al. 2009, p. xi)*

Such a culture, Jenkins and colleagues argued, provides numerous opportunities for learning and sharing, promotes diversification and the cultivation of a wide range of new media literacies' social skills and cultural competencies, and 'a more empowered conception of citizenship' (p. xii).

Complementing Jenkins *et al.*'s (2009) account of participatory culture and the practices it entails are accounts of what was named at the time 'Web 2.0'. Lankshear and Knobel (2006) described Web 2.0 not so much as a set of technological capabilities as 'a developing trend or attitude' (Merchant 2009, p. 108). Merchant highlighted four characteristics of such spaces: what they encouraged, what they made possible, and the kinds of participatory activity and literacy and learning practices they might entail:

1. Presence ('Web 2.0 encourages users to develop an active presence through an online identity, profile or avatar ... Many users develop a sense of self across a number of spaces ... thus performing multiple identities', p. 108);
2. Modification ('Web 2.0 spaces usually allow a degree of personalization such as in the design of the user's home page and personal links. ... Web 2.0 spaces may also be "mashable" or "interoperable"', p. 109);
3. User-generated content ('Web 2.0 spaces are based upon content which is generated within and by the community of users rather than provided by the site itself', p. 109);
4. Social participation ('Web 2.0 spaces provide an invitation to participate. ... Just as user-generated content makes us both producers and consumers, so with social participation we are simultaneously both performers and audience', p. 109).

An important dimension of the work of the Serious Play project was to explore ways to support students in drawing on the knowledge and experience gained through their familiarity with the spaces and opportunities, characteristic of participatory culture, particularly online games, to develop media literacy and new and traditional literacy skills. This was done in diverse ways throughout the project; for instance, through students designing and in some instances creating their own games Chapter 7 (O'Mara); through the analysis of popular games Chapter 5 (Dezuanni and Zagami); and the use of games to develop new and traditional literacies Chapter 9 (Beavis, Prestridge and O'Mara). Much of the classroom work explicitly set out to enable students to put knowledge gained through their out-of-school membership of games-playing communities to use; as, for example, in work with *Minecraft* – Chapter 3 (Dezuanni and O'Mara), Chapter 8 (O'Mara and Robinson), Chapter 10 (Dezuanni); or the study of citizenship through a purpose-built serious game in Chapter 4 (Thompson, Beavis and Zagami).

Defining digital games and gameplay, their qualities and characteristics, is notoriously difficult, given the diversity of games and play. Rather than buying into slippery issues of definition, in particular with respect to diverse forms and platforms, and the nature and style of play (Juul 2005; Burn 2013), the project adopted a view of games that saw them as cultural forms in their own right, as amalgams of text and action, and as encompassing a spectrum ranging from popular commercial 'off the shelf' games (COTS); purpose-built educational or 'serious' games; sandbox and god games; text games; phone games; Xbox games and games made by students themselves using game-making software including *GameMaker* (YoYogames 2016) and *Scratch* (MIT Media Lab 2005).

In recent years there has been considerable interest in the possibilities of digital games as vehicles for learning, and what the use of games in the classroom might achieve. The capacity of computer games (videogames, digital games) to engage players in challenging and complex ways has been explored by educators in many parts of the world, and attempts made to design curriculum and learning materials and opportunities that utilise games engines and possibilities. Many 'serious' games have been developed for educational purposes and introduced into schools (Davidson 2008; Whitton 2014). However, for the most part, despite the promise of the affordances and possibilities offered by games to enhance learning at a deep level, as yet these games appear to have had limited effectiveness. The review by Young *et al.* (2012) of games-based learning research to date found it to be 'inconclusive' (p. 80), with school contexts and institutional expectations and requirements flattening out what might otherwise have been achieved. Perrotta *et al.* (2013), in a similar study, noted the absence of research that 'accounts for the realities of schools' (p. iii).

More positive accounts of the use of games emerge from individual studies undertaken by teachers themselves who are expert in gameplay and passionate games players; they have introduced into the classroom commercial games such as *Myst* (Cyan 1993; see e.g. Rylands 2006, Barrett 2009), *Civilization III* (Meier 2001; see e.g. Squire and Barab 2004), or more recently, on a larger scale, *Minecraft* (e.g. Ito 2015). Semi-formal educational sites such as afterschool clubs have provided opportunities for children to play in virtual worlds such as *Club Penguin* (New Horizon Interactive 2005; see e.g. Marsh 2010) or participation in gaming competitions by students, particularly girls, who might otherwise be marginalised within games culture (Carr 2007; Steinkuehler and King 2009). Such studies attest to the opportunities such participation provides for the development of new and traditional literacies, and the kinds of learning and collaboration that affinity groups such as those around games make possible, as Gee (2007) and others have described.

The Serious Play Project

Facility with technologies, and the resources they offer, and an awareness of the powerful qualities and affordances offered by digital games, are fundamental if schools and teachers are to take up the challenges and opportunities offered by digital games, but not all teachers are equally conversant with digital games, or comfortable in introducing them to the classroom. The Serious Play project set out to learn more about the ways in which digital games might be incorporated into a wide range of areas, across a range of schools, over an extended period of time.

Serious Play was a three-year research project involving collaboration between three Australian universities and teachers in ten schools across two Australian states. Yam San Chee, from the National Institute of Education in Singapore (part of Nanyang Technological University) was a partner investigator in the research. Funded by the Australian Research Council, the project involved university-based researchers working in partnership with the Department of Education and Early Childhood Development (Victoria) and individual Queensland schools. Six primary and four secondary schools took part across the two states, with students ranging in age from five to sixteen.[2] Schools comprised a mix of public and private schools, with diverse populations located in a range of geographic and socioeconomic contexts, and in mixed and single-sex schools. In some instances, schools, and participating teachers within them, were already experienced in working with digital games with students in various ways; in others, teachers had not previously worked in this way, but were open to seeing what games might offer and were interested to learn more about what might be entailed in doing so. All teachers and schools were invited to participate in the project on an opt-in basis.

The teachers ranged in age and seniority, from teachers in their first few years of teaching through to those with many years of classroom teaching experience and senior roles within their schools. An important focus of the project was to recognise the diversity of teachers' knowledge, interest and experience in working with technology and games. In contrast to many studies of games-based learning, or the use of information and communications technology (ICT) in the classroom, the project did not presuppose high levels of technological knowledge or familiarity, but rather, recognised a wide variety of starting points, aiming to support teachers 'where they were', and to build from there. Conversely, the perspectives and experience of teachers in the project already working with games provided valuable insights as well as practical strategies and resources to the work of the project, and to other teachers, students and researchers in the project team.

The aims of the project were to explore:

1. the ways in which students with widely different preferences and experience of games and digital culture approached games-based teaching in the classroom;
2. the ways in which teachers were able to work with games most effectively, and the kinds of pedagogical practices and approaches which best capitalise on the capacities of games to teach;
3. the opportunities that games provide for creativity, production and innovation;
4. digital literacies and the ways in which learning through games challenges and extends multimodal literacy learning;
5. assessment and whether a specific assessment framework was required to identify and support deep learning, creativity and the production and sharing of knowledge online.

Games were introduced across a range of subject areas, as determined by individual teachers in each school. Formal curriculum areas included Literacy, English, Media, Drama, Information Technology, Studies of Society and Environment (Social Studies), Languages (Chinese) and Religion. Games were introduced in classrooms ranging from Year 1 through to Year 10, with some additional involvement in the last year of the project from students in one high school in Year 12, the final year of school. Students changed from year to year, while teachers, for the most part, participated for the full three years. Up to 400 students per year were involved in the project, with a core group of 22 teachers over the three years working in project schools.

The project comprised a mix of whole project and individual school activities. While much activity was undertaken jointly, teachers and students, researchers and schools also worked with relative autonomy, to explore and implement diverse approaches to working with games, within the specificity of their local contexts and priorities. The length of the project, the range of foci, and the diversity of schools, students, teachers and contexts, provided the opportunity to explore the possibilities and practicalities of working with digital games to enhance learning on a large scale, and the messy complexity of doing so. Work undertaken, in individual classrooms and across the project as a whole, allowed the mapping and close study of a range of issues, opportunities and challenges on the ground; of what was possible and what was achieved.

FIGURE 1.2 The use of *Assassin's Creed Unity* in English.

Activities across the schools comprised a mix of whole project undertakings, and individual teacher research projects addressing specific themes and research foci, according to the curriculum areas and year levels at which the teachers worked, and their estimates of games' potential and of their students' interests and needs. Whole project activities included two large-scale student surveys, at the beginning and end of the project; common interview and focus group questions with teachers and students at each school, undertaken at regular intervals and addressing each focus area, in addition to observations, interviews and the collection of student work in specific classrooms individually. Participation also included teachers' postings on the project website and blog, and attendance at six regular project meetings (two per year) – Professional Learning days – at which teachers shared work in progress or recently completed, and reflection on and discussion of issues as they arose. These days were very important in setting the tone, opening up the research space and exploring ideas. Not only did they work to establish the focus and research issues in each instance; they also provided opportunities for teachers to present their work, meet informally and develop ongoing relationships over time. As a form of sustained professional learning, the days, and the project, worked particularly well.

Each Professional Learning day had a specific focus, providing for the introduction and discussion of research issues and project sequencing, together with organisational and management matters. The geographical distance between Queensland and Victoria meant that it was not feasible for all teachers to be physically present at the one event, so Professional Learning days were held separately in each state. To build the sense of commonality and community, and to enable teachers to hear about each other's work and discuss issues of common concern across both states, various strategies were employed. These included simultaneous video links between states for some or all of the day; travel by teachers from one state to the other to present their own and their students' work and join in discussion face to face; and travel by researchers between states to present at both state events. Teachers also created presentations for Professional Learning days, which were shared across the whole group. These included multimodal vignettes using voice thread technology about specific instances of games-based work, and links to teachers' online blogs where they wrote about and displayed what they had done. For the concluding Project Summit, held on separate days in Victoria and Queensland, *WordPress* (WordPress Foundation 2003) snapshots were created to showcase individual schools' work.

Alongside this, the project was organised around school-based projects undertaken by individual teachers or groups of teachers in their schools, supported by the academic team. School-based work was loosely structured into one of three strands: Using Games; Analysing Games; and Making Games. The Using Games strand looked at the use of purpose-built 'serious games' and/or commercially available or free-to-download games to support learning across a range of curriculum areas. In this strand, the focus was on teaching, learning and curriculum. The Analysing Games strand explored approaches to discussing and analysing games as part of the spectrum of texts that might be studied, for example, in English and Media. The focus in this strand was on literature and literacy in the digital context, particularly on narrative, drama, the aesthetic and the imagination, and on critical digital literacy. The third strand, Making Games, explored game-making and design using commercially and free-to-download software – *GameMaker*, *Scratch* and others, as well as building and creating within existing games, particularly *Minecraft*. The focus here was on creativity, imagination and construction.

How the Book Is Organised

The book is organised into five themes, each prefaced by a brief discussion pointing to key ideas. Theme I looks at how students approach games-based learning. In Chapter 2, Beavis, Thompson and Muspratt present a view from across the project, as seen through students' eyes, calling on survey data and interviews from two different cohorts of students undertaken in the first and last year of the project. They discuss findings and implications related to students' attitudes, preferences, expectations and experiences of the use of digital games in school to support learning. Chapter 3 looks at student and teacher work more closely, and specifically work around *Minecraft*, a game warmly welcomed in a number of project schools. Dezuanni and O'Mara explore the game as 'a site of impassioned learning', teasing out 'connections between learning and fandom and the implications for learning with games'.

Theme II turns to the ways gameplay changes in the classroom context. In Chapter 4, Thompson, Beavis and Zagami discuss the ways in which students and teachers in one Queensland school worked with *Statecraft X* (Chee 2010), a citizenship education game. In Chapter 5, Dezuanni and Zagami take up the notion of 'curatorship', and 'the consequences of curriculum curation with digital games when classroom and pedagogic practices change gameplay in unintended or unexpected ways'.

Theme III takes as its focus the ways in which teachers can work effectively with games and the kinds of pedagogical practices that best capitalise on the capacities of the game, and the opportunities that games provide for creativity, production and innovation. In Chapter 6, Prestridge discusses the relationship between teachers' beliefs and their negotiation of identity as they implement games-based learning in their classrooms. In Chapter 7, entitled 'Narratives come to life through coding: Digital game making as language and literacy curriculum', O'Mara focuses on students' creative work in making games. In Chapter 8, O'Mara and Robinson address the core concepts of playfulness and play, and the opportunities these provide, through close analysis of the use of *Minecraft* in an extended environmental education-themed project with Year 6.

Theme IV takes up digital literacies, multimodality and the question of literacies more generally. In Chapter 9, Beavis, Prestridge and O'Mara compare three teachers and their approach to literacy and digital games, calling on understandings of games as text, action and design. In Chapter 10, Dezuanni problematises both traditional and multimodal concepts of literacy, arguing that 'it is necessary to expand beyond socio-cultural and "multimodal" approaches to literacy when aiming to understand how digital literacies are produced through *Minecraft* play'.

Theme V turns to the contentious area of assessment, and to teachers' roles as creative professionals. The teachers' views and experience in assessing qualities and outcomes of students' work with digital games are discussed in Chapter 11 by Rowan and Beavis. This chapter is juxtaposed against 'real world stories and practical examples' from the project in Chapter 12, in which Rowan 'provides fine-grained examples of the ways in which teachers were able to create spaces within which student experiences – be they academic, social or emotional – were enhanced'.

Chapter 13 looks back across the five themes and the project as a whole. Rowan and Prestridge address the risks and possibilities associated with videogames in education for diverse cohorts of students and the opportunities games can provide to help 'at-risk' students experience academic success, social acceptance and, overall, feelings of inclusion and success: feelings that they are the stars. The chapter concludes the book by demonstrating, not the 'magical' or innate capacity of games to enhance learning everywhere, and for everyone, but rather by telling careful stories about the possibilities that creative experimentation with digital games can generate for heterogeneous students and their teachers.

FIGURE 1.3 Making and learning with *Minecraft*.

Areas of Emergence

The project coincided with three key developments that have significantly changed how games may be used in education more broadly. We were well positioned to observe, across those three years, what they offered, how they were taken up by teachers and students, and how they played out in project schools. The first was the emergence of *Minecraft*. Over the course of the project, this extraordinary and highly popular game was taken up in many classrooms, supporting learning of all kinds, in formal curriculum areas like Mathematics, History, Literacy and Geography; it served as a site for game-making and curation, and for developing expertise and interpersonal collaboration, negotiation and autonomy as Chapters 3, 8 and 10, amongst others describe. Teachers' openness to exploring the game's possibilities, and the wealth of out-of-school experience and expertise that students brought as they played, enabled the development of rich understandings and ownership of curriculum areas and activities, inventiveness and creativity; opportunities for those less usually successful at school to take a lead; and the development and display of all manner of 'twenty-first century skills' and creativity. We were able to observe, first hand, the imaginative take-up of the game by both teachers and students – a phenomenon echoed in schools across Australia, North America and the UK, and many other countries in the world – so much so that the game now has the backing of Microsoft and its 'Education Edition' project (Microsoft 2016).

The second development we observed, with profound implications for what became possible and the opportunities they provide, was the emergence of tablets, particularly iPads. Within the classroom, tablets support new ways of gaming and of learning, facilitating active engagement and interaction, understanding, creativity and play. They enable different kinds of pedagogy, different kinds of interactions with 'content' and games, and they challenge definitions of what counts as 'game', with some apps being game-like, but not exactly games. They were widely used in project schools, from even the earliest days, with five- and six-year-old children in Year 1, for example, using tablets as a regular part of their literacy classes, for reading, letter recognition and story writing amongst other things, in print and multimodal forms. Class sets of tablets, or tablets individually owned, allowed students to undertake the kinds of game analysis, design and making described in Chapter 8, for example; the *Minecraft* work described in Chapters 3 and 10; and a wide range of classroom work besides.

The third phenomenon we saw emerge was what Potter (2012) and others have referred to as 'curatorship' or 'curation'. As Dezuanni and Zagami note, according to Potter, 'young people's everyday lived practices within digital culture may be understood as curatorship, leading to complex meaning making processes deeply connected to identify performance' (this volume, Chapter 5). In Chapter 5, Dezuanni and Zagami describe a wide range of classroom work with games viewed through this lens, and show how teachers and students utilised curatorship practices in depth. As they outline, the term provides a 'useful metaphor to describe an emergent literacy practice in new media production', where individuals

> have access to digital artifacts at their fingertips [and] have the means to take and remix content, to publish things that they have made alongside things they have created and establish new relationships between the elements to make new meanings.
>
> *(Potter 2012, p. xvi)*

Curatorship refers both to the collection and compilation of digital resources, whether for teaching, learning or other purposes and to the selection, creation, shaping and maintenance of those resources, for oneself or others. The work of teachers and students across the project described here exemplifies processes of curation, as also of critical and creative pedagogy, an openness to the affordances of games, to new ways of doing things, and to the opportunities opened up for all learners if we can find ways to work effectively with games.

Acknowledgement

This work was supported by the Australian Research Council under Linkage Grant LP110200309: Serious Play: Using digital games in school to promote literacy and learning in the twenty first century. We acknowledge the contribution of our Industry Partners: the Department of Education and Early Childhood Development (Victoria) and six Queensland schools. Particular thanks must also go to the students and teachers who participated in the research. The Serious Play Research Team consisted of Catherine Beavis, Michael Dezuanni, Joanne O'Mara, Leonie Rowan, Sarah Prestridge, Jason Zagami and Yam San Chee. Research Assistance: Roberta Thompson, Christy McGillivray and Colleen Stieler-Hunt. The statistical consultant for the project was Sandy Muspratt.

Notes

1. Serious Play: Using digital games in school to promote literacy and learning in the twenty first century. Australian Research Council LP110200309.
2. Primary and secondary education in Australia corresponds to elementary and high school education in other settings.

References

Barrett, T (2009), 'Using Myst 3 for descriptive writing', *The Curious Creative*. Available from: http://edte.ch/blog/2009/08/08/using-myst-3-for-descriptive-writing/ (Accessed 26 July 2016).

boyd, d (2008), 'Why youth (heart) social networking sites: The role of networked publics in teenage social life', in D Buckingham (ed.), *Youth identity and digital media*, The MacArthur Foundation, Cambridge, MA: The MIT Press, pp. 119–142.

Brand, J E and Todhunter, S (2015), '*Digital Australia 2016 (DA16)*', Interactive Games & Entertainment Association. Available from: www.igea.net/wp-content/uploads/2015/07/Digital-Australia-2016-DA16-Final.pdf (Accessed 16 July 2016).

Buckingham, D (2016), 'Radicalisation, social media and young people: Why we need a more thoughtful approach'. Available from: http://davidbuckingham.net/2016/01/14/radicalisation-social-media-and-young-people-why-we-need-a-more-thoughtful-approach (Accessed 26 January 2016).

Burn, A (2013), 'Computer games in the playground', in R Willett, J Richards, J Marsh, A Burn and J Bishop (eds), *Children, media and playground cultures: Ethnographic studies of school playtimes*, Basingstoke, UK: Palgrave, pp. 120–144.

Carr, D (2007), 'Contexts, pleasures and preferences: Girls playing computer games', in S de Castell and J Jenson (eds), *Worlds in play: International perspectives on digital games research*, New York, NY: Peter Lang, pp. 313–322.

Chee, Y S (2010), *Statecraft X*. Available from: http://cheeyamsan.info/NIEprojects/SCX/SCX2.htm (Accessed 8 August 2016).

Cyan (1993), *Myst*. Available from: http://cyan.com/games/myst/ (Accessed 8 August 2016).

Davidson, D (2008), *Beyond fun: Serious games and media*, Pittsburgh, PA: Entertainment Technology Center, Carnegie Mellon Press. Available from: http://repository.cmu.edu/cgi/viewcontent.cgi?article=1000&context=etcpress (Accessed 16 January 2016).

Davies, J (2013), 'Trainee hairdressers' uses of Facebook as a community of gendered literacy practice', *Pedagogy, Culture and Society*, vol. 21, no. 1, pp. 147–169.

Erstad, O and Sefton-Green, J (2013), *Identity, community and learning lives in the digital age*, Cambridge, UK: Cambridge University Press.

Gee, J (2007), *What videogames have to teach us about learning and literacy*, New York, NY: Palgrave MacMillan.

Ito, M (2015), *Connected camps summer of Minecraft*. Available from: www.itofisher.com/mito/weblog/2015/03/connected_camps_summer_of_mine.html (Accessed 26 July 2016).

Jenkins, H, Purushotma, R, Clinton, K, Weigel, M and Robison, A (2009), *Confronting the challenges of participatory culture: Media education for the 21st century*. An occasional paper on Digital Media and Learning, Building the Field of Digital Media and Learning, The MacArthur Foundation. Cambridge, MA: The MIT Press.

Juul, J (2005), *Half-real: Video games between real rules and fictional worlds*, Cambridge, MA: The MIT Press.

Lankshear, C and Knobel, M (2006), *New literacies: Everyday practices and classroom learning* (2nd ed.), Maidenhead, UK: Open University Press.

Lenhart, A (2015), *Teens, social media and technology overview 2015*, Washington, DC: The Pew Research Center. Available from: www.pewinternet.org/files/2015/04/PI_TeensandTech_Update2015_0409151.pdf (Accessed 16 January 2016).

Livingstone, S (2014), *EU kids online: An introduction to the project*. Available from: www.youtube.com/watch?v=8sU25ZIwy1A&list=PLK4elntcUEy3D2m1WO_tEDJpLVkZ0EGdx (Accessed 16 January 2016).

Marsh, J (2010), 'Young children's play in virtual online worlds', *Journal of Early Childhood Research*, vol. 8, no. 1, pp. 23–39.

Meier, S (2001), *Sid Meier's Civilization III*, Firaxis Games. Available from: www.civilization3.com (Accessed 8 August 2016).

Merchant, G (2009), 'Web 2, new literacies, and the idea of learning through participation', *English Teaching: Practice and Critique*, vol. 8, no. 3, pp. 107–122.

Microsoft (2016), *MinecraftEdu*. Available from: https://education.minecraft.net (Accessed 8 August 2016).

MIT Media Lab (2005), *Scratch*. Available from: https://wiki.scratch.mit.edu/ (Accessed 8 August 2016).

Mojang (2011), *Minecraft*. Available from: https://minecraft.net/en/ (Accessed 8 August 2016).

New Horizon Interactive (2005), *Disney Club Penguin*. Available from: www.clubpenguin.com/ (Accessed 8 August 2016).

Perrotta, C, Featherstone, G, Aston, H and Houghton, E (2013), *Game-based learning: Latest evidence and future directions*, Slough, UK: NFER.

Potter, J (2012), *Digital media and learner identity: The new curatorship*. New York, NY: Palgrave Macmillan.

Raco, E (2014), *Aussie teens online*, Australian Communication and Media Authority. Available from: www.acma.gov.au/theACMA/engage-blogs/engage-blogs/Research-snapshots/Aussie-teens-online (Accessed 26 January 2016).

Rylands, T (2006), *Myst 'Exile' in the classroom*. Available from: www.youtube.com/watch?v=X5xFMmK5Ujs (Accessed 26 July 2016).

Squire, K and Barab, S A (2004), 'Replaying history: Engaging urban underserved students in learning world history through computer simulation games', in *Proceedings of the 6th International Conference of the Learning Sciences*, Santa Monica, CA: UCLA Press, pp. 505–512.

Steinkuehler, C and King, B (2009), 'Digital literacies for the disengaged: Creating after school contexts to support boys' game-based literacy skills', *On the Horizon*, vol. 17, no. 1, pp. 47–59.

Stuart, K (2014), 'UK gamers: More women play games than men, report finds', *The Guardian*. Available from: www.theguardian.com/technology/2014/sep/17/women-video-games-iab (Accessed 26 January 2016).

Whitton, N (2014), *Digital games and learning: Research and theory*, New York, NY: Routledge.

WordPress Foundation (2003), *WordPress*. Available from: https://wordpress.org (Accessed 8 August 2016).

Young, M, Slota, S, Cutter, A, Jalette, G, Mullin, G, Lai, B, Simeoni, Z, Tran, M and Yukhymenko, M (2012), 'Our princess is in another castle: A review of trends in serious gaming', *Review of Educational Research*, vol. 82, no. 1, pp. 61–89.

YoYogames (2016), *GameMaker*. Available from: www.yoyogames.com/gamemaker (Accessed 8 August 2016).

Student Approaches to Games-Based Learning

THEME PREFACE

The student voice is, paradoxically, often missing from studies of games-based learning, yet it is students who are most directly affected and best positioned to comment on the use and effectiveness of games. And while there are numerous accounts of games-based learning in individual classrooms, there are few that canvass students' experience across a wide range of classrooms, age groups, subject areas and teacher familiarity with games. A great strength of the Serious Play project was the number of students, teachers and classrooms we worked with/in over a period of three years. Students ranged from those just entering formal school, through to those in upper and middle secondary, drawing close to the highly challenging final years. Each year, up to 400 students were involved, in schools ranging from inner city government and independent schools; regional independent and government schools serving students in mixed or low socioeconomic status (SES) communities; schools with strong religious affiliations – Anglican, Catholic and Lutheran; and proudly secular schools located within the state education systems in Queensland and Victoria. The states themselves had commonalities in their curriculum and outcome requirements, through the national Australian Curriculum, Assessment and Reporting Authority (ACARA) Curriculum, but they also had their own histories, cultures and traditions, and different ways of doing things. Cumulatively, this meant we were able to hear from students with widely varying experiences: differences of age, of year levels, of school type and of geographical location, as well as a diversity of subject areas and activities, and a diversity of games. In addition, for the most part, students also had some experience of gameplay at home – many were highly expert – and a great deal of experience about how things at school usually go.

Many things struck us from watching students' gameplay, and listening to what they had to say. In Chapter 2, Beavis, Thompson and Muspratt present findings from the student surveys and interviews, many of which reappear in other chapters subsequently. Students were thoughtful and observant critics and reflective research participants. They were astute judges of when games worked best in classrooms, and the purposes that games-based learning activities served. They had views about what they most enjoyed, about what games made possible, about 'getting the balance right', and about what got in the way. The best school-based work connected with and drew on out-of-school experiences of play; valued and was respectful of what students knew; and tapped into deep knowledge, ownership and authority, in the case of experienced players. It opened up the world of games and their mysteries for those less experienced, and for those for whom it was new, but there were also some students who were not convinced, or had other preferences, and it is important for games-based learning research to attend to their voices too. *Minecraft* in particular, but other games too, saw students deeply immersed in 'impassioned learning', acquiring rich curriculum knowledge, and experiencing 'the deep satisfaction of making' as outlined by Dezuanni and O'Mara in Chapter 3. Listening to the student voice and seeing through student eyes has much to offer to school-based work with digital games.

2

'A GAME ISN'T A GAME WITHOUT INTERACTION'

Students' Thoughts About the Use of Digital Games in School

Catherine Beavis, Roberta Thompson and Sandy Muspratt

I think the important things that you should have in a game should be a bit of facts, a bit of fun and a bit of things that are interesting and interaction because a game isn't a game without interaction, it's just a video.

Year 5 student

Introduction

In this chapter, we explore students' thoughts about the use of digital games in school. A great strength of the Serious Play project was the opportunity to hear from students across a wide range of contexts about their actual experience of working with digital games in the classroom. This project was structured in such a way that students from various age groups with differing levels of gaming experience participated in different games-based activities at different schools in Queensland and Victoria, Australia. While united in their common interest in exploring the possibilities of digital games, the teachers, in turn, had varying experience as games players themselves, and with the use of digital games in school. With the exception of the school where Nick and Kynan taught – the site for some of the activities discussed in Chapters 3, 7, 8 and 9 – the study did not take place in specialist games-based learning or technology schools. Rather, it explored the introduction of games into mainstream, non-specialist schools, and the implications of doing so for teaching and learning; for curriculum, pedagogy and assessment. Amongst the raft of studies addressing the use of games in schools, this chapter is one of only a small handful of accounts to seek out and present student views on such a scale, where the context was the integration of games into everyday classrooms by interested teachers in non-specialist schools. Students' answers highlighted the value of digital games for learning, but also pointed to the importance of getting it right and balancing the use of digital games with other pedagogical practices.

Digital Game Experience

As outlined in Chapter 1, the starting point for this project was an interest in the potential of digital games to enhance learning. Teachers joined the project on the basis of their interest in exploring the use of games in this way. Students involved came from a wide range of year levels, depending on where the project teachers taught. They ranged in age from five to sixteen, and from Year 1 to Year 10, with games played across a wide range of curriculum learning areas in schools. This arrangement meant we were in a position to canvass the views of students across different stages of schooling, in diverse contexts, and in multiple disciplinary areas. What had their experience been? In what contexts had they used games at school? What did they think games were good at teaching them, and what not? What made them work? What made them fun? How did they think games fitted in with their other activities in school?

In each year of the project, up to 400 students were involved. Over the three years, this wide spectrum offered the opportunity to observe and ask students questions about what they actually thought about the use of digital games in school. Each year, as teachers began new games-based projects, we observed classes and interviewed students about their use of digital games in particular units of work (e.g. the *Minecraft* [Mojang 2011] classes described in Chapter 3), Nick's game-making work described in Chapter 7, and the use of *Statecraft X* (Chee 2010) in Chapter 4. In 2012 and 2014, we asked most of the students involved in the project to participate in a short survey about their experiences with digital games in school. We did not ask students in the earliest grades (i.e. Years 1 and 2) to answer the survey, but all other students were asked to answer the questions. The 2012 survey comprised 402 students in Year 3 to Year 10. In Victoria, the younger students in Year 3 were scaffolded as they completed this task, with their teachers reading and explaining survey questions on a one-by-one basis, with a break in the middle, so that a wide-ranging and informed set of views could be obtained. The 2014 survey involved 241 students in Year 4 to Year 9. Through these two mechanisms, we were able to hear from more than 600 students across a range of year levels, subject areas and schools. The students in each survey group (2012 and 2014) changed, so we did not collect longitudinal data. Therefore, the feedback does not reflect individual students' experience longitudinally, but it does reflect their views about games in school and, indirectly, their teachers' growing confidence, fluency and facility in working with digital games, and their critical appraisal about how best to do so.

The survey data from 2012 suggested that students' experience of digital games in school varied; that they enjoyed the opportunity to engage and socialise with each other; that they liked the challenge and enjoyed options for accumulation, but were also frustrated and impatient with games which they saw as boring or overly 'educational', or when technological issues got in the way. They valued connections between fun and learning, believed games were good at developing skills such as problem solving, but were astute critics when it came to what games could, and could not, achieve. They were open to the inclusion of games in the classroom, but valued these most when they were integral to the subject area or context, respectful of their age and abilities, and worked effectively as games (Beavis, Muspratt et al. 2015).

By 2014, the third year of the project, changes in policy priorities and staffing in some schools meant that not all students participating in the project took part in the survey that year. As previously, we asked students a variety of questions about themselves as game players, and their experience with digital games in school, including whether or not they played games outside school, and what they liked and didn't like about games-based learning in the classroom. To gain a detailed picture of student preferences and experiences, in addition to tick-the-box answers from the survey, in this chapter we include qualitative responses from the 2014 surveys as well as observations and comments from the 2012 student focus-group discussions. Seventy-five students from Year 1 to Year 9 were involved in the focus-group sessions. They came from a wide range of school contexts and had varying degrees of interest in and experience with playing digital games in and out of school. For some of these students, games were already a familiar feature of classroom learning, while for others, games-based learning was a reasonably new experience. However, all of these students had been using digital games at school in at least one topic or curriculum area and were therefore well positioned to report on their experience of using games in school.

We used a broad-based thematic approach (Boyatzis 1998) in analysing this data to arrive at the central themes, identifying words, groups of words and descriptive patterns in the students' contributions concerned with their experience of games-based learning. We did not set any limits around the number of potential themes that might emerge; nor did we seek to counter or confirm teacher beliefs (Beavis et al. 2014). Simply, we sought to identify the students' perceptions of their experience with digital games in the classroom. As has been noted elsewhere (de Castell 2011; Beavis, Muspratt et al. 2015; Livingstone and Sefton-Green 2016), the possibilities for and constraints of games-based learning at school intersect with the ways in which students experience games outside the classroom. While we were mainly concerned with students' perceptions of games-based learning in school, we were conscious that students' experience of games is both situationally specific and constituted of and by their experience as games players (or non-players) in contexts outside school.

To capture something of this diversity, the survey included questions about favourite games played at home, what students liked best about those games, how often they played games and what they valued most in gameplay, in addition to their views and experiences of working with games in school. Given the teachers' largely optimistic beliefs about the benefits of using digital games in the classroom and the capacity to make maximum use of games' affordances to extend and strengthen learning (Beavis *et al.* 2014), students' perceptions about all aspects of digital gameplay, including comparative comments about in- and out-of-school play, were particularly relevant. Their answers and observations offer insight into the diverse range of experiences they had had with digital games in the classroom. For clarity, the students' answers are grouped into four broad sections: expectations, preferences, possible problems, and recommendations for optimum use of digital games in the classroom.

Student Expectations

In the 2014 survey, close to three-quarters of the students (72 per cent) said they believed that digital games could help them learn in the classroom. We offered a list of options based on existing studies (e.g. Gee 2007; Perrotta *et al.* 2013) and our own previous findings (Muspratt and Apperley 2012; Beavis, Muspratt *et al.* 2015; Beavis, Walsh *et al.* 2015), about what games can do to support learning in the classroom. While answers across the group as a whole show that all items were seen to be important to some degree, the ones students valued most were games' capacity to support 'making things interesting', 'solving problems' and 'using your imagination'. A summary of their responses about what might be learned from using computer games in classrooms is depicted in Figure 2.1. Numbers in each section of the horizontal bar graph (e.g. grey and white areas) represent the actual number of student responses per item, while the horizontal axis at the bottom of the graph shows response percentage per item.

Qualitative comments on the 2014 survey were consistent with student observations from the earlier 2012 focus-group interviews; for example, students agreed that digital games made things more interesting. Three specific themes emerged as relatively important when students were asked to describe their classroom experience in detail – that games should be fun and enjoyable, that interactivity was highly important, and that the games used should be challenging.

Fun and Enjoyable

The majority of students expected games in the classroom to make learning fun. They repeatedly commented on the importance of having fun and how digital games made learning better and more enjoyable.

> It has to be fun and enjoyable.
> Having fun: EXTREMELY IMPORTANT.
> They can make learning about a subject a lot more fun.
> Computer games are good at teaching people how to be happy.
> It would make work and learning more enjoyable.

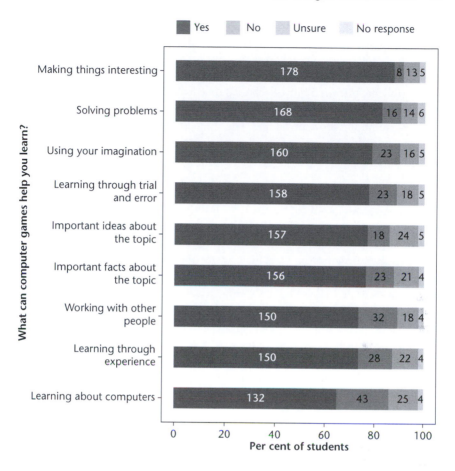

FIGURE 2.1 Summary of student response to survey questions concerned with what can be learned from using computer games in classrooms.

Students often compared the inherently 'fun' character of gameplay with the less interesting practices of 'normal' learning. They described normal learning as 'just reading', 'just watching the teacher', 'doing pen and paper activities' and 'doing board work', and argued that games were a 'much funner' way to learn content because topics and ideas were explained better, hints and helps in the game showed them how to do things properly, they could be a bit more creative, and it was a faster way of solving problems.

Nevertheless, not all students held the view that games in school were fun and engaging. A small number of them described classroom games as boring, repetitive, too easy and childish. As one Year 8 student explained:

> You had to correctly complete a series of questions before you could play the game where you smacked bugs for points. The quicker you completed

the questions, the more time you had to play the bugwhack game. The problem was that the game wasn't fun at all and gave players no motivation to complete the questions.

These students preferred out-of-school games where they 'didn't really have to think that much', had greater freedom of game choice, and could adopt a wider range of communication modes and styles such as typing messages to each other; sharing materials, websites and images; and talking through webcams.

Interactive

Many students associated digital games with sources of action and interaction and high degrees of personal control. Students frequently commented that games enhanced classroom learning experience by providing opportunities to interact with learning materials in ways that were not possible with other types of educational resources such as books and worksheets. Games provided 'things that let you interact, like you click on things, adventure around, and move around and do things' and 'instead of just sitting there and watching, you get to get in yourself and try and solve mysteries and so on'. They associated the active nature of games with authentic engagement, active learning and stronger content retention. 'It gets you more excited about learning so you kind of want to learn more because you can interact with the game. So it can stick with – in your mind what you've learnt.' Another student said, 'I think you realise it better when you're in control of the whole thing.'

Games were also described as an important avenue for building positive relationships with classmates, developing teamwork skills, sharing ideas and getting help from others. The ways in which games provided opportunities for students to work with friends was valued. 'You can actually talk to your friends in the class while you're doing it. You can communicate and work alongside your friends to actually advance in the game to progress to a higher level.' The collaborative benefits of gameplay have been frequently argued (see, for example, Jenkins *et al.* 2009; Takeuchi and Vaala 2014), and certainly the potential for games to develop and encourage communication was important to most of the students in this study. However, some students did express concerns over working with others and claimed that they were 'not really much of a team player'. On the other hand, for most, being able to talk during lessons and share ideas was valued, and opportunities for choosing, creating and building things, and controlling characters, storylines or objects in the game, were identified as important improvements over 'pen and paper' learning.

Challenging

The students commented repeatedly on the need for games to be challenging and progressively more difficult. Challenging games were described as those that were strategic, fast-paced, hard to win, competitive, made you think a lot, were 'knowledge demanding' and involved problem solving.

> I like unexpected surprises. That's my sort of game, where you, it's just like stuff happens and then you've got to see what you can do about it.

> It makes you think carefully about your actions and provides a competitive atmosphere.

The students' desire for gaming activities that were challenging is key to realising the actual potential of games to support and extend learning, by nature of their affordances, the kinds of engagement they foster and their capacity to call on diverse modes of understanding and connection through procedural rhetoric (Bogost 2007), ludic epistemology (de Castell 2011), dialogic activity and performance (Chee 2015). If games are fun, but no more than this, the potential for games to actually build rather than decorate learning is lost. That many students identified the importance of challenge reflects their recognition that in addition to curriculum content, digital games have potential to facilitate, enhance and foster a number of thinking and problem-solving skills including creativity. Where this worked, it was highly valued. However, claims that one and the same game was too easy and boring or too hard and confusing suggested that selecting games which challenged and met the interests of all students equally in a single class was difficult. As one girl put it, 'It's better than main classwork but it's still bad. It's still maths.'

Student Preferences

The games-based learning activities undertaken in project schools took place at different points across the year, depending on schools' curriculum and timetables. When the 2014 survey was administered, more than three-quarters of the students surveyed at that time (78 per cent) had used digital games as part of their classroom learning. Student preferences for in-school games were diverse, as were the responses to individual games. The choice of games, what kinds of games they were, how they were used and how long they were used for, varied widely between schools, so it is not possible to generalise across the group about individual games or game-playing preferences. However, when asked about their favourite game used in school, some interesting patterns appear. The most frequently nominated game by far was *Minecraft*, which emerged during the course of the project and was taken up in a number of classrooms in four of the project schools. On some occasions, as discussed below, the same game was mentioned as either the favourite or least favourite game, by different students within the same cohort.

The key principles and mechanisms claimed for games-based learning, such as learning by doing, self-reliance and autonomy in a fictional setting (Perrotta *et al.* 2013), were reflected in students' tick-the-box responses and free-text comments. Points about why certain games were favoured coincided with the student expectations discussed earlier. Students liked individual games because they were having fun while learning and the games were interactive and challenging. In addition, the open world experience and specific in-game features were identified as important qualities of favourite games.

Open World Experience

The students repeatedly commented on the freedom that games such as *Minecraft* provided for players to 'roam around' and 'pretty much do whatever [they] wanted'. Students valued the open world experience provided by some games where opportunities for creativity, exploration, imagination and independence were emphasised. Students explained:

> I like how you can adventure far and take care of everything. It's like being a grown-up in your own world.

> You don't have to follow instructions; you have the freedom of using your imagination and having lots of fun.

There was considerable variety in terms of how students expressed the experiential aspects of gameplay, but the notions of free choice and personal control were remarkably consistent. Personal ownership of game outcomes was engaging for students even if there were obstacles and disasters along the way. Finding and coming to know new things through discovery were reflected in their claims. While teachers may aim to deliver overt and deliberate educational content through games (Merchant 2013), particularly when using purpose-built 'serious games' to support learning in disciplinary areas, these students preferred games that provided some degree of autonomy and space to 'learn about the outside world'. Students wanted to use 'the creative side of their mind', they wanted to be able to imagine and visualise things. One Year 2 student said:

> If we write a narrative, it makes it so much easier because you've already seen what happens [in the game] and like if we're describing the sand sharks [for example], we can have it in our head because we've seen it. But if we just have to make up a story, it's hard.

Some students viewed games as 'more of an experiment to see how things worked'; it wasn't the real world, but you came to understand the topic 'by engaging your brain', finding things and learning about them through self-discovery: 'I might discover something on the computer that I never knew.' In contrast, games that were overly prescriptive or had a 'skill and drill' focus were not popular.

In-Game Features

Students' game preferences were strongly linked to specific in-game features. These included the graphics, characters, pace of action, storyline, variety in game options and ease of gameplay (e.g. knowing how to use the controls). A particular game was favoured, for example, because:

> It had lots of levels and was fast moving.

> The graphics were well done and the storyline was fantastic.

> It was intelligently designed and loaded continuously.

The ways in which games brought the story alive through graphics and sound were valued. For these students, content delivery in gameplay was important. A Year 5 student explained:

> You realise how much easier it is than reading a script. Just over and over, it's not very exciting but you can listen to music and hear – like when she screams you can actually hear her scream so it is good because you can imagine what her scream was like because it's put in her way.

Not all students valued the same in-game features. For example, the game *Zork* (Infocom 1980) was ranked most favourite by several students and least favourite by several others. Students who favoured this game described it as a 'very interesting old-fashioned game which is fun to play. It does not have pictures so you can use your imagination.' Students who did not like *Zork* claimed that 'it was not very descriptive, a bit dull and slow. It was very hard to do things, difficult to figure out and control.' Views about what made gameplay interesting clearly differed from student to student, and game to game. As one student put it, 'it depends if you're really that type of gamer, like the old fashioned one'. On the whole, reasons for not liking games were reasonably consistent. Games that were repetitive, confusing, not descriptive, slow, hard to use or fiddly, and overly prescriptive were often rated as students' least favourite.

Possible Problems

In the 2014 survey, as in 2012, we offered students a list of options concerned with possible problems using digital games in the classroom. Although the majority of students felt that digital games helped them learn, and believed that they were suitable for school use, many of them also identified with the problems listed in the survey question. Figure 2.2 summarises the list of possible problems offered and the students' response to these options. Student concerns were primarily associated with finishing games in the allocated class time, but other students' gaming practices, abilities and behaviour, and technological issues were also

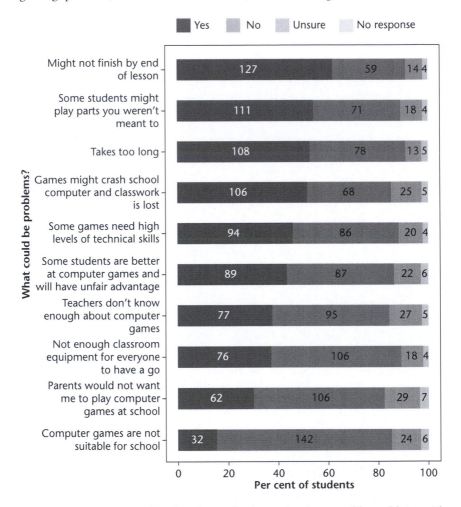

FIGURE 2.2 A summary of students' contributions related to possible problems with digital games in the classroom.

considered somewhat problematic. The stress and strain of gameplay in the classroom were tellingly reflected in interview comments. For example, not everyone liked the physicality and noisy emotion accompanying gameplay. As one Year 2 student said, 'It's really fun but one thing I don't like about it is everyone else screams when you have a go and it makes you stressed. Everybody screams like when you do something wrong.' A similar preoccupation with technical problems and the pressure for success was noticeable in the earlier survey (Beavis, Muspratt *et al.* 2015).

Optimum Use

Claims about the optimum use of digital games in the classroom have frequently linked digital games to increased student interest and motivation. In this project, students' comments were largely supportive of these views, but also supportive of the arguments that games need to do more, actively extending understanding, collaboration and knowledge. Several students claimed that digital games helped with content retention. For example, one Year 5 student said, 'the math equations got stuck in my head so I remembered them more'. On the other hand, a number of students suggested that games-based learning was best balanced with other pedagogical practices.

> You have to find a happy medium.

> There needs to not be too much games in school, otherwise no one will be paying attention and actually learning as well.

> It would get boring after a while; you get sick of playing games.

Student comments about the extent to which games should be used in the classroom echoed findings from an earlier study undertaken by Francis (2006). Francis noted that one of the problems faced by teachers using games-based practice was that students became overly engaged in the gaming activity rather than the educational focus of the lesson. In the free-text comments in the survey, this potential for students to rush their 'serious work' to play the game was raised. A Year 5 student expressed it this way:

> Sometimes [gameplay] might get a bit distracting for your work. If your website is *Mathletics* [3P Learning n. d.], they have avatars that you can create. But if you're going on to do your work, you might not get all your work done because you're just thinking, oh I want to go and create an avatar. Yeah and you wouldn't like take all the learning in and you might not concentrate on the actual subject.

Several students discussed the importance of getting the balance right; that is, 'to get in the middle of serious and fun'. According to these students, a good school game had something serious about it such as a proper set of tasks that helped them to learn, but also something fun, 'sort of like a reward – a reward kind of pumps you up'. Rewards and creative activities did encourage them to work more on set learning tasks, but there needed to be a 'fair share' between 'serious things' and 'fun things'.

For all the enthusiasm of most students, views about the positive influence of digital gameplay on learning were countered by a smaller group of students who expressed an overall disinterest in using digital games in the classroom. For some, gameplay conflicted with their preferred style of learning (e.g. 'I am more of a write-it-down person. I don't really use the computer to type'); and for others, with their preference for more physical activities (e.g. 'I like to be on the ovals running around, I would prefer that'). Still others explained that they 'didn't really learn anything'; instead, gameplay was 'just boring'; that is, 'some of the games just go on and on and on and on'.

Conclusions

In the main, student attitudes towards their academic work had a significant impact on their expectations and preferences for the use of digital games in the classroom. Students who were keen learners and high achievers preferred games that had a clearly defined learning focus and a series of set tasks. Student experience and preference for digital games in the classroom highlight the importance of 'getting it right', 'making it interesting' and balancing the use of games in the classroom with other pedagogical practices. The experiences of these students highlight the value of digital games for facilitating student learning, whether through promoting disciplinary knowledge, providing 'free' space for learning or creating opportunities for collaboration, problem solving, creativity, imagination and play. Their comments also highlight the real-world challenges for systems, teachers and schools in moving beyond seeing games as decorations, entertainment or rewards, to recognising and implementing games as serious learning resources for present and future iterations of pedagogy, learning and curriculum. The presence of games on their own is not sufficient to ensure that learning occurs, and that the rich opportunities they offer are achieved. Rather, as these student perspectives confirm, the success of games in the classroom is as much about the choice of game and the ways in which they are used. In this, pedagogy is central, with learning built around the game in creative and enabling ways. In the chapters that follow, we describe some of this work in project schools, with a range of year levels, subjects and games.

References

3P Learning (n. d.), *Mathletics*. Available from: www.mathletics.com.au/ (Accessed 8 August 2016).

Beavis, C, Rowan, L, Dezuanni, M, McGillivray, C, O'Mara, J, Prestridge, S, Stieler-Hunt, C, Thompson, R and Zagami, J (2014), 'Teachers' beliefs about the possibilities and limitation of digital games in classrooms', *E-Learning and Digital Media*, vol. 11, no. 6, pp. 569–581.

Beavis, C, Muspratt, S and Thompson, R (2015), 'Computer games can get your brain working: Student experience and perceptions of digital games in the classroom', *Learning, Media, and Technology*, vol. 40, no. 1, pp. 21–42.

Beavis, C, Walsh, C, Bradford, C, Gutierrez, A, O'Mara, J and Apperley, T (2015), 'Turning around to the affordances of digital games: English curriculum and students' life worlds', *English in Australia*, vol. 50, no. 2, pp. 30–40.

Bogost, I (2007), *Persuasive games: The expressive power of videogames*, Cambridge, MA: The MIT Press.

Boyatzis, R (1998), *Transforming qualitative information: Thematic analysis and code development*, Thousand Oaks, CA: Sage.

Chee, Y S (2010), *Statecraft X*. Available from: http://cheeyamsan.info/NIEprojects/SCX/SCX2.htm (Accessed 8 August 2016).

Chee, Y S (2015), *Games-to-teach or games-to-learn: Unlocking the power of digital based learning through performance*, London: Springer.

de Castell, S (2011), 'Ludic epistemology: What game-based learning can teach curriculum studies', *Journal of the Canadian Association for Curriculum Studies*, vol. 8, no. 2, pp. 19–27.

Francis, R (2006), 'Towards a theory of a games-based pedagogy', in Proceedings of the *Innovating e-Learning 2006: Transforming Learning Experiences* JISC Online Conference, March 27–31.

Gee, J (2007), *What videogames have to teach us about learning and literacy*, New York, NY: Palgrave MacMillan.

Infocom (1980), *Zork*, personal software. Available from: https://archive.org/details/a2_Zork_I_The_Great_Underground_Empire_1980_Infocom (Accessed 8 August 2016).

Jenkins, H, Purushotma, R, Clinton, K, Weigel, M and Robison, A (2009), *Confronting the challenges of participatory culture: Media education for the 21st century*. An occasional paper on Digital Media and Learning, Building the Field of Digital Media and Learning, The MacArthur Foundation. Cambridge, MA: The MIT Press.

Livingstone, S and Sefton-Green, J (2016), *The class: Living and learning in the digital age*, New York, NY: New York University Press.

Merchant, G (2013), '"I oversee what the children are doing": Challenging literacy pedagogy in virtual worlds', in G Merchant, J Gillen, J Marsh and J Davies (eds), *Virtual literacies: Interactive spaces for children and young people*, London: Routledge, pp. 161–180.

Mojang (2011), *Minecraft*. Available from: https://minecraft.net/en/ (Accessed 8 August 2016).

Muspratt, S and Apperley, T (2012), 'Patterns of digital gameplay in Australian high school students', in *Proceedings of the 8th Australasian Conference on Interactive Entertainment: Playing the System*, New York, NY: ACM Digital Library, pp. 17.1–17.9.

Perrotta, C, Featherstone, G, Aston, H and Houghton, E (2013), *Game-based learning: Latest evidence and future directions*, Slough, UK: NFER.

Takeuchi, L M and Vaala, S (2014), 'Level up learning: A national survey on teaching with digital games', The Joan Ganz Cooney Center at Sesame Workshop. Available from: www.joanganzcooney.center.org (Accessed 25 July 2015).

3

IMPASSIONED LEARNING AND *MINECRAFT*

Michael Dezuanni and Joanne O'Mara

Introduction

This chapter explores the popular game *Minecraft* (Mojang 2011) as a location of 'impassioned learning' both in and out of school. We argue that impassioned learning occurs when individuals are motivated through a deep, interest-driven desire to learn new knowledge and skills within fan culture associated with digital gameplay. Jenkins (2013[1992], 2006) argued that fandom involves individuals in significantly meaningful relationships with popular culture that often lead to intense engagement with the fictional worlds built for narrative engagement and gameplay, and the development of communities of practice. Gee (2003) showed how successful digital games require players to engage intensely with knowledge and that this often leads to the formation of affinity groups in which deep knowledge is created and shared. Through their concept of 'connected learning', Ito *et al.* (2013) argued in favour of learning that is socially embedded and interest-driven, and which occurs when 'a young person is able to pursue a personal interest or passion with the support of friends and caring adults' (p. 4). They suggested that this form of learning can be linked to academic achievement, career success or civic engagement. By building on these concepts of fan participation, affinity group sharing and connected learning, we argue that meaningful and impassioned learning occurs in young people's personal lives in ways that can be harnessed within formal education settings.

We find Lave and Wenger's (1991) communities of practice theory helpful for understanding how young people become passionate about fan-based learning, where learning communities 'are groups of people who share a concern or passion for something they do and learn how to do it better as they interact regularly' (p. x). *Minecraft* provides an exemplary instance of an ecology within which children and young people are passionate about play and learning for play within ever-evolving communities. In this chapter, we draw on interviews with students and teachers, survey and observational data to discuss *Minecraft* play in and out of school. The chapter discusses the ways in which *Minecraft* promotes deep knowledge, problem solving and creativity (Cipollone *et al.* 2014). We explore *Minecraft* as popular culture and popular learning, and we use theory from fan culture and informal learning to explore the connections between learning and fandom.

The examples provided in this chapter come from three Serious Play project schools: two primary schools in Brisbane (one a private girls' school and the other a private boys' school), and a public primary school in Melbourne. Throughout the project, *Minecraft* came up as a regular topic of discussion as we interviewed teachers about their motivations for using games in the classroom, their experiences of using games for learning and what they believed their students were learning from playing games in class. At the beginning of the project and at other points throughout, we also conducted focus-group interviews with students about their experiences of gameplay at home and at school, and again, *Minecraft* was frequently referred to as one of the most popular games for fun and learning. In addition to these interviews, observations of gameplay for learning at school were undertaken on several occasions throughout the project and we collected examples of student work related to their classroom *Minecraft* play.

Impassioned Learning

Our starting point in this chapter is an acceptance of Wenger's (1998) 'communities of practice' (CoP) as a useful way to think about learning and identity formation as everyday socially situated practices. Integral to a CoP approach is a belief that learning is continuous and ongoing and does not start and end at the school gate; furthermore, community, identity, meaning and practice are core elements of learning. We believe these aspects are central to how children and young people learn through and with *Minecraft*, and that the passion many have for the game is integrally connected to the ways in which their practice connects them to community and allows them to undertake identity work. Of course, for most young people, learning is not the end goal of home *Minecraft* play. Most young people play to relax, escape the pressures of school, to hang out with friends and to be creative. On another level, though, *Minecraft* might be thought of as an alternative learning system because the game provides young people with opportunities to develop expertise and skills that will not be assessed and reported to parents. Rather, the game provides challenges, social currency and knowledge valued by friends and other *Minecraft* players, which is less accessible to adults. As popular cultural currency, *Minecraft* becomes part of children's play and talk that exist beyond the official curriculum, potentially providing a sense of control and status in friendship groups and in the schoolyard. As Wenger said:

> Students go to school and, as they come together to deal in their own
> fashion with the agenda of the imposing institution and the unsettling
> mysteries of youth, communities of practice sprout everywhere – in the
> classroom as well as on the playground, officially or in the cracks.
>
> *(Wenger 1998, p. 6)*

School governance structures and curriculum content can be daunting for many
young people and the challenges of becoming socially viable within peer groups
can be just as difficult. Playing *Minecraft* with insight and skill is one way for
young people to gain a sense of achievement and to develop relationships with
others for validation and recognition. In addition, the complexity of *Minecraft*
practice and the opportunities it offers to develop insider knowledge and expertise
extend well beyond gameplay. Young people can also learn how to speak about
Minecraft; how to make something in the game and share it; how to find the best
Minecraft videos on YouTube; how to know as much or more about the game
than their peers; and how to hack and mod the game. All of these forms of
knowing enable various kinds of *Minecraft* practice and require learning which
occurs in socially situated practices in young people's everyday lives.

Impassioned learning, however, does not just originate with a need for
achievement, social acceptance and validation. An aspect of passionate engagement
with *Minecraft* is becoming deeply involved in the game's extensive ecology. To
account for this, we also draw on Sennett's (2008) theorisation that 'making is
thinking' to discuss the ways in which many of the children and young people we
spoke to and observed were intensely immersed in the *Minecraft* experience,
leading to deep learning.

Minecraft Fandom and Popular Learning

It is useful to think of young people's *Minecraft* practices as a form of fandom
because fandom implies a commitment to a media ecology that goes beyond
casual interaction or occasional participation. As Jenkins has argued, media
fandom involves particular modes of reception, encourages forms of activism,
functions as an interpretive and social community and promotes traditions of
cultural production (2013[1992], pp. 1–2). The particularities of how *Minecraft*
invites play and participation, promotes interpretive and pedagogic peer discourse,
encourages specific creative practices and develops community strongly align to
Jenkins's (2006) categories, especially where he reimagines fandom through the
lens of participation within convergence culture. Playing, consuming and
recirculating *Minecraft* through creative practice, talk and the distribution of
knowledge and skills provide an instance of fan-based participatory culture. Of
course, young people probably move in and out of fan communities all the time
as they become engaged in communities of practice around particular sports,
popular music, film and television, popular fiction, fashion and gaming. However,

fandom is seldom used as a way to think about young people as learners and the implications of fandom for classroom practice are typically ignored. There is a sense in which fandom is dismissed within formal education precisely because it is motivated by passionate interest, and because it presents a counter-narrative to the objective, rational and measurable knowledge promoted by the formal curriculum. Passionate interest in 'trivial' pursuits like gameplay represents the kind of practices that educators and parents often steer students away from, because they are considered distractions to learning. For instance, many students indicated to us in interviews that they could play digital games only when their homework was complete. We believe the marginalisation of fan practices is to the detriment of students' learning because educators can learn a great deal from the ways in which young fans engage with new knowledge, circulate knowledge, share practice and solve problems.

Throughout the Serious Play project, students and teachers alluded to *Minecraft* fandom on numerous occasions. For instance, when asked during interviews if they were looking forward to using *Minecraft* in class, the Year 5 students at the private boys' school in Brisbane responded excitedly, with one saying, 'I just like it – it's fun doing multiplayer, building houses and you can play on, like, Hunger Game arenas'; and another suggested, 'it's fun, you create nearly anything you want … and it's endless. You can do so much things'. Yet another suggested, 'everyone in our class likes it, except for like … people who don't have it'. The interviewees also thought that the majority of students in the class would like using *Minecraft*, 'because a lot of people play and … a lot of people have accounts. It's pretty popular on Xbox and all that. I reckon maybe one or two may not like the game in our class or something'. These responses came from interviews conducted at the start of the project prior to the game being used in class, but it was obvious from the responses that most of the students were already talking about *Minecraft* at school as part of their everyday schoolyard conversations. As Willett *et al.* (2013) have argued, media culture is becoming central to children's playground cultures, and it was evident at this school that possessing *Minecraft* knowledge was important to being part of the popular cultural milieu. As a Year 5 teacher said in an interview, *Minecraft* 'is all they talk about'.

The enthusiasm for *Minecraft* was also evident from observations of the students' in–class play. Initially, the teacher of the Year 5 class introduced *Minecraft* as a Friday afternoon 'activities' session, which was not directly aligned to the curriculum. The teacher wanted to explore the game's possibilities for developing the students' collaboration and problem-solving skills, and eventually to create more 'school-like' activities within the game. However, this initial casual approach to using *Minecraft* at school was more like a large free play session and it was particularly interesting to observe the students' excited interactions both within the *Minecraft* world and in the classroom space itself. Play took place in a 'computer room' in the school library in which the *Minecraft*Edu mod was installed. As a researcher in the space, Michael was often approached by students and thanked (they believed he was responsible for the game being installed) and one student reverentially asked him if he was from Mojang, the company that developed the game. At the end of one session, almost every student shook Michael's hand as they left the room. Although conveying these experiences is somewhat embarrassing from a researcher's perspective, it is important to recount them because they point out the extent to which *Minecraft* play disrupted the students' usual expectations of school. During the play sessions, the students spoke loudly and quickly to each other (and typed multiple messages to each other in-game) as they revelled in the opportunity to play as a whole class. Michael was struck during these sessions by the level of passion almost all the students had for *Minecraft*, and the extent to which they were motivated to participate in the game's broader practices.

Young people's enthusiasm for *Minecraft* was also recorded through the Serious Play project survey data from 2014 (Beavis *et al.* 2014), where it was the most popular game both outside school and in the classroom. Wenger's (1998) suggestion that young people develop their own communities of practice outside the official constraints of schooling (p. 6) became evident in the survey responses. For instance, the reasons students gave for *Minecraft* being their favourite game point to the game's openness and the sense of agency and creativity that this enabled. Students appreciated the game's structure and technical affordances because, as one student said, 'it's a sandbox game and you can go anywhere'. Another student liked 'the way it is intelligently designed and loads continuously', which enables creative play without interruption. Some of the comments focused on the building aspects of the game, such as 'you can make and build anything and it makes your imagination go crazy'. Building worlds in *Minecraft* gave the students a sense of ownership. For instance, one suggested, 'I like it how you can try and build things and have your own world' and 'you can build whatever you want'. In contrast to their regular lives, where young people have parents, carers and teachers frequently directing them, there are typically no adults in *Minecraft*, or as one student wrote, 'it's like being a grown up in your own world'. Many of the young people expressed the sense of agency and freedom they felt as a result of the lack of instruction provided by either the game itself or adults, agreeing that, 'you don't have to follow instructions'; 'it is so open you can do whatever you want'; 'you can do what you want and you can build anything in the game' and 'the fact that you can pretty much do whatever you want and explore'.

The freedom and agency seemingly provided by *Minecraft* were also linked to some young people's understandings of creativity and imagination. Several comments identified the affordances of the game which allowed young people to create and imagine what they wanted: as one said, 'I like how it's creative and free roaming'; and another suggested, 'you have the freedom of using your imagination and having lots of fun'; one student argued that an important aspect of playing the game was 'setting my imagination free'. Students also recognised the learning that can occur through working together to create within the game, with a number of students responding to the survey by identifying their favourite aspect of *Minecraft* to be 'creating things and learning to work together'. Overall, students summed up that with *Minecraft*, 'you have to use your imagination and it is a *lot of fun*'; and, 'it is fun because there is lots of things to learn and do'. By capitalising on the passionate fandom these students have for *Minecraft*, the teachers in the project were able to create a learning environment where the students were enthused in ways that went well beyond what is usually described as 'engagement' in education parlance. The teachers connected to key aspects of students' engagement in entertainment and learning outside the classroom to make connections to formal curriculum, as we indicate in the following section of this chapter.

Connected Learning, Problem Solving and Creativity With *Minecraft*

While fandom provides the context for impassioned learning with *Minecraft*, we also want to account for how the game promotes practices leading to connected learning and sustained dispositions towards problem solving and creativity. In doing this, we tease out examples from the Serious Play project to discuss attempts to make these kinds of practices possible in school environments, rather than the family home. *Minecraft* play at school was 'connected' in several ways that educational research argues is necessary for school to become more meaningful for students – being connected to their world outside the classroom (Lingard *et al*. 2003, p. 415) and linking to projected identities (Gee 2003). As popular culture, *Minecraft* connects to young people's lives and their interests beyond the classroom, as shown by the survey responses discussed above. It is a site of connection to repositories of knowledge and skills development, particularly through online communities and resources like YouTube, in a manner that is production-centred, promotes shared purpose, is openly networked and is relevant to academic pursuits (Ito *et al*. 2013; Connected Learning TV 2016). The learning that takes place for *Minecraft* play at home is often more heterarchical and networked than school learning is, typically. Several young avid *Minecraft* players we spoke to shared stories about how they had developed their game expertise through playing alongside older siblings or with friends, and through independently looking up 'how to' videos on YouTube. It was also evident that the students wanted to teach each other about *Minecraft* in class, and we saw many examples of students mentoring less able Minecrafters in class. As discussed in detail in Chapter 13, these mentoring relationships often recast the typical power structures within the class group, providing opportunities for young people who had not always been recognised for their skills and achievements to succeed.

At another level, creativity and problem solving occurred with *Minecraft* as students became immersed in the game through the crafting process. As we observed students playing in class, we saw intense concentration and high levels of active participation as students interacted with each other online, and designed and built structures through negotiation and experimentation. This kind of activity reminded us of Sennett's (2008) conception of 'making is thinking'. In *The Craftsman* (2008, p. 271), Sennett drew on Erik Erikson's 1970s scholarship on children's building-block play to argue for a deep connection between the materiality of childhood play and the development of adult craft skills and dialogue with materials as they are worked with. For Sennett (2008, p. 272), repetition and rule-making in play is a precursor to the development of expertise because it enables trial and error and the perfection of a process. Furthermore, play allows children to undertake more complex tasks as they master processes and seek to make more complex structures and narratives. Sennett's proposals are reflected in students' deep engagement with *Minecraft*, the repeated processes they undertake to mine and craft and the increasing complexity of their builds in the game. From this perspective, a significant part of their passion for the game resides in its complexity as a system for designing, building and creativity that allows young people to master skills and experience the deep satisfaction of *making* in a digital environment.

We saw an example of students' play for the development of expertise in 'The *Minecraft* Challenge' day undertaken at the private girls' school. The *Minecraft* Challenge was conducted over the course of two sessions – a 90-minute planning session, followed by a whole day of gameplay. It involved girls in a combined Years 4 and 5 class (9 and 10 year olds) who were divided into two teams which had to work together to build a series of structures on two separate islands in a *Minecraft* world. The two groups were physically separated in different schoolrooms and 'in world', they were not allowed to visit each other's islands. In addition, there was a series of conditions on the students' building. One group could not mine for coal and the other group could not mine for iron – these items were to be traded through negotiation at a trading post. During the first hour, the students could only build with wood; in the second hour, they could also build with stone; and in the third, they could build with iron. For the final part of the day, they could build with anything they liked. Finally, for the first hour, the game was set to survival/peaceful mode, meaning that the students would not be attacked by monsters at night and they would not become hungry; this gave them a chance to create structures and collect food for survival. From the second hour, it was intended that the game be switched to survival/normal mode, so that monsters and hunger became a threat. The curriculum objective of this challenge focused on the development of collaboration and cooperation skills, as well as knowledge of the social structures required to develop a basic society and design skills.

The *Minecraft* Challenge, which was designed by the research team and the classroom teacher, wasn't an entirely successful activity because it became a rather artificial way to require students to collaborate, which, in some respects, was the antithesis of the kinds of informal connected learning students undertake with *Minecraft* at home. There was little sense in which a community of practice was nurtured, and in some ways, we disrupted the communities of practice the students had already established around the game. Some students found it quite difficult to collaborate, even if they were friends. The structure of the day was altered part of the way through because the students found it difficult to work together under pressure to build shelters and grow food – so the survival/peaceful mode was restored after an initial period of chaos when the survival/normal mode was activated after the first hour. The teaching team's expectations about what the students might achieve in terms of built structures were also refined when it was clear that both groups of students were struggling to collaborate to build. There was a tendency in the initial hour or two for the students to simply want to play in open and creative ways rather than get organised. The activity did not provide an opportunity for 'making as thinking', and the over-engineering of the task did not tap into students' passion for the game. They were not used to playing *Minecraft* with such constraints or time pressures. Despite these constraints, the students enjoyed the day and spoke very highly of it. And they did complete many of the tasks the teachers had expected them to. Figure 3.1, for instance, shows one group's series of structures and also a chat exchange between students arranging to trade items. Each group also created a series of quite successful structures. On reflection, the teaching team agreed that this might have been a more successful task if there had been more time for planning and an altered range of constraints throughout the day, to allow for a more creative response from the students.

Connected learning with *Minecraft* was also a feature at a public primary school in Victoria, where the Years 5 and 6 students and teachers worked together to create a new civilisation in *Minecraft* (described in detail in Chapter 8). This curriculum unit ran in all three years of the project, and one of the significant aspects of this work was the growing enthusiasm of the teachers involved as they fully realised the potential of *Minecraft* in education, and developed their own

FIGURE 3.1 Classroom challenge with *Minecraft*: 'Just say "L1T" if you want to trade.'

passion and enthusiasm for its teaching opportunities. In their discussion of the project, the teachers recognised the power of their curriculum unit in *Minecraft* to tap into fandom and impassioned learning to develop a more connected curriculum. In this section of the chapter, we discuss an interview conducted towards the end of the project with one of the teachers who had been involved with the *Minecraft* project from the beginning. This was his third year with the unit and he had become a passionate advocate for the use of *Minecraft* in school. In describing how *Minecraft* works, he identified some of the particular affordances of the game that he believes foster creativity and learning:

> *Minecraft* is a game that our kids from about grade three and above absolutely adore … It's a very non-traditional game in a sense because there's no defined outcome – they're not playing for points, they don't have to go through different levels. It's a very pixelated world in which they can dig, and once they've dug out a resource they can build something with it. The more they dig, the more they can build, the more they build, the different things they can build, and then they can start to access different materials within the game. And from there they are limited only by their imagination really and what they can build, which for us means they're not limited at all because some of the stuff they create is absolutely fantastic.

This teacher's personal enthusiasm for *Minecraft* seems to stem from his students' passion for the game, the game's lack of instruction and constraint, and the examples of work he has seen his students create in the game. His response reflects Sennett's argument (2008, p. 272) that play enables trial and error and the perfection of a process, and that mastery of processes leads individuals to seek to make more complex structures and narratives. As the teacher notes, the more immersed in the game one is, the more resources and access to resources one accumulates, and the more creative one can be. From this perspective, learning results from passionate participation in a process in which problems are solved because they enable further play and participation. From a teaching perspective, there is an opportunity to connect this impassioned participation to curriculum: as the teacher explains, he and his colleagues have had 'a hundred and fifty odd students working in one world collaboratively; they produced infrastructure, railways, viaducts, aqueducts, they produced schools, museums, farms, nuclear power stations'. But more than this, *Minecraft* building provided an opportunity for classroom discussion and debate, and for the teachers to intervene and subtly steer a 'teachable moment', as occurred when the students had to make a decision about whether or not to include a nuclear power station in their build, because of the risk of a nuclear accident in their virtual community.

> We had some highly scientific minds, [a student of] Russian heritage, very scientific, very intellectual, and he was the one that was pushing for having

nuclear power in this world because his arguments were very convincing. The other students weren't to be swayed, however, so we took it upon ourselves to alter the playing field a little bit and we introduced this new element that had been discovered which just so happened to be ideal for providing nuclear power and not very good for anything else. So we kind of led them down this path, so the rest of the cohort relented and he was permitted to build his nuclear power station, but it was buried deep, deep, deep underground just in case something should go wrong. But it was fantastic; he then looked into all the kinds of things that he would need to build to put into this power station and it was absolutely huge by the time they'd finished it.

This event provided an example of connecting play to real-life contexts in a manner that utilises the 'productive pedagogy' of 'connectedness to the world' for authentic learning (Lingard *et al.* 2003, pp. 416–417). Lingard and colleagues suggested that connectedness is one of four crucial pedagogies that lead to high-quality learning, the other three being 'intellectual quality', 'supportive classroom environment' and 'engagement with difference'. By making a direct link to broader public policy, the teachers were able to introduce a public policy debate in Australia where there are no nuclear power stations (despite the fact that Australia sells uranium to other countries to power their nuclear power stations) and public opinion is set against nuclear energy. The students as a class group echoed public sentiment, but the teachers recognised the research work the pro-nuclear student had completed, including amassing articles about the environmentally positive arguments for building the nuclear station. The teachers helped the building of the nuclear station by adding an element to the world, but again the students had to research how this might be achieved safely. The teachers enabled student-centred problem solving, where the students worked on ideas that emerged from the class. The students were driven in their research due to their deep engagement with the curriculum unit and the passion they felt for their arguments and positions.

Another way in which the teachers made a direct connection to students' broader experience of digital culture was through the use of a Wikispace to replicate some of the paratextual practices commonly associated with media fandom. *Minecraft* is experienced by young people not just as a game, but in spaces like the *Minecraft* Wikia (http://minecraft.wikia.com/wiki/Minecraft_Wiki), where the Wikia has the subtitle 'The home of fandom'; and in the official *Minecraft* Wiki in Gamepedia (http://minecraft.gamepedia.com/Minecraft_Wiki). These Wikis provide information exchange and community interaction. In the following vignette, the teacher described how the school-based Wiki was used:

So we set them up, we had a Wikispace, [this] was a central hub for us, so there was an online presence and that meant that we weren't confined by the classroom boundaries. We've got downstairs classrooms, we got upstairs classrooms, a hundred and fifty something children. They could all log on and have this discourse in an online space both at home and at school, which was great because it did take the learning back into their home environments.

The Wiki allowed the students to connect not only to the classroom information about the project, but also to each other in ways that would otherwise not be possible. Perhaps most importantly, the Wiki provided the teachers with a way to alter their pedagogy and to introduce practices that are successful within sections of the *Minecraft* information-sharing community. In this sense, the teachers made a connection to informal pedagogic practices sometimes associated with the social software movement and often discussed within digital media studies as 'folksonomies' (Bruns 2008, p. 181). A folksonomy is more dialogic, pluralistic and user-driven than formal information-sharing systems that rely on taxonomies for knowledge categorisation and transfer. The teacher said:

> They had to keep all their research on there, decisions they were making had to be justified through that, and it was a nice centralised place where we could say, 'There's been a new task set', or 'New challenges have come up and you need to solve this problem now'. So rather than teaching, standing up at the front of your classroom and setting out the day's work, it could be conveyed through the Wikispace. They would've read it at home – by the time they come to school, they're already talking about it and they're ready to work through it.

The pedagogy enabled by the Wiki was a more appropriate avenue to involve students with impassioned learning through *Minecraft* because it somewhat de-centred the teachers as the classroom experts and allowed the students to engage more directly with each other in the learning process. Of course, this is not to suggest that the teachers were able faithfully to reproduce informal learning within the confines of the formal learning system in place at the school. However, by making connections to the students' passion for *Minecraft* and by finding ways to enable communication in less formal ways, the teachers made themselves much less central to the students' overall learning experience, and this seems to represent a successful example of the inclusion of a digital game in the classroom in an authentic way.

Conclusion

This chapter has argued that impassioned learning occurs as individuals become involved in deep, interest-driven learning motivated by a desire to participate in communities of practice. We have argued that *Minecraft* fandom involves participation, interpretation and pedagogic peer discourse associated with creative practice and community development. 'Impassioned learning', as we have called it, is motivated by personal interest and is rewarded through recognition and status within peer groups, opportunities to undertake identity work and opportunities to connect learning to tasks that are personally meaningful. This kind of learning is often not valued by schooling systems and yet it is sustained and makes a deep connection to young people's everyday lives. In the case of *Minecraft*, at least, impassioned learning provides opportunities for creativity, skills development, problem solving and peer tutoring at increasingly complex levels. Throughout the Serious Play project, we watched as young people revelled in the opportunity to play *Minecraft*, to collaborate with their peers in formal classroom environments to play and learn together. We listened to children and young people telling us about the long hours they dedicate to playing *Minecraft* outside school hours, which often involves forms of research, problem solving and creative practice. We also heard from teachers who recognised the potential of involving young people's enthusiasm for *Minecraft* in various classroom learning opportunities. Some of these projects were more successful than others, but it was evident that the teachers were convinced that *Minecraft* provided opportunities to connect their students' learning to the world around them. In the best cases we saw, the teachers were themselves passionate about *Minecraft*'s potential, and were excited about the opportunities the game presents to involve students in authentic learning experiences. It seems to us that impassioned learning is a crucial element of young people's successful participation in their communities and broader society, and it is important that formal education systems provide opportunities to foster this kind of learning. From this perspective, *Minecraft* fandom should be recognised as a potentially powerful resource for young people's learning.

References

Beavis, C, Dezuanni, M, O'Mara, J, Prestridge, S, Rowan, L, Zagami, J, Muspratt, S and Thompson, R (2014), Serious Play student survey report (unpublished internal report).

Bruns, A (2008), *Blogs, Wikipedia, Second Life and beyond: From production to produsage*, New York, NY: Peter Lang.

Cipollone, M, Schifter, C C and Moffat, R A (2014), 'Minecraft as a creative tool: A case study', *International Journal of Game-Based Learning*, vol. 4, no. 2, pp. 1–14.

Connected Learning TV (2016), *What is Connected Learning?* Available from: http://connectedlearning.tv/what-is-connected-learning (Accessed 5 August 2016).

Gee, J P (2003), *What video games have to teach us about learning and literacy*, New York, NY: Palgrave Macmillan.

Ito, M, Gutiérrez, K, Livingstone, S, Penuel, B, Rhodes, J, Salen, K, Schor, J, Sefton-Green, J and Watkins, C S (2013), *Connected learning: An agenda for research and design*, Irvine, CA: Digital Media and Learning Research Hub.

Jenkins, H (2006), *Convergence culture: Where old and new media collide*, New York, NY: NYU Press.

Jenkins, H (2013[1992]), *Textual poachers: Television fans and participatory culture*, New York, NY: Routledge.

Lave, J and Wenger, E (1991), *Situated learning: Legitimate peripheral participation*, Cambridge, UK: Cambridge University Press.

Lingard, B, Haynes, D and Mills, M (2003), 'Teachers and productive pedagogies: Contextualising, conceptualising, utilising', *Pedagogy, Culture and Society*, vol. 11, no. 3, pp. 399–424.

Mojang (2011), *Minecraft*. Available from: https://minecraft.net/en/ (Accessed 8 August 2016).

Sennett, R (2008), *The craftsman*, New Haven, CT: Yale University Press.

Wenger, E (1998), *Communities of practice: Learning, meaning and identity*, New York, NY: Cambridge University Press.

Willett, R, Richards, C, Marsh, J, Burn, A and Bishop, J C (2013), *Children, media and playground cultures: Ethnographic studies of school playtimes*, London: Palgrave McMillan.

THEME II

Changing Gameplay for the Classroom Context

THEME PREFACE

Some of the most persuasive arguments for the use of games in school come from observations of the sophistication and complexity of out-of-school, leisure-time gameplay, and a recognition of players' enthusiasm and commitment, together with games' capacities to provide deep experiential insights and conceptual understandings of complex kinds.

But playing games in school is not the same as leisure-time play. Contexts and purposes for play, and games themselves, may be significantly different, with the effective use of games needing to take account of factors such as these. The situated nature of learning and the ways in which context shapes learning are particularly evident in gameplay. Playing at home, at a friend's place, in internet cafés, on public transport, or wandering the streets with *Pokémon Go*, is very different from most school-based classroom play. Different relationships, different expectations, different outcomes and time frames are likely to obtain, with out-of-school play serving purposes including skill demonstration and mastery, the development of new relationships and the performance of identity, in addition to such matters as satisfaction, competition or pleasure. When games are brought into school, different parameters may apply, overlying the experience of games elsewhere. At times, this potentially creates conflict, requiring skilful negotiation from students and teachers, as Chapters 4 and 5 describe. Conversely, time and again we saw students, who struggled with traditional work but were adept or expert players out of school, have the chance to succeed when work in class was built around games.

The logic and design of games themselves are also likely to be organised differently, particularly in the case of 'serious games'. *Statecraft X*, for example, discussed in Chapter 4, was structured so that students played in out-of-school locations, in their own time, consistent with an 'anytime, anywhere' philosophy, with formal teaching sessions relying on immersion and commitment similar to that associated with out-of-school play. The game had built-in points of intervention beyond which play could not continue, such as the arrival of refugees seeking entrance at the town gate. Gameplay was structured to build in pause points such as these, which were mapped against classroom discussion of key issues and principles at preprogrammed stages. And crucially, the ways in which students engage with games, the knowledge they call on and the ways they present themselves are also differently inflected in the classroom compared to leisure-time play. In Chapter 4, Thompson, Beavis and Zagami discuss the use of *Statecraft X* in a Year 8 Studies of Society and Environment classroom to explore the ways in which students and the teacher interacted with the game to take up different roles and manage their classroom gaming experience.

Teachers are central to the successful use of games, in the knowledge they bring and the choices they make. Characteristically, inviting games into the classroom enabled teachers and students to capitalise on knowledge and skills already acquired by many students to serve curricular purposes, with teachers guided by students' expertise. The skilful adaptation and use of games calls on deep disciplinary and pedagogical knowledge: insight, creativity and imagination. Dezuanni and Zagami call on the concept of 'curatorship' in discussing this in Chapter 5, with curatorship enabling and requiring 'expert epistemic practice to mobilise the production of knowledge in meaningful ways'.

4

NEGOTIATING PEDAGOGICAL TRANSFORMATION AND IDENTITY PERFORMANCE THROUGH GAMEPLAY IN *STATECRAFT X*

Roberta Thompson, Catherine Beavis and Jason Zagami

Introduction

In this chapter, we explore how the roles of teacher and student are taken up, enacted and negotiated through gameplay. This perspective is used to consider how pre-existing relationships and already established rules of conduct for interaction frame or shape games-based learning. We use Goffman's (1959, 1967) notion of impression management and identity performance to consider how the challenges and subsets of interaction that naturally emerge in classroom settings come together to influence the ways in which students play digital games for learning. Impression management is understood as the practices, actions and strategies used by individuals to shape, shift or maintain their social identity in day-to-day interactions. The view holds that regardless of gaming options and curricular demands, players are likely to mediate their own experience by deploying individual strategies to perform their social identity (i.e. maintain or save face). These concepts are explored by focusing on data from the Year 8 Studies of Society and Environment class in which the students played *Statecraft X* (Chee 2010). *Statecraft X* is a citizenship game developed by Chee and colleagues at the National Institute of Education, Singapore. Because gameplay in *Statecraft X* emphasises strategy, collaboration and teamwork, it provides an opportunity to observe and explore how students negotiated existing rules of conduct and established their identity in this games-based learning context. Deeper understanding of processes such as these provide insight into the ways in which existing sociocultural dynamics influence both individual and group participation when digital games are used for learning. Drawing on teacher and student interview data, the chapter demonstrates how the teacher, individual students and groups of students operated within a specific frame of gameplay to co-construct learning about the processes and practice of good citizenship.

The Game

Statecraft X is an online multiplayer game that is played on an iOS device such as an iPod or iPhone (see Figures 4.1 and 4.2). In the game, the king of Velar has passed away leaving no adult heir. A competition to rule the kingdom until the child prince comes of age arises. Four factions – Dragons, Griffin, Phoenix and Pegasus – compete for this leadership. Each faction is led by a team of players. Individual players start out governing a single town, although they can make attempts to take over other townships. The ultimate goal is leadership of the kingdom's capital city, Bellalonia. However, along the way, players must manage their town's economy, resources, defence and healthcare system. They must protect their township from attack and, more importantly, they must build trust within their community and develop diplomatic ties with other factions. Each faction shares a common pool of money and players therefore need to coordinate resource development and allocation, consumption of resources, defence strategies and financial expenditures with fellow faction members. A series of scheduled events, including attacks by bandits, arrival of refugees and invasions from a neighbouring kingdom, increasingly challenge individual players, factions and the group as a whole.

Students played the game on 5th Generation iPod Touch mini tablets that were supplied by the project. They did not play during class time; instead, the game was played outside class at home before and after school, and in some instances, during school breaks, to replicate as far as possible the out-of-school experience of leisure-time gameplay. A night-time curfew between 11 pm and 6 am was established to manage potential problems and interruption to daily routines. In each turn of play, students were faced with a strictly limited number of interactions with game mechanics, within the constructs, rules and methods designed for interaction within the game. For example, players could trade resources with other players/factions (one interaction) or train a villager for defence purposes (one interaction) in each turn. Once the allocated interactions were exhausted, players had to wait 30 minutes for another round of play.

The progressive introduction of unknown events and challenges encouraged students to move away from heavy reliance on gameplay mechanics to take up

FIGURES 4.1 AND 4.2 Splash page and screen shot of gameplay in *Statecraft X*.
Source: Nanyang Technological University.

more collaborative interactions to optimise outcomes. For many, a balanced approach to gameplay was quickly identified as necessary for survival. Those players who attempted to play the game around a specific element of game mechanics (e.g. building armies or attacking villages) were subsequently less able to respond to unplanned challenges. Inter-player military aggression was possible and experimented with by a few players. However, in the main, domestic concerns and external threats appeared to limit this aspect of gameplay. The game closed with successful resistance of the long-anticipated attack from Salfreda, a neighbouring kingdom, and, in this instance, the declaration of Griffin faction as the new ruler of Velar. Elsewhere, one of us has explored these students' use of multimodal literacies and twenty-first-century skills as they played *Statecraft X* (Beavis 2015). In this chapter, we focus on pedagogical transformation and identity performance through gameplay.

Impression Management and Identity Performance

Goffman (1967) has argued that identity is enacted or performed by individuals to impress, manage or shape how their actions are read or interpreted by others. We use this notion of performance to consider how the teacher and his students used their identity work to negotiate gameplay activities in *Statecraft X*, while simultaneously managing the rules of conduct implicit to their classroom identity. The implication here is that interactions with classmates (including anecdotal stories of experience) establish a set of expectations and rules of conduct for each individual and each faction. That is, what students see and hear in the classroom shapes and defines the actions and practices they expect from their teacher and other students. For example, a student who is successful with gameplay at home might be expected to perform well in classroom gaming situations. In contrast, a student who shows little or no interest in digital games at home might be expected to perform poorly in games-based learning contexts. A teacher who always uses chalk-and-talk methods to introduce new topics will be expected to continue to do so. It is argued that these ideas or expectations have the potential to shape and guide interactions between the teacher and students regardless of whether or not they replicate actual everyday occurrences. At the same time, because games such as *Statecraft X* mandate new ways of defining and performing teacher and student identities (Chee *et al.* 2010; Chee 2013, 2015), gameplay has the potential to shift or disrupt identity performances in the classroom. Lasky (2005) suggested that critical to negotiating a new performance is an open willingness to take risks, experience loss and reconstitute understandings and expectations for learning. Such transitions are likely to require considerable personal adjustment and, as pointed out by Akkerman and Bakker (2011), shared understandings and common goals regarding the activity. However, they argue that the ways in which new and productive identities are constructed under conditions of learning have much to do with the efficacy with which individuals embrace change. We argue that this process not only involves strategies for managing impressions, but also questions both the rules of conduct for 'proper' learning (Goffman 1967) and the specific subject positions (Albrechtslund 2008) that define and shape what it means to be a teacher or student in the games-based classroom.

To apply these ideas, we suggest that part of the gameplay process involves manufacturing impressions specific to classroom positions associated with particular levels of achievement, ability or motivation such as expert gamer, inexperienced gamer, winner, loser, non-competitive person and so forth. By deploying actions and practices associated with these particular identities or positions, students manage and shape their social presence. In the case of the *Statecraft X* classroom, following the rules for appropriate classroom conduct (e.g. being a 'good' student) facilitated a willingness to learn and experiment, build trust with peers and encourage collaboration in gameplay. These practices helped individuals to fit in and be proactive members of their faction. However, individuals who did not accept or identify with the mandates and obligations that shaped *Statecraft X* gameplay were less likely to generate positive gaming outcomes. Shifts in the rules of conduct (e.g. moving from independent seatwork to games-based teamwork) and fluctuating states of being (e.g. moving from a position of academic excellence to that of inexperienced gamer) seem to act as critical prompts for negotiating interactions and managing identity (Goffman 1967; Lasky 2005; Akkerman and Bakker 2011). Understanding how pre-existing relationships, normative rules for classroom conduct and established identity positions influence teacher and student interaction has significance for considering how gameplay can enhance student learning of complex concepts such as citizenship and governance.

Playing *Statecraft X*

Data drawn on for this chapter included classroom observation notes and recordings, student focus-group interviews, teacher interviews and the teacher's project blog. The actual words, text accounts, and actions and practices of the teacher and students were analysed in relation to thematic units concerned with impression management practice and identity performance. A cyclic process of interpretation (Asvoll 2014) highlighted the interrelationship between content learning (i.e. citizenship and governance), gameplay, impression management and identity performance.

Both the students and the teacher felt that students had gained deeper insight into the issues of citizenship and governance than they might under different pedagogical conditions. In the main, students described the *Statecraft X* activity as a better option for learning about such issues. Playing the game was more fun and engaging than 'just reading from a textbook' or 'writing down words'. The five qualities they valued most were:

1. being involved and controlling outcomes;
2. strategising, manoeuvring and negotiating;
3. discussing and sharing ideas alongside friends;
4. discovering things through first-hand experience;
5. learning about technology.

Clay, for example, found that the game gave him a sense of control:

> It gives you sort of, like, control over your own learning and it's really fun to do instead of just listening to a teacher tell you, you know, what makes a good society, what you should do, what you shouldn't do, you can discover for yourself.

Students identified several citizenship skills and capacities which they felt that *Statecraft X* enhanced. These included acting responsibly, working as a team, building rapport and managing opportunities to maximise outcomes. Some students explained how these understandings influenced their interactions with classmates outside the game itself. For example, Anna found it valuable that:

> you could interact with all the other people in your class … you can talk about it at lunch, you know, what you should do, what you shouldn't do … you could actually outside of the game try and win people's affection so that they could give you resources and all that if you needed it.

Other capacities called upon through gameplay involved dealing with uncertainty and disappointment, managing personal disposition and controlling emotions, decision-making and problem-solving skills and the recognition that personal actions are value-laden and consequential for others. For Jim, the game pushed him to make hard decisions about others' well-being:

> There are some hard decisions in the game. I don't know. There's, for example, a sick kid and I have to decide whether to treat him, but the medicine costs heaps of money to treat him and I don't know … yeah and then … then other people with medical problems that aren't as big as his and it costs less money to treat, so I'm just, like, who am I going to have to treat – lots of people or just one sick kid? So I'm going to feel bad for the sick kid, but I have to do that.

Another boy, David, described how *Statecraft X* had helped him to understand the complex process of managing people and making decisions about their lives:

> You learn how hard it is. So normally you'd just be, like, all these problems and carrying on with this, and then you'd be, like, wow, that must really

suck for those people. But when you're a person in the town, you're, like, wow, what am I going to do? I've got all these people's lives in my hands, how am I supposed to take care of them? It's stressful, but yeah, it teaches us how hard it really is and instead of just saying these problems are occurring and such and such, you actually get to think of different ways to fix them and different ways to handle them.

Students nominated a number of areas where *Statecraft X* supported their learning about governance specifically. These included managing defences and building armies, understanding taxation, building and developing resources, understanding trade practices, understanding cost–ratio benefits, managing population size, dealing with multicultural expansion and understanding power relations. Experiencing these actions first-hand was important, even though several students found the learning curve quite challenging. For example, dealing with power relations was described as hard: 'it's harder having the capital city because everyone is out to get you, you've got to try and warn more people with all the diseases and such and such', said one student. Another described resource management as difficult: 'it was a lot harder to keep everyone in my town happy; I had other responsibilities because I was the only person in our faction that began with wood'. While a small number of students limited their actions to building armies to take over the capital, many agreed that through gameplay they came to understand what makes a good society. Kylie summarised it this way:

I think that you learn what it takes to control a society – it's a lot of work, you know, you have to control the people and you have to build up the forces, and you have to make sure that your city doesn't get over taken by other cities, and it's ... it's really crazy, but ... it's also a really fun game that keeps you thinking while you're playing.

The teacher's observations about the benefits of *Statecraft X* for teaching citizenship and governance paralleled student comments. He, too, felt that the outcomes were positive and that student performance had improved over previous offerings of the course. Students had approached assessment tasks related to these curricular elements with more detailed communication and insight than in previous years. Moreover, the dialogic engagement involved in *Statecraft X* provided students with a better conceptual awareness of 'why a state employs things like healthcare systems and educational systems'. He concluded, 'I really do think the discussions that came from the game enabled them to see that in a much more conceptual light'. Drawing discussion topics from the game's narrative provided a stimulus for encouraging students to be more expressive and communicative in classroom activities. In particular, he noted shifts in classroom interaction. Students who often sat back in class became more involved, and this shift in participation resulted in a wider range of detailed communication and insight into issues of citizenship and governance: 'Students were actually talking about processes and systems.' Beyond talking about content knowledge, he also noted that they were more self-directed, confident and expressive in their written work. He explained:

> It enabled kids, particularly with their writing, to really expand on points and they became much more confident about writing about abstract concepts than if you'd just given them a question and explained it in class. Because they'd experience it and they knew what they were talking about.

Although classroom discussion 'petered off towards the end', on the whole, he concluded that the experiential quality and activities of *Statecraft X* had provided students with many opportunities to expand their understandings of citizenship and governance: 'I was very impressed with the way the kids could draw on the game experience and compare and contrast them against systems within the state and the country.'

Negotiating Pedagogical Renewal

Deviating from tried-and-tested teaching practices to negotiate games-based learning was described by the teacher as both challenging and enlightening. He shared his early thoughts:

> I was very sceptical at the start of the project [laughs]. I suppose that's something that you're going to get a lot of. I wasn't sure how I was going to be able to make it work within my classroom. I wasn't sure if the [activity] was going to work. I didn't know what the kids were going to get out of it. It was just the whole cloud of unsureness that did make me uneasy about starting the project. But once you've moved through that first phase of uneasiness, you can actually really see that you do lose control, but the benefits of that outweigh the negatives.

Concerns about meeting educational responsibilities and curricular demands while engaging student interest sat at the forefront of early discussions. He was concerned about how to access students' gaming experiences to help them make sense of curricular content and, more importantly, how to produce a meaningful tool for collecting student thoughts to assess content learning. Worry about being a game technician rather than a teacher of content was also a concern. Retrospectively, he described the biggest challenge as 'just letting go':

> I am used to preparing my lessons, knowing what my lesson objectives are, and creating up my series of questions to stimulate the discussion ... What this game forced me to do was become much more reactive to classrooms ... and let them unfold the way the kids wanted them to unfold and just

> sort of … be much more gentle on the steering wheel … as opposed to, you know, trying to drive a truck, I suppose.

As the unit unfolded, initial scepticism and worries about games-based learning were replaced by high levels of personal satisfaction and pedagogical renewal. He became more comfortable about letting go. He described six significant ways in which the *Statecraft X* unit advanced his practice and renewed his pedagogy. These comprised:

1. improved lesson-planning skills;
2. becoming more realistic about lesson objectives;
3. improved questioning technique;
4. developing better insight into student interaction;
5. developing strengths in group-work practice;
6. expanding strategies for teaching complex concepts.

He summarised his experience by saying:

> The number one thing I took away from it and I would encourage other teachers to do is, you know, let go of the control that you think you might have over the classroom, and let the kids explore the knowledge that they can get from these types of instruments in the ways that they want to explore it … and then become more … much more flexible … It is harder, but you get more out of it.

Like the teacher, some students expressed early concerns about the use of *Statecraft X* for learning about citizenship and governance. Several expected the teamwork needed to successfully progress through the game to be challenging. These students claimed that they did not like working with other people because they were not good communicators: 'Teamwork is going to be hard.' At the same time, several other students said that working together and controlling the lives of the villagers was something they looked forward to. There were plenty of opportunities to learn and 'think things through'. Even though some students felt that they were left to make decisions on their own a bit too much, each team easily identified aspects of class discussions that acted as stimulus for gameplay. Maria, for example, clearly linked her motivation for budgeting team money to classroom discussions about managing economies:

> Well, Mr M said that we only started with a certain amount of money, so what immediately popped into my head was if we run out of money, all our people are going to die. So we had to find a system that would enable us to build houses and healing centres, but not lose all our money. So I got

a book and put all the names down, what they were spending, who had an army so other people didn't have to get one, so we'd budget.

While students offered some recommendations about how *Statecraft X* as a game could be made more exciting (e.g. add more functions and roles as the game progresses to keep it interesting), most students described gameplay as 'better than normal work' and a process that 'really engages your brain'. It 'enabled you', 'kept you thinking' and 'got you talking about social diversity and how to build trust'. 'You've done it firsthand, you've run a town. It's not like you've just listened to someone telling you about what it's like, you've actually done it'. On the whole, student comments strongly suggested that the *Statecraft X* experience and teacher-facilitated lessons enhanced their understanding of citizenship and governance. On the other hand, the pedagogical opportunities offered by *Statecraft X* also emphasised competing frames concerned with gameplay, impression management and identity performance.

Gameplay, Impression Management and Identity Performance

As discussed earlier, students were divided into four groups, or factions, called Dragons, Griffin, Phoenix and Pegasus. While students did not choose their own group, they did have some freedom to choose their own in-game character. Although character attributes were limited to gender and race, the game did give students some control over their avatar's identity (see Figures 4.3 and 4.4, Choose your own character). However, in the main, students constructed their in-game identity by assuming particular roles (e.g. prime minister or financial controller) and taking up certain gameplay actions (e.g. defence practices and resource development). These attributes often paralleled discourses concerned with good citizenship such as being supportive, building trust and acting responsibly. By taking up these positive attributes, teamwork was strengthened and overall outcomes improved. In some instances, however, gameplay actions did not coincide with conventional notions of smooth governance. Gameplay of this kind was often self-driven and frequently disruptive to the progress and well-being of both faction and game. For example, Chan, one of the most experienced and competitive gamers in the class, and a member of the Dragons faction, lived up to his reputation as an expert gamer by building armies so fast and efficiently that he wiped out many opposing villages before the other factions could build their defences. While Chan's expertise was not unexpected, his focus on conquering neighbouring territories (as one student said, 'he went very Rambo in the game') shifted the agenda of play away from strict adherence to the governing roles inherent to the game. Instead, positions experienced in students' previous classroom interactions outside the game emerged. For instance, when Chan attacked and ransacked one of the Pegasus villages, team members of the Pegasus faction became disillusioned. They did not respond with strategic or

FIGURES 4.3 AND 4.4 Choose your own character.
Source: Nanyang Technological University.

disciplined action. Members progressively lost interest in the game and, in the end, they all stopped playing. The performance of the Pegasus faction was closely aligned to their self-described identity as non-competitive individuals. In contrast, the Griffin faction embraced the challenges of gameplay. They systematically and strategically planned manoeuvres to block the attacks by Chan and his team. They relied on their strong friendship ties to help them establish trust and strengthen communication practices. Self-described as 'good communicators' and a group who 'always win', they worked together to overcome the challenge of controlling the capital and defending against Chan and his faction, the Dragons.

While student comments strongly suggested that gameplay in *Statecraft X* was influenced by roles and positions inherent to good citizenship and governance, each faction appeared nonetheless to develop its own 'modus operandi' for gameplay (Goffman 1967) which characterised and influenced their performance.

Group Performance

An analysis of the interactions within the four factions (see Table 4.1, Summary of the attributes and practices of the factions) showed that each group had a loosely defined set of practices and expectations which guided gameplay and shaped their group performance. The efficacy of group performance clearly determined the degree to which citizenship and governance were understood and enacted during gameplay. Factions that were internally cooperative, communicative and organised were also more strategic and systematic. Clear plans, strong teamwork and cooperation provided greater opportunity for experiential learning and skill development. Two groups, Griffin and Phoenix, exhibited these co-constructive practices. They also generated a degree of autonomy from dependence on teacher directives and were clearly able to direct and become involved in their own learning.

In contrast, the Dragons took up a more competitive individualistic approach. This approach set up internal priorities (e.g. building armies to debilitate other factions) that conflicted with the more engaging collaborative approach of Griffin

TABLE 4.1 Summary of the attributes and practices of the factions

Faction	Attributes and practice
 Dragons	• competitive experienced gamers outside school • members were often grouped together for class activities • self-described as 'best group ever' • individual roles emerged through the natural process of gameplay rather than through strategic planning • communication and planning between members were limited (e.g. 'we spoke a little bit but not much') • the main aim was to 'pretty much take over the capital' • individual members expressed frustration over various aspects of gameplay (e.g. 'I hated when I had my army there and I went to dinner and when I got back all my army was dead') • reliance on one member's defence capabilities appeared to cloud their efforts for balanced teamwork and healthy governance of their faction • dissatisfaction and annoyance expressed at loss to the Griffin faction ('they were like, hard core')
 Griffin	• mixed experience with digital games outside school • good friends inside and outside class • self-described as 'good communicators' • confident in their ability to play the game successfully (e.g. 'we always win') • demonstrated strong teamwork characterised by systematic, strategic and goal-oriented gameplay (e.g., strategic manoeuvres included staying up late and playing the game when others were finished or in 'cool down') • enjoyed the unexpected surprises of gameplay, overcoming things, and finishing challenges • agreed that discussing issues in class and strong teamwork helped them to understand governance better and ultimately win the game
 Phoenix	• mixed experience with digital games outside school • described as responsible team players who often worked together • struggled early on to sustain faction until roles became more clearly defined and teamwork was established • showed awareness of individual responsibility, fair management, and team support, but found communication hard work when difficult situations emerged • members struggled to fight against other factions' defence practices • they concluded that 'the military was a compulsory item in the success of your town'; 'the military was your bait, your stick to hit everyone, you either won or lost by your military' • with the aim of preventing Griffin from winning, they formed a loose alliance with the Dragons; this tactic was unsuccessful
 Pegasus	• experience with playing digital games and working as a group was less clear • self-described as 'non-competitive' • members shared a somewhat laissez-faire orientation towards role allocation and task division • interest in game quickly faded when events became challenging • resourcing wood was the main activity undertaken but they did not follow any basic principles or enlist any strategies to successfully trade resources or manage defences • the faction was not strategic or disciplined in their gameplay and towards the end, all members stopped playing and inevitably they came last

Source: Nanyang Technological University.

and Phoenix. A focus on independent priorities seemed to challenge or interrupt group capacity for conversation, sharing ideas, planning strategies and building group rapport and trust. This rigid and competitive approach seemed to cloud their ability to balance the teamwork needed to be successful at the game. While the Dragons proclaimed themselves to be 'the best team ever', they acknowledged that the 'hard core' practices of Griffin helped that team to take over the capital. At the same time, a certain degree of competitiveness seemed to be essential for progressing through *Statecraft X* gameplay. Both Griffin and Phoenix acknowledged the importance of taking up challenges in a fairly assertive or defensive way. The least successful faction, Pegasus, agreed that they were not as competitive as the other groups. They had a somewhat laissez-faire attitude towards events as they unfolded. By their own admission, they were not strategic or disciplined in their actions and, inevitably, the faction came last.

On the whole, the ways in which the factions performed or played the game together demonstrated the effects of pre-existing relationships and experiences, rituals of everyday practice and codes of conduct in influencing outcomes and opportunities for learning in this games-based context. While some students were clearly able to generate a cooperative relationship that was conducive to co-constructing learning, others struggled with the interdependence required for successful teamwork. In light of these findings, it seems reasonable to suggest that the opportunities for pedagogical renewal provided by *Statecraft X* operated in tandem with the interpersonal relationships, impression management practices and identity positions taken up by game players. That is, their gameplay appeared to operate within a specific frame of experience bounded by pre-existing expectations, routines and rules of conduct that were articulated through individual and group participation. Group interaction emerged as a significant component of this games-based teaching and learning. This suggests that impression management and identity performance offer useful theoretical devices for coming to understand how teachers and students interact and engage with new pedagogical resources such as the game *Statecraft X*.

Conclusions

On the whole, both the teacher and his students agreed that games-based learning offered a useful and effective resource and approach for learning complex concepts such as citizenship and governance. Students enthusiastically supported the use of digital games over 'just reading from a textbook' or 'writing down words'. The teacher concluded that the experiential quality and activities of *Statecraft X* provided students with many opportunities to improve their understanding of citizenship education.

The example of *Statecraft X* also highlighted the ways in which games-based pedagogy can ratify transformative tensions around pedagogical practices. The teacher described some aspects of implementing *Statecraft X* as challenging, but he also acknowledged the positive ways in which he felt his teaching had been transformed. In particular, he said that the experience had helped him to overcome the limitations of more prescriptive methods of teaching complex concepts (e.g. direct teaching). The introduction of *Statecraft X* provided him with opportunities to broaden his lesson planning, to become more realistic about lesson objectives, and to take up activities that transformed his professional thinking. Overall, he was very much encouraged by the ways in which the students were more conceptually aware and expressive in their classroom work concerned with citizenship and governance.

Both the teacher and his students highlighted the value of their games-based experience with *Statecraft X* in learning about this area of the curriculum. In addition, they pointed to other aspects of gameplay and classroom interaction that were relevant to how both teacher and students interacted with and engaged in impression management and identity performance. Individual, group and teacher identities played out in the ways they each performed the roles and took up the actions dictated by gameplay to achieve the aims of the game. The students appeared to perform their in-game role and their group identity through the lens of expectations, routines and rules of conduct constructed from subjective patterns of previous experience (e.g. expert gamer or always winning). While some students were able to negotiate these boundaries effectively (e.g. 'I'm sitting there like I'm going to be terrible at this game … then we were first … I'm okay'), other students' gameplay was restricted by either their own performance (e.g. 'I don't like working with other people') or the performance of others (e.g. 'he didn't really do anything'). These experiences highlighted how 'the expressive and communicative properties of students' identity construction' (Chee 2011, p. 117) and the obligations, expectations and rules of conduct central to locally developed curricular demands influenced the ebbs and flows of games-based pedagogy in the everyday classroom. For the teacher and his students, this games-based unit enabled them to explore new approaches to teaching and learning and to develop deeper curricular understandings through the interpersonal dynamics and everyday roles and experiences that shape the everyday classroom.

References

Akkerman, S F and Bakker, A (2011), 'Boundary crossing and boundary objects', *Review of Educational Research*, vol. 81, no. 2, pp. 132–169.

Albrechtslund, A (2008), 'Online social networking as participatory surveillance', *First Monday*, vol. 13, no. 3. Available from: http://journals.uic.edu/ojs/index.php/fm/article/view/2142/1949 (Accessed 8 April 2016).

Asvoll, H (2014), 'Abduction, deduction and induction: Can these concepts be used for an understanding of methodological processes in interpretative case studies?', *International Journal of Qualitative Studies in Education,* vol. 27, no. 3, pp. 289–307.

Beavis, C (2015), 'Multimodal literacy, digital games and curriculum', in T Lowrie and R Jorgensen (eds), *Digital games and mathematics learning: Potential, promises and pitfalls*, Dordrecht, The Netherlands: Springer, pp. 109–122.

Chee, Y S (2010), *Statecraft X*. Available from: http://cheeyamsan.info/NIEprojects/SCX/SCX2.htm (Accessed 8 August 2016).

Chee, Y S (2011), 'Learning as becoming through performance, play, and dialog: A model of game-based learning with the game Legends of Alkhimia', *Digital Culture & Education*, vol. 3, no. 2, pp. 98–122.

Chee, Y S (2013), 'Video games for "deep learning": Game-based learning as performance in the Statecraft X curriculum', in C B Lee and D H Jonassen (eds), *Fostering conceptual change with technology: Asian perspectives*, Singapore: Cengage Learning, pp. 199–224.

Chee, Y S (2015), *Games-to-teach or games-to-learn? Unlocking the power of digital game-based learning through performance*, Singapore: Springer.

Chee, Y S, Tan, E M and Lui, Q (2010), 'Statecraft X: Enacting citizenship education using a mobile learning game played on Apple iPhones', in *WMUTE 2010: The 6th IEEE International Conference on Wireless, Mobile and Ubiquitous Technologies in Education*, 12–16 April, , pp. 222–224. Available from: doi:10.1109/WMUTE.2010.16 (Accessed 8 April 2016).

Goffman, E (1959), *The presentation of self in everyday life*, London: Penguin Books.

Goffman, E (1967), *Interaction ritual: Essays on face-to-face behaviour*, Ringwood, Victoria, Australia: Penguin Books Australia.

Lasky, S (2005), 'A sociocultural approach to understanding teacher identity, agency, and professional vulnerability in a context of secondary school reform', *Teaching and Teacher Education*, vol. 21, no. 8, pp. 899–916.

5

CURATING THE CURRICULUM WITH DIGITAL GAMES

Michael Dezuanni and Jason Zagami

Introduction

This chapter introduces curatorship as a concept to explore how teachers in the Serious Play project deployed digital games to assemble curriculum experiences for students. In this chapter, we argue that curatorship may help us understand how teachers use games in the curriculum design process to provide students with learning pathways. Curatorship has come into focus because digital media provide new ways of selecting and making content and circulating it to others (Hogan 2010), and the concept has been applied as a pedagogical tool in media education research in digital contexts (Andrews and McDougall 2012; Potter 2012; Mihailidis and Cohen 2013). Historically, centralised broadcasters and publishers have controlled the circulation of media and educational resources for use in the classroom, including television programs, films, documentaries, textbooks and software. Today, however, a multitude of rich educational content can be accessed, produced and shared by anyone with computer access. Teachers have the ability to choose from a multitude of digital resources, including digital games, to enhance their students' learning experiences and this includes repurposing digital games for educational outcomes. For this reason, we believe curatorship has classroom implications well beyond media studies and provides a productive framework for thinking about the use of digital games across the curriculum.

Drawing on Serious Play project data, we consider how games were used in the English, Science, Studies of Society and Environment, and Religious Education curriculum areas. We explore examples of the use of digital games in specific curriculum experiences, including *Angry Birds* (Rovio Entertainment 2010) and *Cut the Rope* (ZeptoLab 2010) in primary school Science; *Minecraft* (Mojang 2011) in primary school English; the 'educational' game *Statecraft X*

(Chee 2010) in Studies of Society and Environment; and the classic 1980s game *Secret Agent: Mission One* (Kolbe 1988) in Religious Education. The chapter draws on classroom observation, student and teacher interviews and student work samples. We argue that it is important to recognise the consequences of curriculum curatorship with digital games when classroom and pedagogic practices change gameplay in unintended or unexpected ways. Introducing digital games into the formal classroom setting presents both opportunities and challenges for fostering student learning. Gameplay inevitably differs in the contexts of home and school, and educators should recognise that students may respond to games variously in these different contexts. Curriculum curatorship is not, therefore, an innocent or trouble-free process, and the success of learning experiences created through curating digital games into the curriculum depends on teacher expertise and the knowledge teachers have of their students' learning needs.

Curating the Curriculum in Digital Contexts

Curatorship is a useful way to think about teachers' expert coordination of various classroom resources to provide curriculum-aligned learning experiences. Bigum (2014, p. 4) has suggested that 'curation' can be adapted from the Galleries, Libraries, Art Galleries and Museums (GLAM) sector to help us understand how disparate objects, texts, resources, concepts and people are brought together to provide individuals with new perspectives or experiences to assemble knowledge. According to Bigum (2014), within digital culture, resource scarcity has been replaced by a plethora of content available to educators to help their students develop expertise in specific knowledge fields. Like GLAM sector curators, teachers expertly draw together physical objects and spaces, print texts, conceptual resources, still and moving images, interaction and learners to mobilise knowledge production. With a focus on young people's media literacies, Potter (2012, p. xv) argued that curatorship is a 'useful metaphor to describe an emergent literacy practice in new media production'. He suggested that individuals:

> have access to digital artifacts at their fingertips [and] have the means to take and remix content, to publish things that they have made alongside things they have created and establish new relationships between the elements to make new meanings.
>
> *(Potter 2012, p. xvi)*

Potter (2012) suggested that young people's everyday lived practices within digital culture may be understood as curatorship, leading to complex meaning-making processes deeply connected to identity performance. He argued that curatorship is more complex than authorship, because it is 'a form of metaauthorship, understanding the relationship between texts of all kinds: moving image, still images, print and more' (Potter 2012, p. xvi). For Potter, curatorship includes combining digital culture elements through arranging and assembling so that elements come to be in dialogue with one another (p. 163). While Potter focuses primarily on young people's digital culture practices, we believe it is also important to understand teachers' use of digital culture elements, brought into dialogue with each other, digital experiences and non-digital artefacts to assemble 'the classroom' as a learning space.

Teacher curators arrange and assemble, classify and juxtapose within socially and technologically situated time, space and relationships. Time is a factor because learning episodes in schools are segmented and temporally controlled. Space is central because classrooms (physical and digital) are arranged in various ways to coordinate interaction between individuals and objects of various kinds in the room. Relationships between individuals, objects and experiences are central to socially situated knowledge production. For instance, Bigum (2014, p. 4) argued that effective classrooms operating in digital contexts enable students to become curators of each other's experiences, in support of the teacher as expert curator.

Teacher curatorship has become more visible in digital culture as teachers combine 'found' resources from across the internet to construct learning opportunities for their students. This is made possible due to the availability of digital technologies in the classroom. In the classrooms we visited for the Serious Play project, all the teachers had access to a laptop computer and digital projector, and the students had regular access to digital technologies in the form of laptop computers, handheld devices or desktop computers. As a result, teachers regularly arranged for students to interact with a range of digital materials as part of their learning. But the successful use of digital technologies and the contexts they make available relies on far more than mere access, as we found throughout the Serious Play project. Curatorship requires expert epistemic practice to mobilise the production of knowledge in meaningful ways. Teacher expertise includes the ability to make judgments about when and how it is appropriate to provide students with new opportunities to produce knowledge. Teachers possess deep disciplinary knowledge that allows them to effectively curate the curriculum (Bigum 2014). Successful curatorship requires an ability to provide students with pedagogical experiences, including direct instruction, facilitated instruction, individual and group tasks, challenges, problem solving, research opportunities, simulations and creative responses. Introducing digital games to provide these kinds of pedagogical opportunities has consequences for how students both produce knowledge and experience gameplay. Furthermore, digital games present their own internal logics that invite individuals to play and produce knowledge in particular ways. When digital games are reappropriated for classroom use, this internal logic is inherently challenged, for better or worse. When a teacher introduces a digital game into their students' overall learning experience, he or she chooses to change the way the game is usually played, and this has consequences for the player's experience of the game and the kind of 'dialogues' that may be established as knowledge is assembled within disciplinary fields.

Investigating Curatorship in the Serious Play Project

In the following examples, we draw on observational, interview and student artefact data in three schools. The first two examples come from a private girls' primary school in a middle-class Brisbane community. In the Year 3 classroom in this school, the students undertook a range of activities across the curriculum with the popular game *Minecraft*. While playing the game, the students were asked to complete English curriculum activities in their writing books, including descriptive reports about their gameplay, reflections on their own learning in the game, and planning for a collaborative design task. Several student workbooks have been analysed to provide insights into teacher-curated learning with and around *Minecraft*. In addition, interviews with the teacher and students are discussed. The second example from the same girls' school comes from a combined Year 4/5 class in which students were learning about physics concepts like gravity, resistance, force and friction. As a knowledge-enhancement activity, the teacher introduced a range of iPad games with underlying physics properties such as *Angry Birds*, *Cut the Rope* and *Feed Me Oil* (Chillingo Ltd 2011). The students analysed these games, captured still images from the games, and then imported these into an eBook app called *Book Creator* (Red Jumper 2011), where they added explanations of the physics concepts they had identified in the games. The third example discusses the use of the game *Statecraft X*, which was specifically designed for civics education. A Year 8 class at a public secondary school located on Queensland's Gold Coast used this multiplayer game to learn social studies concepts, as discussed in Chapter 4. The final example of curation discusses a teacher's use of the game *Secret Agent: Mission One* in a Year 9 Religious Education class at a private boys' school. The students discussed the ethical choices required by the game and then went on to design their own games to curate a similar experience for other young people.

Curating English Curriculum in Year 3, Using *Minecraft*

The teacher of a Year 3 class in an all-girls' school chose to introduce the popular game *Minecraft*, initially as a way to engage the students with writing for English curriculum; she later went on to use the game as an aspect of design and mathematics curricula experiences, as discussed in Chapter 10. The use of *Minecraft* for writing stimulus is an interesting example of curriculum curatorship because it makes explicit the construction of an intentionally arranged dialogue between the students, the digital game and the development of written composition knowledge and skill. The teacher set a series of writing tasks in response to classroom *Minecraft* play, and the students were required to keep a dedicated writing journal to complete these tasks. The students practised neat handwriting, correct spelling, punctuation and grammar, and aimed to extend their vocabulary as they wrote about their play sessions. This was a decidedly non-digital response to a highly digital experience, with specific curriculum objectives about formal writing and the development of pencil grip and physical writing taking precedence over a digital response. The students could just as easily have written their responses on their individually allocated laptop computers, but the teacher's goal was to develop physical writing skills using digital gameplay as a means to stimulate a response. The students' writing was scaffolded because they were provided with specific topics to discuss. For instance, Figure 5.1 provides the opening response from one student's diary in which she responds to her feelings about playing *Minecraft* at school, following the first play session.

The students' written artefacts also became the site of intervention from the teacher because she provided corrections with red pen and affirmations in the form of 'ticks' and initialling. In this sense, then, the students' overall learning experience traversed conventional literacy learning and innovative digital games' use.

The teacher expertly combined several elements to develop this learning experience for the students. She made a judgment about the students' interest in a

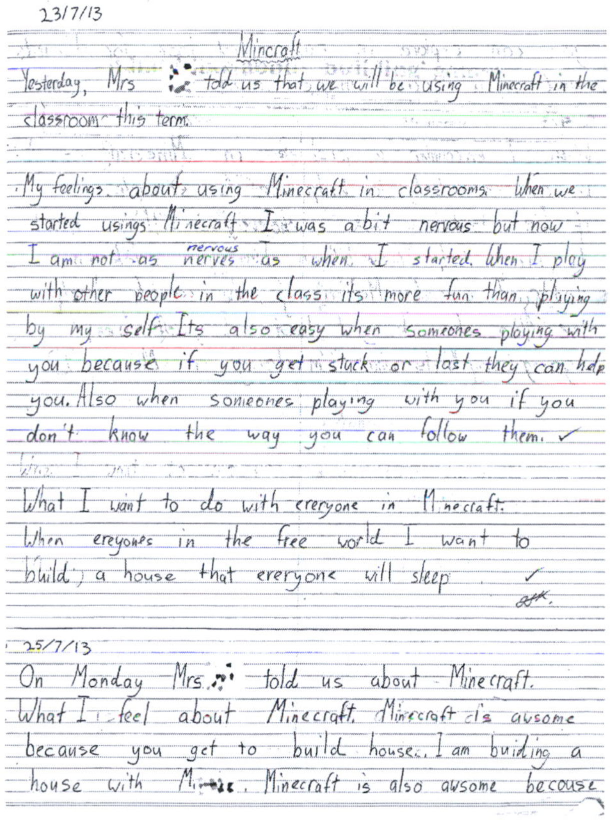

FIGURE 5.1 Student *Minecraft* writing sample.

highly popular digital game, which she knew many of her students were playing at home, due to classroom and playground discussion about the game. A digital resource was made available to the students in the form of laptop computers, which the students were familiar with using for classroom tasks, but which had rarely been used for gameplay. The teacher arranged for the educational version of *Minecraft* to be installed on the school system to enable the students to play the game in a safe multiplayer environment, which allowed the girls to use the game in ways that most had not previously experienced at home. Finally, the teacher brought her expert knowledge of teaching English as part of the Australian Curriculum to bear on the arrangement and set particular tasks for the students to complete in a highly directed way in their workbooks. This overall arrangement is a highly sophisticated example of curatorship in which a multiplayer digital game becomes central to very traditional written literacy development. The teacher made numerous decisions about her students' learning needs and the series of mediations and dialogues in which she would involve them, in order to assemble new knowledge. In addition, she took a risk because she was not an experienced *Minecraft* player, and she relied on her students' knowledge of the game and their ability to teach each other as a significant component of the experience. This combination of elements was highly successful in the teacher's view, especially for students who often struggled with more standard classroom approaches:

> [I]t was those girls who didn't experience a lot of the traditional book-based success that did better at *Minecraft*, because it was just – they thought it was fun … Whereas the girls that were the better students felt a bit uneasy, like, hang on, this is not really work. This is play. They had no way – they're used to getting best mark in the class or something to measure their success. This was an unfamiliar thing for them – how do I measure my success when I'm in *Minecraft*? So I liked the way that they were unsure. They still came around to it, but it just gave those who were less successful traditionally to have that feeling of what it feels like [to succeed]. Once you've got that feeling, you know you can do it and, yeah, you can keep up the momentum.

The arrangement of elements in this curated experience and the ways in which it invites learning raise some important questions about the use of digital games in the classroom. The student's written response (Figure 5.1) indicates that she was concerned about the introduction of *Minecraft* into the classroom, but this gives way to relief when she is able to rely on her classmates to assist her in the game. As the teacher indicates, *Minecraft* disrupted the usual flow of the classroom experience and the order of expectation about achievement and classroom status. This would seem to be a positive development, especially for those students who are often failed by traditional pedagogies. And yet, the need for students to respond in a very traditional way during the initial phases of the use of *Minecraft* in this classroom, through bookwork assessed against formal conventions, points to an inherent tension when digital games and the formal curriculum are brought into dialogue with each other. In this sense, curriculum curatorship involving digital games requires deft balancing of disciplinary normativity and preparation for assessment with a desire to engage students in meaningful, fun and challenging learning experiences. As the teacher of this class argued:

> I've got nothing against assessment and monitoring growth. I mean absolutely, that's the core of what we do, but this constantly bringing it back to the old ways of, you're an A, B, C or a D. I think we're killing – you know we, on one hand, we're saying, Oh look at this, I'll let you play with that, you can use this. Then we still say, Oh but you didn't cut the mustard here. I've got to give you a C or a D or whatever. I just think that the fact that there's this conflict and I think that's a really big issue.

Curriculum curatorship is not therefore a benign process of arranging activities, but rather involves judgments about students' individual learning needs and the requirements of governmental processes.

Curating Physics Experiences With Digital Games for Year 4/5 Science

The second example of curriculum curatorship with digital games that we wish to discuss in this chapter also comes from the all-girls' school, but this time from a Year 4/5 combined class. In this case, the teacher worked with a member of the Serious Play research team to introduce iPad games to consolidate his students' knowledge about physics concepts such as motion and forces. The students had already spent several weeks learning about these concepts in a relatively conventional manner, and the teacher wanted to provide an opportunity for the students to assemble the same knowledge in a different way. Over the course of four classes, the students initially experimented with 'found' physical objects to make games to test various aspects of force and motion (Figure 5.2). The students were required to develop rules for their games and the students then played each other's games. Next, the students worked in small groups to play the iPad games *Angry Birds*, *Cut the Rope* and *Feed Me Oil*, which are all programmed to simulate realistic physical properties including gravity, velocity, resistance and force. The students were required to record screen shots of key moments in the games to illustrate specific physics concepts, which they added to a *Book Creator* app (Figure 5.3). After adding digital text to explain the physics concepts illustrated by the images, the students then plugged the iPads into the classroom projection system and presented their representations of the physics concepts to the rest of the class. In the final session, the students were able to play an iPad game called *Monster Physics* (Freecloud Design Inc. 2012) that was specifically designed to teach physics concepts.

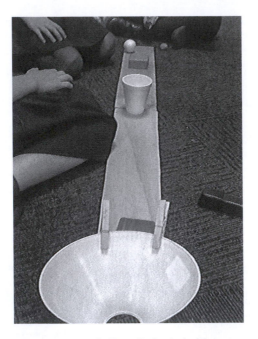

FIGURE 5.2 Students experiment with 'found' physical objects.

FIGURE 5.3 Students used the *Book Creator* app to represent physics concepts used in the digital games.

Source: Feed Me Oil image courtesy of Alexander Ilin, developer and creator, Chillingo. Cut the Rope image courtesy of ZeptoLab UK Ltd © 2010–2016.

Through these examples, the teacher curated an experience that allowed the students to experience physics concepts in three different ways: as book knowledge; as physical interaction with found objects; and as physical interaction with digital materials in the form of games as physics simulations. The games were woven into the overall flow of the students' experience of physics concepts and are brought into 'dialogue' with both abstract concepts and the physical presence of the found objects. The games were repurposed away from their primary entertainment function to act as educational resources, and the students quite literally deconstructed the games by grabbing images from key moments to write about them using disciplinary knowledge. The teacher made a series of decisions about his students' learning needs, the role of games as entertainment, the availability of iPads as a publishing platform, and the time and space available to provide his students with a rich learning experience. From the teacher's perspective, the main objective was to provide a new and engaging experience for the students.

> [T]hey don't see it as another sort of normal standard lesson. It's a bit different and a bit more engaging. I think that's the biggest thing. It just captures a little bit more excitement and interest from them. Another outlet to show their understanding, rather than the standard sort of test or a little project or a little quiz or whatever it might be.

The teacher's aim to provide his students with a non-standard classroom experience by using digital games' structures and concepts allowed the students to apply physics concepts to a familiar form, as most of the students in this class indicated that they played iPad or iPhone games at home. But more than this, they also experimented with physics concepts by playing both physical and digital games, and wrote and reflected on this. The students connected their book knowledge to real-world experiences. It was interesting to note, for instance, the similarities between the contraptions the students built with their found objects and the iPad games. In general discussion during the making of the physical games, students commented on how their game was like an iPad game, and the teacher was overheard discussing this further with the students. This kind of connectedness is crucial for what Luke (2003) has described as 'productive pedagogies' that move beyond superficial classroom experiences to create authenticity and rich learning. Curatorship drawing on expert teacher judgment is a crucial component of the provision of rich educational experiences. Despite the authenticity of the physics games experience, the teacher commented, in reflection about the students' learning, that he believed he needed to more fully integrate the games into the overall unit structure, to have them present from the beginning, so that the students did not simply experience them as an 'add on'. A significant reason for using the games at the end of the unit was because the teacher wanted to ensure that the core unit learning was achieved first, but he could see that this undermined the value of the games for learning. He suggested in a follow-up interview that time was always a factor, and that it was not always possible to provide the students with rich learning experiences.

Curating Social Capital Knowledge in Year 8 Studies of Society and Environment With *Statecraft X*

This example of curatorship outlines how a teacher in a Year 8 Studies of Society and Environment class at a large co-educational state secondary school collaborated with the Serious Play research team to use an educational game, *Statecraft X*, which is outlined in more detail in Chapter 4. *Statecraft X* was introduced into the Year 8 class to provide a rich online group gameplay environment using an iPod Touch mini tablet system. This system accessed a multiplayer server to facilitate an online social studies simulation in which students individually managed a small town as members of one of four collective factions, each vying to rule a kingdom. The first element of curation of this learning experience involved problem solving to arrange expertise, hardware, software and procedures to conduct the online multiplayer game within the school environment. This was not straightforward, and drew attention to the complexities of introducing such a game into a classroom environment, especially one that was to be played across school and home contexts. Several issues arose with loaning iPod Touch mini tablets to students in order to allow them to access the game across formal and informal learning contexts.

Classroom gameplay, particularly with devices enabling multiplayer gaming, required addressing a wide range of issues beyond the curriculum and the computer game itself. Curation of resources, expertise, access and rules of use were some of the elements that required management for school use, and many such issues were not identified or resolved prior to the provision of the devices, requiring timely management in order for successful gameplay to occur. The first challenge was hosting the game on a server accessible to both students and the research team, which was eventually made available via a researcher's home broadband account. It was also necessary to prepare 30 iPod Touch mini tablets, and each required a series of set-up responses, account creation, battery charging and the deployment of development software onto the iPods. The software could not be deployed through the online App Store because the software was still in development. In addition, internet access at the school had to be changed to open up Queensland Department of Education firewalls to an external server. Two students who did not have home internet access were provided with 3G Hotspot Modems to be able to play after school hours. Another important aspect of curation was time management. The game was shut down between 11 pm and 6 am to prevent excessive after-hours gaming. A core premise of the game design was that students would learn through immersing themselves in the game, undertaking actions and making decisions in role, to foster deep learning and enable them to experience citizenship principles and values 'from the inside'. A fundamental feature of the game design, therefore, was to replicate, as far as possible, young people's leisure-time experience of play, where play occurs anywhere, anytime, and is not constrained within the time-bound, physical and locational frameworks of the school (Chee 2013). Class time would be used to draw on issues and challenges that had arisen in the intervening periods of gameplay to deepen understandings of specific aspects of the social studies curriculum.

There was also a challenge related to the blending of the formal and informal learning environments and students' expectations of after-hours play. For instance, students did not initially realise that their in-game communications, including chat, was sent to the administrator/researcher's account. This caused the students some embarrassment as they realised that their usual informal gaming banter needed to be altered for this more formal, albeit after-hours, environment.

The second element of curation that emerged from the multiplayer game *Statecraft X* was socially oriented. The game system itself curated aspects of the experience, providing information about how to play the game, resource collection and trading and management of virtual commodities. The game's broader dynamics also played a curatorial role on a more complex level, and students found that they needed to cope with the new social structures that the game required for success. They were placed into four factions that may or may not have included members of their normal friendship groups. The game's internal logics invited a version of social capital (Hanifan 1916) which became more dynamic as game structures reallocated existing social capital, and students with gameplay experience found unexpected credibility in this new social dynamic that was different from their usual peer interactions. The ability of factions of students to build consensus on their collective gaming strategies might be seen as a positive measure of their development of social capital (Arefi 2003), forming networks of trust and reciprocity negotiated by students. Over the three weeks of gameplay, however, pre-existing social groupings seemed to reassert themselves, and many gameplay decisions were made based on friendships rather than those criteria that would benefit game factions. In some cases, students put considerable pressure on their friends to do things within the game that were not in the best interests of their faction.

This arrangement of the formal and informal presents an important challenge to educators in curating learning experiences using multiplayer games in the classroom. While a game may encourage students to take on various roles and perspectives, external forces, particularly in multiplayer games played over any length of time, may influence students out of these roles. As noted earlier, curation is not a benign process, and the mediations and dialogues that occur between digital games, teachers, students and conceptual and material resources require ongoing negotiation. Curating digital games within the formal space of the classroom necessarily changes the nature of play. Curation of social capital is an important element of multiplayer games, and young people playing multiplayer online games outside school rely on elements such as their player's name, their avatar, game scores and league tables, knowledge of the game and its rules, their ability to communicate in game chat forums, and reputation for playing the game that they build within online gaming communities. Within a school environment, such anonymous elements are combined with their relationships within their school and classroom communities. Curation of anonymous personas in online game environments is a skill developed over time by gamers, and even within single-player games, players often have the option of reframing their identity, changing its name and avatar. This is less possible in a school context, rendering anonymity less possible, with consequences for the gameplay experience.

Students playing games in school may come with skills in curation of their online gaming persona, but the less anonymous nature of classroom gameplay can present additional challenges in curating a classroom gaming persona. Classroom games can often be anonymised, but social pressures to share details between students make this difficult to sustain. Weaving the social nature of multiplayer gaming into an educational game is a challenge when the learning outcomes are dependent on particular roles and priorities. While games provide a rich Secondary World (Zagami 2014) in which students are encouraged to sustain such roles, immersing themselves in the game narrative and basing their decisions upon their in-game persona, the Primary World of their friendship groupings creates a complex dynamic for such immersion, and this needs to be incorporated into the curation of games for teaching.

Curating Ethical Dilemmas in Year 9 Religious Education with *Secret Agent: Mission One*

The final example of curation we wish to discuss presents a good example of the arrangement of a teacher's deep disciplinary knowledge with students curating the learning experience for themselves and each other (Bigum 2014, p. 4). This took place at a private boys' school, where the teacher introduced games for teaching moral values in a Religious Education course. In this example, games, ethical concepts, student knowledge and game-making software were arranged with the goal of students exploring their ethical stances and perspectives on various issues.

The teacher began the course by drawing upon a computer game he was familiar with from his youth, a text-based adventure game *Secret Agent: Mission One*. Using an online re-creation of this 1980s Apple II classic, the game presented students with a range of ethical dilemmas concerning lying, theft and murder (Figures 5.4 and 5.5). As the game progresses, the player is asked to make a series of decisions that have ethical and moral implications. The teacher wanted his students to think about each decision they were asked to make in the game, and initially, they played as a class with the teacher in control of the game. Each decision was made by consensus, after discussion of the ethical implications involved.

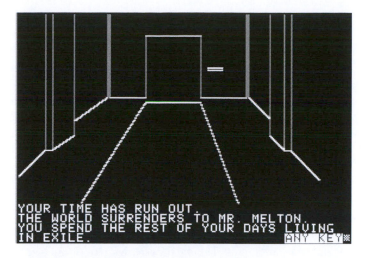

FIGURE 5.4 Starting scene of *Secret Agent: Mission One.*

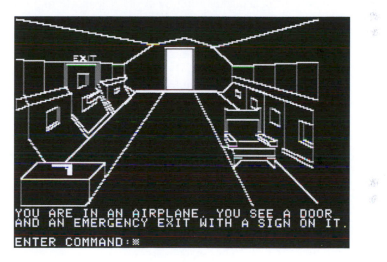

FIGURE 5.5 Ending scene of *Secret Agent: Mission One.*

Students then individually played through the game, noting their personal ethical and moral choices in response to the game; this, in effect, curated a series of dilemmas and personal responses within a game environment.

After the students had played through the game, a discussion followed about the ethics involved in games that students played at home. As the teacher was not sufficiently familiar with the wide range of game genres and specific games currently played by students to direct discussion on their ethical elements, he set this task as a collective student activity. At this point, the students began to curate their own and other students' learning under the teacher's guidance. As apprentice curators (Bigum 2014), the students identified and categorised a wide range of game-based examples of ethical dilemmas and elements to inform subsequent classroom discussion on ethics, morality and values.

For teachers who are not active game players themselves, providing students with the opportunity to curate from their experiences outside the classroom is important and often necessary. As we noted earlier in the chapter, through the *Minecraft* example, students' games expertise can transform the status and arrangement of 'expertise' in the classroom. While the Year 9 teacher was not able to explicitly curate in advance the wide range of experiences that students recounted arising from their personal ethical dilemmas while playing computer games, subsequent student curation provided rich collective resources for class discussion and could potentially be used as a resource for future classes.

Next, the students embarked on creating their own games using a range of game-making tools, including PowerPoint for 'choose your own adventure'-style games, and specialised game-making software that introduced more complex graphics and interfaces such as *GoAnimate* (GoAnimate Inc. 2011) and *GameMaker* (YoYogames 2016). The students were given the task of creating games that engage players in ethical decision making, which progressed from critical discussion of games that they played, to the challenges of designing their own games within moral constraints. In effect, the students were asked to create games that would curate other people's thinking about ethics and morality. This proved difficult for many students, who opted for demonstrations of morality through what not to do, as this fitted more closely to the games they were familiar with, rather than rising to the challenge of creating games that remained within a positive moral framework. The process did, however, create a worthwhile dialogue with the students' previous critique of the morality and values expressed in digital games.

Curation of knowledge, resources, materials and experiences for both the teacher and students presents new frames of reference for learning activities and learning outcomes. For the teacher, all learning resources, activities, artefacts and pedagogies contribute to the mix that they can draw upon for a unit, lesson, or most flexible, the dynamic classroom interactive experience. Experienced teachers have a significant repertoire to draw upon, and are able to select elements to arrange into effective and differentiated learning experiences. From a student perspective, learning can be seen as a process of curation that involves collecting and organising ideas, experiences and resources, drawing links and building an increasingly complex set of knowledge and practices. Students are also able to curate each other's learning in meaningful ways; this adds a great deal to the process of learning with digital games. The interplay between the curation efforts of teachers and learners is well represented in this case, where some elements were provided by the teacher, but many were also provided by the students, drawing on their own prior understandings, which allowed them to contribute to the learning process.

Conclusion

In this chapter, we have used curatorship as a concept to consider how teachers introduced digital games into their classrooms for the Serious Play project. Curatorship productively describes the processes that teachers undertake as they expertly create 'dialogues' between conceptual materials (such as curriculum knowledge), physical materials and classroom spaces, the time available to them and their students, various technologies and games as digital experiences. The advantage of using curatorship in this way is that it recognises teachers' expert role in making these arrangements in response to their students' learning needs. We came to appreciate the complexity which teachers face in balancing a host of competing demands for their own and their students' attention in any school situation, including curriculum, extra-curricula and interpersonal demands. Curatorship draws attention to the challenges of bringing digital games into these arrangements, which inevitably challenges students' expectations of how they usually play digital games and teachers' expectations of how they usually teach.

We have also identified the opportunities that curatorship provides, particularly in digital contexts, where gameplay can be woven into students' learning experiences, to enhance their engagement with curriculum concepts and learning. The Year 3 students enjoyed writing about *Minecraft* and were excited to be able to play *Minecraft* at school. The teacher of the Year 4/5 combined class believed that his students' knowledge of physics concepts was enhanced by their engagement with digital games. *Statecraft X* provided Year 8 students with a new way to engage with civics concepts; and *Secret Agent: Mission One* allowed the Year 9 Religious Education teacher to completely reconceive his approach to ethics education. In digital contexts where available resources are ever expanding, the curatorial role of teachers is likely to become ever more important as they bring to bear their expertise to arrange curriculum, student needs and the competing demands of contemporary schools.

References

Andrews, B and McDougall, J (2012), 'Curation pedagogy for Media Studies: (Further) towards the inexpert', *Medijske Studije*, vol. 3, no. 6, pp. 152–166.

Arefi, M (2003), 'Revisiting the Los Angeles Neighborhood Initiative (LANI): Lessons for planners', *Journal of Planning Education and Research*, vol. 22, no. 4, pp. 384–399.

Bigum, C (2014), 'Thinking beyond massive, open and online programmed instruction', Working Paper No. 3, EdExEd Working Paper Series. Available from: http://chrisbigum.com/downloads/MOOPI.pdf (Accessed 14 July 2016).

Chee, Y S (2010), *Statecraft X*. Available from: http://cheeyamsan.info/NIEprojects/SCX/SCX2.htm (Accessed 8 August 2016).

Chee, Y S (2013), 'Video games for "deep learning": Game-based learning as performance in the Statecraft X curriculum', in C B Lee and D H Jonassen (eds), *Fostering conceptual change with technology: Asian perspectives*, Singapore: Cengage Learning, pp. 199–224.

Chillingo Ltd (2011), *Feed Me Oil (iOS)*. Available from: https://play.google.com/store/apps/details?id=com.chillingo.feedmeoilfree.android.row&hl=en (Accessed 10 August 2016).

Freecloud Design Inc. (2012), *Monster Physics*. Available from: https://dan-russell-pinson.com (Accessed 10 August 2016).

GoAnimate Inc. (2011), *GoAnimate*. Available from: https://goanimate.com/ (Accessed 10 August 2016).

Hanifan, L J (1916), 'The rural school community center', *Annals of the American Academy of Political and Social Science*, vol. 67, pp. 130–138.

Hogan, B (2010), 'The presentation of self in the age of social media: Distinguishing performances and exhibitions online', *Bulletin of Science, Technology & Society*, vol. 30, no. 2, pp. 377–386.

Kolbe, B (1988), *Secret Agent: Mission One*. Available from: www.gameswin.org/gameen.php?id=1142 (Accessed 14 July 2016).

Luke, A (2003), 'Making literacy policy and practice with a difference: Generational change, professionalization and literate futures', *Australian Journal of Language and Literacy*, vol. 26, no. 3, pp. 58–82.

Mihailidis, P and Cohen, J (2013), 'Exploring curation as a core competency in digital and media literacy education', *Journal of Interactive Media in Education*, vol. 2013, no. 1, pp. 1–19.

Mojang (2011), *Minecraft*. Available from: https://minecraft.net/en/ (Accessed 8 August 2016).

Potter, J (2012), *Digital media and learner identity: The new curatorship*, New York, NY: Palgrave Macmillan.

Red Jumper (2011), *Book Creator (iOS)*. Available from: www.redjumper.net/ (Accessed 10 August 2016).

Rovio Entertainment (2010), *Angry Birds (iOS)*. Available from: https://itunes.apple.com/au/app/angry-birds/id343200656?mt=8 (Accessed 10 August 2016).

YoYogames (2016), *GameMaker*. Available from: www.yoyogames.com/gamemaker (Accessed 8 August 2016).

Zagami, J (2014), 'Secondary Worlds and computer gaming in education', paper presented at the Australian Council for Computers in Education Conference, Adelaide, Australia. Available from: http://acec2014.acce.edu.au/sites/2014/files/attachmentsACEC 2014%20Secondary%20Worlds%20and%20computer%20gaming%20in%20Education.docx (Accessed 14 July 2016).

ZeptoLab (2010), *Cut the Rope (iOS)*. Available from: www.zeptolab.com/games/cut_the_rope/ (Accessed 10 August 2016).

Teachers' Work and Games-Based Pedagogies

THEME PREFACE

Accounts of games-based learning are often reports of spectacular success where student engagement and achievement have been turned around by the introduction of games into the classroom by leading-edge teachers. A unique and important aspect of the Serious Play project was that we worked with teachers who often had little experience with games-based pedagogies. The project aimed to move beyond providing accounts of 'early adopters' – those teachers who are often the first to try out new things or to lead pedagogical change. Coming into the project, we were aware that teachers' work is complex and necessitates negotiation of a host of requirements beyond the implementation of curriculum. Teachers deal with constant technological change, frequent policy changes at State and Federal government levels, increasing focus on student achievement against standards, and many internal school initiatives and priorities. The teachers we worked with were expert at meeting their individual students' needs as they responded to these complexities. An important consideration for us, though, was that digital games were likely to be just one of many possible tools that teachers might use to curate their students' learning experiences.

The Serious Play teachers possessed various levels of experience with games-based learning from very little to quite extensive experience. A few teachers were involved in a previous games-in-education research project and already had several years of classroom experience with games, while others were very new to games-based learning. Many of the teachers had mostly used 'skill and drill'-style games, or no games at all. In some schools, teachers were recruited after a school leader negotiated involvement in the project, and although all teachers consented to be involved with the research, a few were initially quite unconvinced about the potential advantages of using games in the classroom.

The chapters in this theme provide accounts of teachers' beliefs about games-based learning, and how, in most cases, their beliefs and practices evolved during the project as teachers at all points on the experience continuum tried out new games and pedagogical approaches. In Chapter 6, Prestridge outlines the experiences of three teachers across four 'types', used as generative categories, to think about how teachers respond to new experiences and adjust (or not) their pedagogies accordingly. In Chapter 7, O'Mara provides an account of how a teacher introduced his students to games production and coding using *Scratch*. The adjustments the teacher makes to the unit across three years of the project provide insight into his processes of reflection about his students' learning needs. In Chapter 8, O'Mara and Robinson provide a detailed account of a completely immersive and integrated unit of work completed across multiple classes and curriculum areas, with *Minecraft* production at its centre. These chapters, along with several others in this book, provide insights into teachers' work with games-based pedagogies from small-scale experiments through to complex and spectacular projects. All these projects provide important insights into how teachers make expert decisions to meet their students' learning needs.

6

THE NON-GAMER TEACHER, THE QUIZ AND POP TEACHER AND THE KINECT TEACHER

Sarah Prestridge

Introduction

This chapter will explore the relationship between teachers' beliefs about the use of digital games in the classroom, their choice of digital games and the pedagogical practices they use to implement digital games. A number of factors have previously been demonstrated to influence teachers' use of games, including student motivation; social growth such as teamwork, communication and self-regulation; and cognitive gains in problem solving, content understanding and procedural knowledge (Garris *et al.* 2002; O'Neil *et al.* 2005; Pozo 2008; Lacasa 2011). What a teacher thinks or believes the use of a digital game can achieve, such as these social and intellectual benefits, can influence and shape how digital games are 'played' by the students in their classrooms. This chapter will focus on why and how teachers use games and the effect this has on their own perceptions of who they are as teachers in the twenty-first century.

Within the field of educational technology, teachers' pedagogical beliefs have typically been expressed in three ways (Ertmer *et al.* 2012):

1. to develop computer skills;
2. to teach the content of the curriculum;
3. to enact change or explore new ways of teaching and learning.

These pedagogical beliefs have characteristically transferred to traditional transmission modes of instruction or towards constructivist-compatible instruction. With regard to the use of digital games, traditional approaches tend to emphasise the use of 'drill and practice'-type games and/or tutors with the use of positive and negative reinforcement to strengthen or practise foundational subject skills. Alternatively, constructive pedagogical approaches often emphasise digital games that enable authentic learning opportunities, where students are creating or problem solving within complex, sandbox or construction-like game environments (Mama and Hennessy 2013).

Teachers form beliefs about digital games and their role in student learning, and they choose a type of digital game that aligns with their beliefs which usually 'fits' within their approach to teaching (Prestridge and de Aldama 2016). In other words, teachers are not inclined to change their teaching to accommodate the use of a digital game, at least initially (Kim *et al.* 2013; Kordaki 2013). They are likely to use the same pedagogical practices for the use of this tool like any other tool or resource in their classroom. However, during digital gameplay in the classroom, interesting things can happen. For example, what a teacher believes can be reinforced, altered, shifted or even disrupted, depending on a number of 'triggers' for change. These 'triggers' have been identified in previous research as relating to a teacher's technological disposition; that is, knowing which tool (digital game) is right for the task and knowing that it is alright to be less competent than the students; adoption of a 'praxis' approach to teaching; curriculum alignment, student engagement or disengagement and student learning outcomes (Prestridge 2017). A teacher's existing beliefs may be confirmed to validate their existing practices; or their beliefs may be disrupted by the introduction of digital games, providing the opportunity for both beliefs and practices to change. Change may result from a redefinition of the way teachers think about digital games and their craft, the relevancy and authenticity of their practice and their fundamental beliefs about how the 'new generation' learns.

This chapter explores the journey of three teachers as they experiment with implementing digital games in their classrooms, uncovering the principles by which they chose the particular digital game; the beliefs they hold; the practices they used; and how, why and if these changed over their appropriation of this technological tool. Four categories developed by Donnelly *et al.* (2011) are adopted to explore the level of digital technology integration into teachers' practices. These categories comprise:

1. the 'Contented Traditionalist' – who teaches towards curriculum and assessment requirements and adopts technologies using traditional practices to adhere to the prevailing school culture;
2. the 'Selective Adopter' – who selects technologies for competency of specific curriculum content and can vary pedagogical practices to ensure better assessment outcomes;
3. the 'Creative Adapter' – who has a strong focus on student-centred approaches that facilitate meaningful learning;
4. the 'Inadvertent User' – who is more oriented to using technologies if it is perceived as a school requirement, rather than to seek out their use.

These categories give us one way of understanding a snapshot of teacher practice, acknowledging that boundaries merge. For this chapter, however, categories can provide a way of describing different approaches to using digital games that are helpful in assisting us in recognising the 'whys' and the 'hows' of teacher practice.

This chapter will explore the case of Lucy, the non-gamer, who started with a reading tutorial game, but ended up having great success with a sandbox game. She demonstrated the greatest change in her pedagogical beliefs and practices, moving from being a Contented Traditionalist to a Creative Adapter over the period of the Serious Play project. Malcolm, the quiz and pop teacher, was a Selective Adopter, as he honoured the requirements of the curriculum and was focused on choosing games to achieve better assessment outcomes for his students. Janet, the Kinect teacher, is a Creative Adapter, as she sought out something completely different – Xbox Kinect – to embrace student activity and engagement. The following recounts of these teachers' journeys provide insight into their professional learning and the construction of their pedagogical beliefs and practices associated with the use of digital games.

Lucy: the Non-Gamer Teacher

With more than 20 years' teaching experience across the primary school years, high levels of confidence and deep knowledge of the curriculum, Lucy was initially not that eager to use digital games in her classroom. By her own account, she had lots of experience playing board games, but no personal experience of or interest in digital games: 'I don't ever play computer games, not even on my phone. I think I'd be bored.' She is a 'non-gamer' teacher.

Lucy decided to trial a computer tutorial, *Reading Quest* (Merrick 2012), to support reading competency in her Year 1 (6 year olds) class. Even though she stated that digital games were good for 'problem solving and higher-order thinking', she believed these were most appropriate for older learners. In the foundational years, her role was to 'get them to read really well before they leave. I'm setting them up for the future'. *Reading Quest* has four worlds in which children advance by completing activities in phonics, word structure, sight words, and vocabulary and comprehension. Like most computer tutorials, students' achievement records are kept, so Lucy could monitor student progress. This, plus the fact that children could 'shoot them up [the words], a bit like an actual gaming park and then to achieve things', meant that the children would be having fun, the game was challenging and it matched both curriculum and age/developmental needs. Lucy had strong beliefs in the computer game as a tool for foundational knowledge and skill development to supplement the required curriculum (Ertmer *et al.* 2012; Prestridge 2012), because it would reinforce vocabulary skills through rote-learning activities.

Lucy had set up a station approach in her Year 1 classroom where there was a line of computers down one side of the room and working spaces of tables and chairs around the room. Children were broken into groups of three, one station being the digital game, another station being guided reading and activity-sheet work supported by a teacher's aide. By her own admission, she used teacher-centred instructional practices to introduce any new activity or concept. She describes this as the '"I do, we do, you do" approach. So I model; then we do it together; then they have a go. So I think that, to me, is best practice. I think that allows for all types of learners.' At the start of the unit, as she herself saw it, Lucy portrayed the pedagogical characteristics described by Donnelly *et al.* (2011) that typically represent the Contented Traditionalist – those teachers who focus on curriculum and assessment and adopt ICT using traditional practices. Lucy demonstrated the computer game in front of the class, the step-by-step procedure for engagement was important and emphasised, and she was in total control of gameplay. She then asked a child to demonstrate the next activity in the game under her guidance, following which she implemented her rotational station approach. She monitored the children's progress in the game by using the learning analytics feature that was available in the teacher dashboard of the game. Her motivation for using *Reading Quest* was to increase her students' vocabulary, spelling and word recognition. In the early years, Lucy considers reading to be one of the most important skills and this game would support that development in her students.

Interestingly, however, when Lucy found that some children were getting bored, she changed her approach and directed these children to start at the top level. She stated that, 'when they could go where they wanted, they loved it'. Lucy described one child in particular, Ashley, who was a poor reader who re-engaged once she was allowed to start at the top level because she felt capable. Once children became self-directed learners, there was more interest and engagement in the game. This change in Lucy's pedagogical approach initiated a change in her belief about using digital games, in that digital games could be used in educational ways not necessarily consistent with the intention of the game. As the children were disengaging, Lucy had to quickly rethink how she was using the game in her classroom. It was quite a surprise to Lucy that digital games could be boring! From this point on, Lucy was open to trying different types of digital games. The disengagement by the children was her 'trigger' to try something new.

Lucy wanted to try something different, but it had to interest her students and be relevant to their learning needs. There were two competing ideals here for Lucy: the external force of curriculum requirements; and the internal force of student interest and needs. Donnelly *et al.* (2011) distinguished between assessment-focused and learner-focused approaches to pedagogy and the use of digital resources. In this instance, such distinctions might be seen as driving game choice. Lucy decided to trial *Minecraft* (Mojang 2011) the following year with her Year 3 class because her students were interested in it and played it a lot at home. This indicates an evolution in Lucy's beliefs, from the Contented Traditionalist driven by curriculum to a more student-needs-based approach.

As Lucy didn't know how to play *Minecraft*, she implemented an exploratory period, calling on a couple of children who knew about the game to share their expertise as group leaders. She did not use her instructional pedagogy of 'I do, we do, you do'; as she said, 'it wouldn't work and I had no idea of what I was doing'. Twice weekly in the afternoon session, children played freely within *Minecraft*. To relate it to curriculum outcomes, the children wrote recounts of what they were doing in *Minecraft*. At this stage, Lucy's use of *Minecraft* demonstrated the need to 'enrich existing curriculum' (Ertmer *et al.* 2012) rather than the previous use of the reading tutorial as a reinforcement or supplementary task. In other words, there was greater curriculum alignment through the use of recounts with a greater focus on student interest. Her pedagogy was more open and experimental, but with relevance to subject-content outcomes.

The following term, Lucy designed and implemented a multidisciplinary unit of work that required the children to learn about the local area and to build their own community space in *Minecraft*. There were two parts to the unit: the development of knowledge of the local area through teacher-directed instruction, research and short tasks; and an experimental 'creative' part where the children built their replica local area in *Minecraft*. The knowledge gained from study of the local area informed the creation of the 'penultimate' local area for each group. They learnt about historical settlements and developments over time, characteristics of different environments and basic requirements for communities. As a culminating activity, the students created a walk-through *QuickTime* video (Softonic International 2016) to campaign for the 'most liveable' community (see Figure 6.1). Upon reflection on the multidisciplinary unit, Lucy stated:

> I am embarrassed to say that I still do not know a lot about *Minecraft*. For the children to be successful using this technology, it was not vital that I know anywhere near as much as them. They taught each other. As I am not one to sit and play computer games of any kind, the learning that evolved amazed me. The ability to work together for a common goal, the many links to the curriculum and the 'fun' that the children had [were] both rewarding and productive.

When the children were using *Minecraft*, Lucy adopted student-centred pedagogies as she didn't know how to play or even felt she had to know how *Minecraft* worked. Her role was in enabling group collaboration and the development of curriculum concepts through gameplay. At this point, Lucy was able to appropriate *Minecraft* as a tool to leverage curriculum outcomes by providing students with a space to apply their knowledge of the local area. The shift in thinking over her journey with digital games moved from using them as a reinforcement tool, to enriching the curriculum, to using them as a tool that facilitates opportunity for deep engagement and application of knowledge (see Ertmer *et al.* 2012, pp. 429–431 for the description of each category).

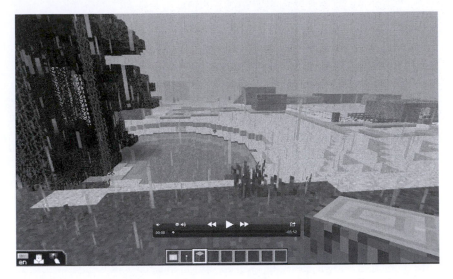

FIGURE 6.1 Screen capture of Terabithia Community produced in *Minecraft*.

Lucy changed her beliefs about using games from needing to 'fit' the curriculum to a premise that positioned student interest and learning at the forefront. She stated that, 'I don't like to fail at anything and I felt I didn't do it right the first time'. This indicates that she would be categorised by Donnelly *et al.* (2011) as moving towards the Creative Adapter. There were two new principles she was becoming more conscious of for rich digital game appropriation as part of the reformation of her beliefs. First, 'teamwork', using digital games which allow children to work towards a common goal. Second, not restricting the choice of game to those you are familiar with or competent in. As Lucy says, 'just allowing the kids to know more, and understanding that that's just the way the world's going, and that's teaching really'.

Malcolm: the Quiz and Pop Teacher

Malcolm is a confident and dedicated teacher with more than 30 years' experience in the classroom. During his involvement in the Serious Play project, he was teaching middle primary (9 to 10 year olds). His class was a mix of boys and girls each with their own laptop computer. He recounted playing computer games like *Pac-Man* (Namco Bandai Games Inc. 1980) at the local milk bar in his youth. Now he plays *Angry Birds* (Rovio Entertainment 2010) with his 7-year-old daughter when they have some relaxation time. Reflecting on the digital game *Angry Birds*, he stated:

> I'd love to know how to play it better, to use a protractor or pull up an online thing so you could work it – estimate where it's going to land – the distance it's projected. I think that would be pretty interesting.

His previous experiences with digital games in the classroom focused on 'drill and practice' software and tutorials that develop specific subject skills such as *Mathletics* (3P Learning n. d.) which provides positive and negative feedback on mathematical computations. His interest in these types of games led to the name of 'quiz and pop' teacher.

In interviews and classroom visits with Malcolm over the course of the project, he continued to use 'drill and practice' games in his classroom. His favourite was *MangaHigh* (Blue Duck Entertainment Ltd 2016), an online game that provides 60,000 mathematics quizzes in Number, Algebra, Shape and Data, with full reporting and learning analytics (see Figure 6.2). It does not need to be downloaded and can be played online on any device. All student data are retained onsite and can be easily accessed by the teacher. Students do the quizzes by themselves and move through at their own pace. This has been considered a 'popular' game with over 6,000 'likes'. As Malcolm had never tried anything other than 'drill and practice' games, though he thought about it (which will be explored later), he could be considered the Selective Adapter (Donnelly *et al.* 2011), as he chose particular games that ensured the most successful outcomes for his students in exams. Malcolm's beliefs about the use of games were associated with 'learning for assessment' where efficiency and output were highly valued. Returning to Malcolm's discussion of *Angry Birds* provides insight into these kinds of beliefs about the use of digital games.

FIGURE 6.2 Students in Malcolm's class independently learning with 'drill and practice' software.

Previously, Malcolm had identified that there were some pretty interesting learning opportunities that could come out of examining *Angry Birds* in mathematics lessons; that is, the use of protractors, estimation and distance. When asked to explore this further, Malcolm stated that:

> You could possibly use it as a prediction-type exercise. If I angle the shot at a particular angle and if you can measure that – predicting how far – and you could be talking about distances and metres – if you could translate that distance into some sort of unit, that would be all right.

Using *Angry Birds* in this way would be considered an authentic appropriation that enriches curriculum content and higher-order thinking skills (Ertmer *et al.* 2012; Prestridge 2012). However, even though this use of *Angry Birds* was considered beneficial, Malcolm never actualised this opportunity as he was constrained by two pedagogical beliefs: 'it wouldn't be something that you would spend huge amounts of time on'; and if it were to be used, it would need to be used instantly, and in a tightly focused way: 'you might have just taught and have been talking about angles. Let's use it now'. To Malcolm, the use of the digital game represented an extended use, playing over time for a purpose, rather than a short application of a concept like angles. A digital game was not conceptualised like other teaching and learning resources. Additionally, to appropriate digital games at the 'right time' for short illustrations or application of content would require an extensive knowledge of the Apps or games available so they could be drawn upon when required. Plus there was the question of the validity of using a game such as *Angry Birds* to practise Angles – was it worth the time? These ideas seemed to present barriers for Malcolm. Tallvid (2016) identified these ideas as barriers to using technology, and called it 'not worth effort', namely:

> teachers' estimation of how much the design of the task would be enhanced and the quality of the task would be improved by using ICT, in relation to the amount of effort put into searching for material and preparing it for classroom use.
>
> *(Tallvid 2016, p. 510)*

Malcolm's response was, 'I'd have to think about it', but nothing progressed during the course of the project.

Understanding Malcolm's perspective on the use of digital games provides deeper insights into processes needing to take place to enable teachers to appropriate this technology in ways that leverage better learning opportunities for their students. One challenge for Malcolm was simply the ability to imagine how digital games might be used in the classroom. For instance, at the beginning of the project, Malcolm stated:

> I don't even know a lot of times what I am meant to be doing. I need to see it, and then once you see one idea, you bounce ideas off. I found it – as a single class – I found that really hard. It would have been a lot easier, I think, if other people on my level were doing something.

Within the project, teachers had uploaded examples of what they were doing to the Serious Play website, but Malcolm didn't look at these, instead searching YouTube videos for story-book-like games: 'I've had a lot of trouble finding something different to skill and drill. I've been trawling through YouTube clips. I've been going through things like Khan Academy, but that's not really anything like it.' This raises a number of issues. Malcolm didn't know of a 'good' game, he was teaching by himself and felt isolated and he was spending a lot of time searching for the 'right' game. He just wanted to be told of a 'good' game and then he'd use it. As previously explained in Lucy's case, the project oriented teachers towards thinking about 'using', 'analysing' or 'making' games and did not prescribe a digital game. The idea of a 'good' game is dependent upon the context and how it is used. As previously stated, *Angry Birds* could be an authentic appropriation of a digital game for experimenting with angles.

From a pedagogical perspective, Malcolm was focused on an exact 'fit' with the curriculum and a 'pay-off' in relation to the amount of time his students would spend on a game for what they would get out of it. Malcolm stated that:

> to weigh up the cost and benefits, you've invested a lot of time and energy getting the children exploring the game, getting their head around how they use it for a tiny little recount that they could do in many other ways.

He explained that a stimulus like a picture or news report would work just as well as a stimulus for a recount, so there needed to be greater educational value during gameplay. He explained that:

> If I could find the right game, and if it was clearly mapped to curriculum, then I could see that. I could say, I'm looking at my English curriculum and I want to cover this, this and this. We've got this game that by kids being immersed in the game, they'll learn about pronouns; they'll learn about conjunctions. Their writing will improve. At the end of the day, if their writing doesn't improve, it's not really achieved the goal.

Malcolm believed that the digital game played a major role in teaching and learning. Games were considered the 'tutors'. By playing a game, the child learnt something, with what they learnt, as far as possible, related directly to the required assessment outcomes. If the game did not teach the child something, or the child did not know more after playing the game, then the investment in time was wasted. Malcolm did not believe that the digital game could be analysed in itself, as a text or for specific qualities; nor could it be an open sandbox-type environment where his students could build something or create, as with Lucy's *Minecraft* appropriation. His pedagogical beliefs directed his search for a game that more or less ensured clear alignment with the curriculum and a measurable outcome. The reinforcement of content skills within a digital game mirrored Malcolm's instructional pedagogy. Moving beyond the drill-type games challenged his control to ensure that if 'I'm going to invest 10 hours – where is my 10 hours of learning demonstrated somewhere?'

Janet: the Kinect Teacher

'I want to do something different, something no one else is doing. What do you think about Xbox Kinect? Anyone doing that?' Janet is an experienced teacher librarian at a junior girls' college. In this role, she advocates strongly to develop the love of literature and joy of reading for her girls. She is a self-confessed energetic and highly competitive person who loves to try anything, and games of any type interest her. Previous to this project, Janet encouraged the children to complete the games or quizzes in story books (on the CD-ROM), as this was 'promoting literature, because it gets them involved and then they'd often go off and read the books'. Other than reading tutors, Janet had little experience of using digital games in her teaching. Her main interest lay in using a game, rather than analysing or making games, as she was restricted to working with her Year 5 class during their library time; but more importantly, she believed in playing a game with her girls first to see how it aligned to the curriculum: 'I want to start off by watching girls playing it and then I'll be able to see how it will fit into the curriculum.' Additionally, Janet wanted to see what the children got out of gameplay. She was interested to see if games could develop literacies, especially digital literacies and problem solving.

Janet's teaching is underpinned by a constructivist orientation (Schunk 2008). Janet prefers working with small groups, and her library lessons have three rotations: focus task, borrowing a book and library skills. She believes that all learning should be active and fun, and that students need to be doing something while collaborating with their peers on an authentic task. Students need to be part of the decision making, with whole-class pre- and post-discussions and directing their learning with self-generated questions that drive inquiries. She affirms that the more engagement in learning, the better the outcomes. These types of belief statements about how children learn evidence relativistic views of knowledge generation (Perry 1970), supported by her pedagogy which illustrates conjectural models (Kemmis *et al.* 1977) that enable students to manipulate ideas and hypotheses to develop knowledge. Janet says, 'there's a lot of movement in the library, a lot of action going on, there's a lot of interaction, it's not a quiet place'. With regard to her appropriation of a digital game, she chose *Kinectimals* (Frontier Developments 2011), an Xbox Kinect game where children could explore animals and their habitats. The principle reason for her choice of an Xbox Kinect game was that it enabled physical action, and it was a 'quest'-like game where the children could go on adventures. This demonstrates the alignment between the choice of game and Janet's pedagogical beliefs. She implemented the gameplay during focus time within her rotation system. Janet soon found this game to be too young for her students as it didn't have much content in it and wasn't challenging enough for her Year 5 girls. With her students' support, Janet spent the term as experimental time on the game, during which she worked out with her girls how to play, and how to move around the game using the sensors with physical actions.

After some searching over the vacation break for a more demanding game, she found *America the Wild* (Relentless Software 2012), an National Geographic Xbox Kinect game that was age-appropriate and more complex in that it allowed the children to be avatars in the virtual space, and to assume features of particular animals such as animal's heads, limbs or wings. Through exploratory gameplay with the girls, Janet began to notice what learning outcomes were being achieved (see Figure 6.3). Initially she said, 'I can't see much educational value at all, but when I sat and analysed ...', she began to notice the literacies, the teamwork, the thinking skills and the strategic play through the interactions between the girls.

> It was interesting to hear the other girls supporting them saying, 'Oh no, you get more if you do this, or if you use your head, or if you use your left arm, use your right arm'. There's a lot of interaction and communication with the girls.

FIGURE 6.3 Girls taking turns playing the Xbox Kinect.

Because of this, she was not worried about the US content and the misalignment to specific Australian curriculum content. Her justification lay in the value of using physical action as engagement, the communication between the girls entailed in interacting with the virtual environment, and the development of digital literacies.

Using the Xbox Kinect as a drawcard to get children into the library, so that once there, 'you can push books on them', was one of the initial reasons for choosing the hardware. Tension for Janet existed between her 'core' business to engender the 'love of books', the need to do something different in the project, and her student-centred pedagogical beliefs. Janet was still unclear about the actual educational value of the Xbox Kinect game. The turning point came as an 'aha! moment' in the development of her professional understanding of digital games. Janet explained:

> [B]y playing the game and by listening to them [the girls], it suddenly clicked on me, oh my gosh, this is an information book. The game is a non-fiction book in the library because you can select chapters (the different episodes in the game), you can select items from it to read. You don't read a book from cover to cover, you just read – you take a chapter you want to read or something interesting, but that's what an information book does. The girls have been selecting episodes that they are interested in. One might do an owl, one group might do wolves, and so on. The more I thought about it, because I didn't – we've seen it more as a gamey-type thing. So I sort of changed my feelings and thoughts about it. I actually see so many benefits to it now.

To Janet, the *America the Wild* Xbox Kinect game is an information text. Two additional events were pivotal in reforming Janet's beliefs about digital games. The first event focused on how students were interacting physically with the game. Using the Kinect feature, the girls were able to take on the façade of the animal, to hunt like the animal, getting a deeper, more authentic understanding of its behaviours and habitat. As Janet stated, 'they were getting closer than you can in a book or at the zoo, they're actually being that animal'. The second event involved the game acting as a stimulus for further reading, in that a student who had played the wolf episode wanted to learn more about wolves, so she read the classic novel by Jack London. Janet thought this was 'fantastic'.

Students' engagement with literature and literacies is Janet's barometer to assigning the educational value of digital games. She passionately loves books and reading, and through her appropriation of *America the Wild* Xbox Kinect, a non-fiction text came alive. She was not focused on the curriculum 'fit' or 'product' per se, but rather a way to enact the process of learning. Through gameplay, the girls were actioning learning, focused more on the process than she had seen before. Janet could be categorised as the Creative Adapter (Donnelly *et al.* 2011) with regard to her approach to integrating technologies, as she has a strong focus on student-centred learning, combined with a high degree of self-efficacy and empowerment to try something new and not be totally controlled by curriculum requirements. The digital game enabled her girls to actively engage in actioning information, exploring and collaborating in a virtual environment. They were communicating, problem solving, making decisions, taking risks, making learning active, which aligned to her constructivist teaching orientations plus the fact that it stimulated the girls' reading of the 'classics'.

Looking Forward

This chapter has examined both the underlying beliefs and the pedagogies these three teachers used to appropriate digital games in their classrooms. Some interesting conclusions can be drawn. First, when faced with the challenge to 'use', 'analyse' or 'make' a game within project boundaries, these teachers chose to 'use' games. Using games was the most common approach to digital game implementation among all teachers in this project. Furthermore, these teachers initially chose a game that aligned to their pedagogical beliefs. Lucy and Malcolm chose 'drill and practice'- type games, Lucy for reading development and Malcolm for proficiency with mathematics. Janet chose a game that was a little different and made learning active for her girls. For their first trial of a game, the pedagogy they employed did not change. Lucy initially used her familiar strategy of 'I do, we do, you do'; Malcolm supported individual work on laptops that replicated direct instruction; while Janet employed rotations. For these teachers, it can be said that their first foray into working with digital games drew on the same beliefs and replicated practices used with other teaching and learning resources. In other words, at the onset or the first go, the inclusion of digital games did not allow them to implement or experiment with new approaches to teaching and learning.

For Lucy and Janet, though, new ways of thinking about digital games and using them in their classrooms did occur. Through a process of trial and error as well as a research context of 'experimentation', Lucy was able to challenge herself to try something new. The initial 'trigger' was the dissatisfaction the children had with the game, the understanding that she wasn't doing anything 'new or exciting' with games, and then the insight that she didn't have to be the game guru, that her students could be more competent than she was. She was coming to believe what other innovative teachers believe: '[y]ou cannot use traditional methods to teach the new student, the 21st century student ... [it was about] enacting an approach that more deeply engaged students' (Garcia, a Middle Years Science teacher cited in Ertmer *et al.* 2012, p. 429). Janet also, on finding that the content and structure of her first game were pitched too young for her students, searched for a game that matched the cognitive level and needs of her girls. However, it wasn't until she observed the learning taking place – learning that could not be obtained from another resource – that her beliefs changed with regard to the educational value of an interactive game. Additionally, she came to conceptualise the Xbox Kinect adventure games as an information text. This had a significant impact on Janet's beliefs about the value of digital games. For Malcolm, the barrier of both his beliefs and pedagogical practices limited his use of digital games to treating them as a functional resource, an opportunity for students to practise and to become more proficient at mathematics. His beliefs about accountability for assessment, time required for student engagement, curriculum fit and best tool for the given task restricted both his exploration of different types of games and of their applications.

In moving forward, as the experiences of Lucy, Malcolm and Janet suggest, teacher beliefs and the pedagogies used to appropriate digital games into the classroom have a major impact on how effective these can be as learning tools. Clearly, teachers will choose a type of digital game that represents what they believe as having educational value in the classroom. As they implement this game, what proceeds is most important. Challenges, disruptions of both the positive and negative kind will trigger and shape change. It is when teachers are trialling and experimenting with games over an extended period of time that new understandings can be reached. Even though the trialling of a digital game may start with something more familiar to the teacher, as in each case here, change in belief and practice did occur when the teacher experimented with a different type of digital game. Educational leaders and professional development facilitators can seek to harness the fundamental role that beliefs play in ensuing practices associated with any technology as part of the process in breaking down the barriers connected with innovative digital game appropriation.

References

3P Learning (n. d.), *Mathletics*. Available from: www.mathletics.com.au/ (Accessed 8 August 2016).

Blue Duck Entertainment Ltd (2016), *MangaHigh*. Available from: www.mangahigh.com/en-au/ (Accessed 10 August 2016).

Donnelly, D, McGarr, O and O'Reilly, J (2011), 'A framework for teachers' integration of ICT into their classroom practice', *Computers & Education,* vol. 57, no. 2, pp. 1469–1483.

Ertmer, P A, Ottenbreit-Leftwich, A, Sadik, O, Sendurur, E and Sendurur, P (2012), 'Teacher beliefs and technology integration practices: A critical relationship', *Computers & Education*, vol. 59, no. 2, pp. 423–435.

Frontier Developments (2011), *Kinectimals* (Xbox Kinect), Redmond, WA: Microsoft Studios.

Garris, R, Ahlers, R and Driskell, J E (2002), 'Games, motivation, and learning: A research and practical model', *Simulation & Gaming*, vol. 33, no. 4, pp. 441–467.

Kemmis, S, Atkin, R and Wright, E (1977), *How do students learn?* Occasional Publications No. 5, University of East Anglia, Norwich: Centre for Applied Research in Education.

Kim, C, Kim, M, Lee, C, Spector, J and DeMeester, K (2013), 'Teacher beliefs and technology integration', *Teaching and Teacher Education*, vol. 29, January, pp. 76–85.

Kordaki, M (2013), 'High school computing teachers' beliefs and practices: A case study', *Computers & Education*, vol. 68, October, pp. 141–152.

Lacasa, P (2011), *The videogames. Learning in real and virtual worlds*. Madrid: Morata.

Mama, M and Hennessy, S (2013), 'Developing a typology of teacher beliefs and practices concerning classroom use of ICT', *Computers & Education*, vol. 68, October, pp. 380–387.

Merrick, M (2012), *Reading Quest* (electronic resource), Clayton, Victoria, Australia: Blake Education. Available from: www.blake.com.au (Accessed 15 August 2016).

Mojang (2011), *Minecraft*. Available from: https://minecraft.net/en/ (Accessed 8 August 2016).

Namco Bandai Games Inc. (1980), *Pac-Man* (arcade game). Available from: http://pacman.com/en/ (Accessed 15 November 2016).

O'Neil, H F, Wainess, R and Baker, E L (2005), 'Classification of learning outcomes: Evidence from the computer games literature', *The Curriculum Journal*, vol. 16, no. 4, pp. 455–474.

Perry, W (1970), *Forms of intellectual and ethical development in the college years: A scheme*. New York, NY: Holt, Rinehart and Winston.

Pozo, J I (2008), *Learners and teachers. The cognitive psychology of learning*, Madrid: Alianza Editorial.

Prestridge, S (2012), 'The beliefs behind the teacher that influences their ICT practices', *Computers & Education*, vol. 58, no. 1, pp. 449–458.

Prestridge, S (2017), 'Examining the shaping of a teacher's pedagogical orientation for the use of technology', *Technology, Pedagogy and Education*.

Prestridge, S and de Aldama, C (2016), 'A classification framework for exploring technology enabled practice – FrameTEP', *Journal of Educational Computing Research*. Available from: doi:10.1177/0735633116636767 (Accessed 28 July 2016).

Relentless Software (2012), *National Geographic: America the Wild* (Xbox Kinect), Redmond, WA: Microsoft Studios.

Rovio Entertainment (2010), *Angry Birds (iOS)*. Available from: https://itunes.apple.com/au/app/angry-birds/id343200656?mt=8 (Accessed 10 August 2016).

Schunk, D (2008), *Learning theories: An educational perspective* (5th ed.), Upper Saddle River, NJ: Pearson Merrill Prentice Hall.

Softonic International (2016), *QuickTime*. Available from: http://quicktime.en.softonic.com/ (Accessed 10 August 2016).

Tallvid, M (2016), 'Understanding teachers' reluctance to the pedagogical use of ICT in the 1:1 classroom', *Education and Information Technologies*, vol. 2, no. 3, pp. 503–519.

7

NARRATIVES COME TO LIFE THROUGH CODING

Digital Game Making as Language and Literacy Curriculum

Joanne O'Mara

> *One day an ordinary rock was sitting under a tree and the rock heard a loud noise. He looked up to find a big spaceship. The door of the big spaceship opened and standing inside was a vampire. 'I'm Vampire Queen,' said the Vampire Queen. 'I'm here to take you away'.*
>
> (Opening of a Year 3/4 *Scratch* game story)

> *I learnt that the Grade 3/4 curriculum has 'upped the ante' and primary school children are learning about things that high school kids are only just now learning about.*
>
> (Comment from a Year 9 student who visited the Year 3/4s and played their computer games)

Introduction: Game Making as Language and Literacy Curriculum

Children are often positioned as consumers of digital games, but what happens when they become the creators and producers of their own games? This chapter describes a digital game-making project in a Year 3/4 classroom where young students made their own digital games using the block coding program *Scratch*. While this project cuts across several curriculum areas, it was primarily designed as a Language and Literacies project with written composition at the centre.

Scratch is free 'visual' programming software developed by the Lifelong Kindergarten Group (2003) at the MIT Media Lab. They described *Scratch* as 'a programming language and online community where you can create your own interactive stories, games, and animations – and share your creations with others around the world'. Instead of typing commands in this language, users join together visual blocks of coding instruction. The process has been described as 'snapping those color-coded blocks together as you would puzzle pieces or

LEGO bricks' (Marji 2014, p. 21). *Scratch* is based upon constructionist educational principles, as explicated by Papert (1980). Papert later explained in *Mindstorms* (1993) how it builds upon the earlier work of MIT Media Labs, with the development of *LOGO* in the 1970s (Papert 1979). However, in creating *Scratch*, the developers followed a set of design principles to make it 'more tinkerable, more meaningful and more social than other programming environments' (Resnick *et al.* 2009, n. p.). This is a significant structural change to the design of this programming language that sets it apart from the previous constructionist approaches. *Scratch* is ideal for use in Language and Literacies curriculum for a cross-curriculum unit, as narrative-based games can be produced with it, and the design and syntax of the program enable children to build their games using the logic of programming without the need to learn programming. Additionally, there is a shift in the use of the term 'literacy' that accompanies this. When Resnick describes coding as 'the new literacy', he is emphasising coding as a skill as important as literacy, rather than using the term to mean 'basic skills'.[1] *Scratch* as both a language and a programming environment can be seen as a set of resources for communicating, composing and writing, for the concept metaphor described by Bill Green (2001) as composITing or as enabling writing – as produced in the example discussed in this chapter – as a 'multimodal technoliterate practice' (Edwards-Groves 2012, p. 108).

Beyond Surface Features: Understanding Literacy as Thinking and Cognition

Literacy is often understood as 'basics skills', and the debate around literacies tends to focus on the development of basic skills rather than complex meaning making. Green (2012) pointed out that a major problem in the ways in which literacy is theorised is the tendency to limit what is understood to be 'literacy' to written language, rather than conceiving it as thinking and cognition. Green has drawn upon a range of literacy theories (Vygotsky *et al.* 1962; Halliday 1975; Moffett 1981; Kress 1982) to develop the '3D Model of L(IT)eracy', with a focus on text composition. Green reminded us of Moffet's (1981) work, where speaking and thinking were the basics of literacy (verbalisation and conceptualisation), not spelling, punctuation and grammar, the 'surface features' of the text.

Green's model (1988; 2012) conceptualised literacy as working across the three dimensions of 'cultural-discursive', 'operational-technical' and 'critical-reflexive'. These three dimensions of literacies practice work together simultaneously, rather than sequentially or developmentally (see Figure 7.1) and the model can be used pedagogically, conceptually and rhetorically (Beavis and Green 2012). In this chapter, the model is used as a conceptual tool to frame the literacies analysis of the students' projects to consider what game making brings to the students' compositional skills, particularly in terms of their understanding of narrative.

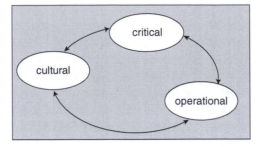

FIGURE 7.1 3D Model of L(IT)eracy.
Source: Green (1988).

Bringing Narratives to Life Through Coding

The case-study data used in this chapter were collected from one teacher, Nick, and his Year 3/4 classes over a three-year period. While coding work in schools is generally located in Science, Technology and Mathematics (STEM) education, Nick drew upon the affordances of *Scratch* to develop a strong language arts/literacies focus through a game-making unit. In this way, the unit cuts across the curriculum, addressing many of the STEM standards in addition to those of Language and Literacy.

Nick reworked the project in an ongoing way over several years, based upon his reflections on his own and his students' classroom practices (Schön 1983), so that each year, the digital game-making project became more refined and the language and literacies outcomes were more clearly articulated. In this case, the game making develops skills of traditional literacy and composition as well as developing what Resnick *et al.* (2009 n. p.) called 'digital fluency ... designing, creating, and remixing, not just browsing, chatting, and interacting'. To show the evolution of the project, the chapter focuses on its first and third years. It considers how this highly skilled teacher developed the curriculum over the three-year period. Finally, the chapter analyses the language and literacies outcomes for students in the final year of the project. The language and literacies tasks are mapped onto Green's 3D Model of L(IT)eracy (1988; 2012), a useful resource to draw upon when analysing complex multimodal texts and experiences, such as those created and experienced by the children through the game-making curriculum.

Evolution of a Task: The Decision to Use *Scratch*

In the first year of the project, Nick, the teacher, gave all the Year 3/4 students the roles of different employees in a games company: programmers, designers, marketing executives. In this initial year, the students could choose between the programs *Scratch* and *Sploder* (Sploder™ n. d.) to make their games. I interviewed the students in small groups about their experiences, and their concerns surrounding the trials and tribulations they experienced in making their teams, keeping their teams together and trying to agree on a topic or story for their games. I was very impressed with the quality of the completed games, but noticed that there was a hierarchy around the use of the two programs, with *Scratch* being seen by the students as much more sophisticated. Nick recognised quickly that the possibilities for sophisticated outcomes were much higher with *Scratch*, and as he became more confident with the software himself, he only used *Scratch* in the subsequent years of the project.

In this first year, all of the choices were very open for the students, and it was up to them to choose the program. Nick was learning the programs alongside the students, and an older boy from a combined Year 5/6 class was teaching both Nick and the younger students how to make digital games. Because he was new to the programming as well, Nick found that learning how to code became the focus for both him and the class, rather than the other curriculum outcomes he had hoped to achieve. At the end of the first iteration of the unit, Nick was really pleased with the students' efforts. He reflected, '*Scratch* is far superior to *Sploder* for the task' and he explained that the students learnt more from using it. He particularly valued the coding aspects of the program and the links to the Mathematics curriculum. He was, however, very dissatisfied with the ways in which these children took on specific gender roles in the class. The boys tended to take on coding identities and the girls mostly took on designing identities. He was really surprised that this happened, as he had not seen such strongly gendered

FIGURE 7.2 Students making a digital game using *Scratch*.

identities in other group work. He also noted that the students spent a lot of time negotiating and renegotiating their teams and roles which led to a significant amount of friction in the class, resulting in group changes and less being achieved as a result.

The students reflected on their experience in a similar way when I interviewed them. They described having hitherto very little experience of game usage or design in school, so at the beginning of the unit, they did not have any real expectations about making digital games in school. Most of them were very excited about the idea of making games, and only two students in the class had ever tried to make a digital game before. Many of the students spoke at length about the instabilities in their groups and the difficulties in coming to agreement about different aspects of the narrative and game design.

The games made in the first year of the project were mostly fairly simple, with progress made in playing the game through unlocking keys (to treasure chests and doors) and collecting items (such as coins, gold or other treasures). The stories that the students created in this first year seemed to be fairly loosely connected to the games, with the stories often telling a dramatic tale and the game might have one element of the story (such as unlocking a chest) represented in it, but the game did not progress the story or seem to alter it significantly. However, the students themselves felt that the stories were important to the games, and this was a common theme across the interviews. Students described aspects of the narrative as being very important to the game structure. There were a number of students, such as Peter, who had imagined all the narrative elements of the story so vividly that the game narrative was a complete imagined virtual world, even though all aspects of the narrative were not clearly rendered across the game texts. Peter was aware of this himself. In an interview with him, while he was 'walking' me through the game, he noted: 'So basically there's the robot there. And it has the aliens in it, and it has the brave guy who has to save people. Well we didn't mention the Alien King in the book …'. He described how it was difficult to work out 'how to put what we draw into the game … 'cause in the game we have all the aliens, so I really do think that the story connects to the game'.

Peter and his team imagined all aspects of the game so vividly that they 'filled in the missing gaps' in their imagination, even though, as he describes here, the Alien King of their imagined text is not present in either the game or the accompanying storybook, but is present in the students' understanding of the story. Nick took note of this, and in the subsequent iterations of the program, he provided more time and help to students to allow them to shape their narratives, so that by the third year, the unit of work had evolved from a STEM-focused unit into one with a greater language and literacies focus.

In this first year of the project, a number of students expressed dissatisfaction with using *Scratch* as exemplified by the following exchange:

Jo: Oh, so do you have to go all the way back to level one?

Tom: Yeah, because we have some glitches and it doesn't really work.

Jo: So do you want it to be that you go back to the beginning of the level that you're in? Or back to the beginning of the game?

Chris: No, we want it to go 'game over', but it's just … Scratch can mess up a lot.

Tom: We'll try it tomorrow. Tomorrow it should work.

This example shows the students blaming the limitations of the game. In the second and third years of the project, when there was a higher level of expertise in using *Scratch* by the teacher as well as by the students, and there was a range of students from other year levels who had developed skills and were available to assist, then the game software itself was not blamed for errors. Overall, this first year of the project was a great success. While Nick identified many things he wished to refine in the game-making curriculum, the students had all had a successful experience and made playable games.

Bringing Composition to the Centre

By the third year of the project, Nick instituted far more preparation for students before making the actual games, and had broadened out the project to become a much more complete and nuanced inquiry-based unit of work with a strong language and literacies focus. Student expectations of the unit were high – helped by the history of it having run for the previous two years and older siblings and friends having talked to the students about what they might achieve. Nick overcame the group-work problems that had existed in the first year by choosing the teams himself – putting equal numbers of girls and boys in each team as far as possible. The students were given the task of negotiating with each other within their groups, and he challenged all students to take on all roles at different times during the project. This was a major turnaround from the free-floating approach some of the students had with their groups in the first year, and this 'enabling constraint' (Davis *et al.* 2000, p. 193) meant that the students were focused more on making their teams work rather than renegotiating the groups on a whim.

Nick took this redeveloped program and added to it a much stronger literacies focus, specifically a focus on composition. There are many standard language and literacies activities that the students have completed in the process of producing these games. In this section of the chapter, I describe the stages of the project. I have divided the activities into four stages:

1.   reviewing commercial games;
2.   narrative development;
3.   designing and coding games;
4.   games production.

After the description of what occurs in each stage of the project, I then analyse each stage in terms of the language and literacy outcomes, using Green's 3D Model of L(IT)eracy (1988; 2012) introduced above.

Reviewing Commercial Games

The students analysed how storylines worked in digital games. They considered a range of games that they played and thought about – some games having multiple routes and many possible ways of playing through the game, and other games working through sequential stages. As they played games together in class, they discussed the elements of each game. They investigated how the elements of the games came together to create the experience of the gameplay, and tried to isolate the aspects of this that would help them in their game making.

The students examined the different ways games were promoted and marketed. They researched 'in-app purchases' and thought about the ways games were structured to make money. They deconstructed game packaging, and noted what was present on the box, including company logos and persuasive texts encouraging people to buy and play the game. The students also considered what worked in terms of promoting games, and thought about how the game marketing was connected to the story of the game.

Narrative Development

The students prepared a narrative storyboard of their game in their groups. Most of these storyboards consisted of frames with pictures, showing the design of the characters, and a written description of what happens in that phase of the story and the game. The initial storyboards included an overall narrative.

Once the students had made the storyboards, they drafted their narrative. These stories were worked over and refined, and eventually 'published' as story booklets that accompanied the games. The task was to incorporate the digital gameplay during some part of the overall narrative. In most cases, the students wrote the opening sections of the narrative as a prequel to the game experience. Many commercial games present the narrative in this way, as a backstory to the game narrative. The students illustrated their stories, and these illustrations were initial designs for characters in the game.

Designing and Coding Games

In the design of the game, the students had to try to continue the narrative elements of the story that they had set up and to have the dilemmas and actions of the story plot continue through the game. They also had to try to portray and represent the characters that they had created in their storyboards and booklets as well as they could through the coding. They drew their characters and used these drawings as the animations. They were very inventive at this and made decisions about whether the character would hop or leap or jump depending on their personality. They found it difficult to program the narrative events into the game, but most of them managed to program in some of their storyline (for instance, a cupcake monster getting bigger and bigger).

There is a complexity in continuing the narrative design through both the narrative storyboard and story text, and then inscribing the story within the mechanics and physical structures and designs of the game. This is the central problem to be solved in the game creation, as the fun and enjoyment of the game comes from this intersection of mechanics and storyline. In interviews with the students, many of them talked about the difficulty of making the story come alive in the game and working out what aspects of the game mechanics would make the story work best.

Games Production

The students wrote instructions for their game – which they tested by asking others to play their game by following the instructions. This testing meant that students were reviewing each other's work and then providing feedback about the clarity of the instructions. They redrafted their instructions until they could easily be followed.

The students designed a box cover for their game. They designed a logo for the company that produced the game, and this appeared on the box. The students wrote persuasive texts for their boxes to 'sell' the game. They designed graphics to appear on the cover. Nick put all of the games on CD and the games were 'published' in their boxes. The publication of the games in this way meant that the students perceived the entire unit as an authentic task where they wrote, designed and produced a real computer game.

All of the students received a copy of their game and the game booklet at the end of the unit. They presented their games to an audience of players, as well as playing the games themselves.

Mapping the Language and Literacy Activities to the 3D Model of L(IT)eracy

In Table 7.1, I have taken the activities completed in the game-making unit, and mapped them across the dimensions of the model. Working across this table, the connectedness of aspects of the 3D Model of L(IT)eracy (Green 1988; 2012) and the multiple outcomes from the unit of work become apparent.

TABLE 7.1 Phases of game-making project mapped against 3D Model of L(IT)eracy (Green 1988)

	Operational-Technical	Cultural-Discursive	Critical-Reflexive
Reviewing commercial games	Articulating the 'how to' of playing digital games including: • loading up and starting the game; • aims of the game: i.e. how to win; • making choices about the playing out of the game; • identifying the elements of the game.	• Drawing upon and making explicit cultural knowledge of games. • Discussing the ways that different genres of games work. • Analysing how different storylines and paths create different meanings. • Considering game context (historical, audience).	• Examining the different ways games are promoted and marketed. • Researching 'in-app purchases'. Critical analysis of how games are designed to sell. • Textual analysis of game boxes, noting what is present on the box. • Consideration of how players and narratives are positioned by game marketers.
Narrative development	• Understanding and using the generic structure of the storyboard frames: pictures, character design. • Understanding and structural features of the narrative.	• Knowing and using cultural genres and forms of game types and backstories. • Drawing on cultural conventions and narrative structures to write contextually located game narratives. • Understanding the cultural form of games, and ways in which gameplay interacts with game narrative.	• Understanding that texts have a purpose and position readers /viewers/players in particular ways. • Structuring the game narratives to position the player in particular ways, to feel and experience specific things.
Designing and coding	• Understanding and using coding blocks in the *Scratch* program.	• Inscribing the story within the mechanics and physical structures and designs of the game.	• Designing for affective impact upon the payer during play.
Game production	• Understanding and using the textual features of game instructions. • Understanding and using the features of logo design. • Understanding the form and features of persuasive texts used to promote games in packaging. • Knowing how to use the CD.	• Utilising digital game instruction conventions. • Testing and providing feedback for others. • Designing logo, drawing on cultural knowledge of forms. • Playing and presenting completed games to an audience of players, as well as playing the games themselves.	• Critiquing games and reflecting on feedback given. • Writing text to try to persuade others.

Digital Fluency, Fun, Cooperation and Achieving Testable Outcomes

In this project, the students completed a range of complex literacies-based activities, where the operational, cultural and critical aspects of literacies occurred simultaneously. While game making can be positioned as a 'coding' or Technology activity, Nick's unit clearly teaches sophisticated literacies. Making the games was the creation of an authentic product for the students – a real, playable game that could be shared and enjoyed by others. The production of such an authentic task provides a context for both the literacy and the coding tasks to be completed, for a worthwhile purpose, and not just as a series of exercises. The production of the games developed the students' perception, enjoyment and ability to critique not only their own games, but also the games produced by others in the class and commercially. In the discussions of the games, the children could identify the essence of the aesthetic experience in gameplay, as well as the rules and some understanding of the mechanics and coding shapes of the game. Many of the students told me that it was quite difficult to build a game that was fun – that is, a game where the experience for the player was fun. They could articulate the way in which it was important to have a challenge in the game while simultaneously being at a level where it was playable, as well as some of the difficulties bringing together the elements of the experience. Many students found that actually making the games was more fun than playing them once they were finished, and part of this lay in the communication of the point of the game, and the instructions on play.

FIGURE 7.3 *Scratch* cat.
Source: Scratch is developed by the Lifelong Kindergarten Group at the MIT Media Lab. See https:// scratch.mit.edu.

The project aligns strongly with the Language and Literacies curriculum in Australia, where the operational, critical and cultural aspects of literacies are required through the varied approaches to text: as writer, reader, speaker, listener, viewer, producer, critic and connoisseur. However, like many jurisdictions, since the early 2000s, Australia has had an increasing focus on standardised literacy testing, which has tended to strengthen the emphasis on the easily testable, the operational-technical, at the expense of the critical-reflexive and cultural-discursive. In other work I have done, we have collected data from schools which tell us directly that they are focusing on basic skills because they have to improve their test results (see O'Mara 2014). I can feel the boredom emanating from the walls and just long for these children to be released into creative, innovative, happy classrooms like Nick's, where their basic skills are developed through the creation and reading of complex texts. For Nick, the development of the unit enabled him to strengthen his own skills not only in game making, but also in sophisticated curriculum development. He said, in his final interview for the project, that being involved in the project gave him permission to try the game making. This game-making unit helps the students towards 'digital fluency' (Resnick *et al.* 2009) and inspires 'impassioned learning' (as described by Dezuanni and O'Mara in Chapter 3 of this volume). Making the games steers students into both production and delight – the students develop connoisseurship of what makes for a good game and begin to recognise that creating something that is fun is hard work.

Note

1. See Mitch Resnick, director of the MIT Media lab, discussing this at: www.ted.com/talks/mitch_resnick_let_s_teach_kids_to_code?language=en (accessed 1 March 2016).

References

Beavis, C and Green, B (2012), 'The 3D Model in action: A review', in B Green and C Beavis (eds), *Literacy in 3D: An integrated perspective in theory and practice*, Camberwell, Victoria, Australia: ACER, pp. 39–60.

Davis, B, Sumara, D J and Luce-Kapler, R (2000), *Engaging minds: Learning and teaching in a complex world*, Mahwah, NJ: Lawrence Erlbaum Associates.

Edwards-Groves, C (2012), 'Interactive creative technologies: Changing learning practice and pedagogies in the writing classroom', *Australian Journal of Language and Literacy*, vol. 35, no. 1, pp. 99–113.

Green, B (1988), 'Subject-specific literacy and school learning: A focus on writing', *Australian Journal of Education*, vol. 32, no. 2, pp. 156–179.

Green, B (2001), 'English teaching, "Literacy" and the post-age: On compos(IT)ing and other new times metaphors', in C Durrant and C Beavis (eds), *P(ICT)ures of English: English teaching, literacy and new technologies*, Kent Town, South Australia: Wakefield Press, pp. 249–271.

Green, B (2012), 'Subject-specific literacy, writing and school learning: A revised account', in B Green and C Beavis (eds), *Literacy in 3D: An integrated perspective in theory and practice*, Camberwell, Victoria, Australia: ACER, pp. 2–21.

Halliday, M A K (1975), *Learning how to mean: Explorations in the development of language*, London: Edward Arnold.

Kress, G R (1982), *Learning to write*, London: Routledge.

Lifelong Kindergarten Group (2003), *Scratch*, MIT Media Lab. Available from: https://scratch.mit.edu (Accessed 9 August 2016).

Marji, M (2014), *Learn to program with Scratch: A visual introduction to programming with games, Art, Science, and Math*, San Francisco, CA: No Starch Press.

Moffett, J (1981), *Coming on center: English education in evolution*, Montclair, NJ: Boynton/Cook Publishers.

O'Mara, J (2014), 'Closing the emergency facility: Moving schools from literacy triage to better literacy outcomes', *English Teaching: Practice and Critique*, vol. 13, no. 16, pp. 8–23.

Papert, S (1979), *Final report of the Brookline LOGO Project*, Cambridge, MA: Massachusetts Institute of Technology, Artificial Intelligence Laboratory.

Papert, S (1980), *Mindstorms: Children, computers, and powerful ideas.* New York, NY: Basic Books.

Papert, S (1993), *Mindstorms: Children, computers, and powerful ideas* (2nd ed.), New York, NY: Basic Books.

Resnick, M, Maloney, J, Monroy-Hernández, A, Rusk, N, Eastmond, E, Brennan, K, Millner, A, Rosenbaum, E, Silver, J, Silverman, B and Kafai, Y (2009), 'Scratch: Programming for all', *Communications of the ACM*, vol. 52, no. 11, pp. 60–67. Available from: http://cacm.acm.org/magazines/2009/11/48421-scratch-programming-for-all/fulltext (Accessed 28 November 2016).

Schön, D A (1983), *The reflective practitioner: How professionals think in action*, New York, NY: Basic Books.

Sploder™ (n. d.), *Sploder*. Available from: www.sploder.com/termsofservice.php (Accessed 12 August 2016).

Vygotsky, L, Hanfmann, E and Vakar, G (1962), *Thought and language*, Cambridge, MA: The MIT Press.

8

MINING THE CLI-FI WORLD

Renegotiating the Curriculum Using *Minecraft*

Joanne O'Mara and Kynan Robinson

> **The planet Earth is in chaos…**
> *Climate Change has ravaged the land, with food and drinking water now in short supply.*
> *Civil unrest, extreme poverty and disease are rampant, as global warming has caused sickness,*
> *famine and a 5000% increase in the occurrence of natural disasters. Fossil fuels are all but*
> *gone, crisis talks are held by the New World Order.*
>
> *The New World Order has asked you to form* **The Districts** *and provided you with the last*
> *of its available resources so that you may attempt to terraform the planet Aurora56z: the*
> *closest planet with atmosphere composition similar to Earth. You must reach Aurora56z,*
> *and, equipped with the creative tools at your disposal, your mission is to Terraform Aurora56z,*
> *to create a colony for the human race.*
>
> *Good luck. The future of the human race is in your hands …* **No pressure**.
> (Brief given to a Year 5/6 primary school group)

Introduction

Places Real and Virtual

'The planet Earth is in chaos … no pressure' was the brief given to a Year 5/6 primary school group (across several classes), at the launch of a 10-week unit of project-based curriculum in the classroom. A group of teachers from the school were undertaking their own research into digital pedagogies, how they might be changing the way students learn and the implications of this for teacher and student practices. Additionally, the school had a focus on developing creative approaches to learning, and had received a large grant from the state Department of Education to develop a computer games curriculum. This unit was developed to bring all of these elements together, with 136 young people, five individual teachers and Kynan (co-author of this chapter) working together to negotiate the curriculum. This work became the focus of Kynan's PhD study (Robinson 2017) and a key site in the research project, Serious Play (Beavis *et al.* 2011–2015).

From the beginning, this primary school was actively involved in the Serious Play project, with strong engagement from eight staff members who were highly supported by their principal. The ambitious *Minecraft* (Mojang 2011) project described in this chapter was first conducted in 2012, when it was very new and innovative to use *Minecraft* for educational purposes. Since then, the curriculum unit has been replicated and further developed each year as a cross-curriculum project. This approach to curriculum covers the 'Sustainability' and 'Biospheres' aspects of the Science curriculum; and, as young people negotiate their co-construction of the new world, Social Education issues such as 'Sustainable Living' and the 'Social Effects of Climate Change' are examined and experienced. These young people work together to create this virtual world – developing skills of composition, imagination, creativity and thinking, through role-play. They design their own spacecraft using Google SketchUp; develop an argument for why their design should be selected to be manufactured; and participate in a drama activity, where they move from the classroom to a dramatic virtual world of a spacecraft made of classroom chairs, and 'land' in a new digital virtual world in the *Minecraft* server! They also embark on their own further investigations of science, researching nuclear power, solar energy, wind power and sustainability so that they can uphold their positions in debate with classmates about what to build in Aurora56z.

Researching the 'Ruins' of Aurora56z

In researching the project, we used conventional data-generation methods, including student interviews, teacher interviews, classroom observation and collection of work samples and artefacts; the most significant of these were the *Minecraft* server and student-produced Wikis. What has been particularly interesting about the process of researching the Aurora56z project is 'mining' the huge volume of data collected through the preservation of the *Minecraft* server as well as the student Wikis which recorded the thinking and negotiations through the construction of the new world, Aurora56z. Kynan immersed himself in this world as he wrote his doctoral thesis, and this has led to the development of his exploratory and practice-led approach to the data analysis. In his process of analysing the server data, Kynan wrote a novel set in Aurora56z, casting the young people as the characters and the 'ruins' of the server as the setting. This immersion in the world of Aurora56z, and reinterpretation of the stagnant server by creating a lively text based upon what he found in the server and the students' Wiki pages, helped him to understand the creative learning process of the curriculum unit more deeply. Somerville (2007) has described emergence in research and the ontological view that researchers 'become' their research through 'opening the mind expansion, seeking to know the unknown, being uncertain, not proving but wandering' (p. 228). In becoming this research, we draw upon our own experiences of fictional virtual worlds, in understanding young people's conceptualisations as we 'mine the data'. The ability to capture data so easily from the entire *Minecraft* server for later examination, as well as the complete set of student blogs, means that the architectures of the virtual world remain as a complete set of 'ruins' for us to work (St Pierre and Pillow 2000).

In this chapter, we focus on the curriculum design of this project-based unit, our understandings and findings about the project, as well as the tensions and opportunities that the project opens up and enables. There was a genuine desire by the teaching staff initially involved for the project-based unit to be open and emergent (Johnson 2002), thinking of the *Minecraft* server and the students' work in it as a dynamic, living system. In this way, *Minecraft* enabled an open approach to the curriculum that differs from many digital games for educational purposes which tend to have more of a fixed or closed approach to the curriculum. The teachers working on the initial curriculum design incorporated aspects of a framework drawn from educational approaches to complexity theory (Waldrop 1992; Davis *et al.* 2000; Doll *et al.* 2005; Mason 2008; Laidlaw and So-Har Wong 2016). A complexity approach to education can value open systems, self-organisation, lack of top-down control and the value of the collective for knowledge production. The most influential ideas on the planning of this unit were to aim for self-organisation within the *Minecraft* world, trying to create a curriculum unit that worked on this idea of an open system, developing structures and spaces for internal communication within Aurora56z and remembering the value of all students contributing to create collective knowledge. The addition of the *Minecraft* Wiki as an adjunct to the world created inside the server was made so that the Wiki would operate as an open communication tool. The teachers also attempted to avoid hierarchical controls over the system, but this proved difficult given the teacher–student hierarchy built into the organisation of the schooling system. Because of this, the curriculum remained partially closed, and in many ways, relations between teachers and young people were still 'business as usual'. Within the classroom, there was a tension for the teachers between the openness of *Minecraft*, their desires to be open and enable creativity, and their duties and roles as classroom teachers.

Throughout the project we documented many examples of young people playing with the resources and openness of *Minecraft*, making new games and exploring ways to play inside the environments that *Minecraft* provides. The young people did this within the classroom environment – as an aside to the world of the classroom project, as well as within it.

Creating a 'Cli-Fi' Virtual World

The concept of creating a virtual world for space colonisation is not a new one, and there are established examples used in process drama (see e.g. Morgan and Saxton 1989). There also exists a plethora of commercial space colonisation games (e.g. *Civilization: Beyond Earth* [Meier 2014], *Homeworld Remastered* [Sierra Entertainment 2015] and *Alpha Centauri* [Meier 1999]). Textually, these games and approaches follow ideas that have become popular in what is known as ecotopian fiction – science fiction following climate-change themes, dubbed climate fiction or 'Cli-Fi' by Dan Bloom in 2008 (Holmes 2014). This sub-genre of science fiction explores the consequences of human-induced climate change – social changes, environmental changes on Earth and/or the establishment of new societies after Earth's destruction. Both authors of this chapter are readers of Cli-Fi, and we can trace the influences of this fiction and our own commitments to raising awareness about human-induced climate change on Kynan's leadership of the project, our subsequent readings of the work the young people did in building Aurora56z and Kynan's writing of the novel set in the *Minecraft* server of Aurora56z (extracts of this writing are discussed later in this chapter). Kynan has previously composed and performed music to accompany readings of sections from *The Road* by Cormac McCarthy (2006), a dystopian Cli-Fi novel that explores the relationship between a father and son in the landscape of a dystopic future. For Kynan, the experience of walking through and inhabiting the *Minecraft* server, after the young people had left, felt like the walk through the remnants of the dystopic America described in McCarthy's *The Road*. This Cli-Fi framing of the curriculum was also shared and shaped by all the teachers in the project. The young people were also committed as a group to the importance of action for climate change. The school is located in the only political seat in Australia held at present by the Greens political party, and climate change is an important issue for this community. All of these perspectives were important to the shaping of Aurora56z and our research, and represent the funds of knowledge (Moll *et al.* 1992) that the Year 5/6 community brought to the server and the shaping of the curriculum unit.

Choosing Minecraft and Developing the Wiki

Minecraft was chosen as the game platform because of its immense popularity with the students as well as the openness of its design. The teachers and Kynan noted its open structure and lack of hierarchy and the fact that its architecture allowed for adaptation and evolution. *Minecraft* also allows for a diverse and large range of participants to play at the same time (thus adding to its complexity) and by so doing, it seems to sit somewhere between order and disorder. It also enables the students to self-organise. The absence of any strict rules of predetermining agenda and the ability of the player to build anything have led to the creation of many outstanding and original styles of play. We have noted both with the play of our own children and with the students in this study that these new modes of playing and additional artefacts, such as 'skins' (which transform the look of characters), are shared between players through paratexts (Genette 1997; Consalvo 2007) such as YouTube videos and blogs. These new styles of play and creations emerge as players constantly shift the ways of playing that take advantage of the affordances of *Minecraft*. This openness made it ideal for the development of the project-based unit.

Minecraft players can choose between two modes: 'creative' and 'survival'. In creative mode, players have access to unlimited resources and tools needed to build. Creative mode is totally uninhabited on entry. In survival mode, skills and resources have to be learnt and earned, and a host of predators roams the world, destroying things and killing people. The teachers decided to simplify the *Minecraft* usage and focus on the curriculum outcomes by playing in *creative mode*. Even then, there were times when several of the students went around 'griefing' other people's work – destroying things that other people had built.

A Wikispace was developed in conjunction with the *Minecraft* server. The Wiki enabled both students and teachers to upload content, comment on each other's content, modify content and collaborate in the context of this project. It was a central place where students' research, discoveries, reflections on learning and ideas could be presented. The Wiki was viewable and editable by everybody: teachers and students could read each other's reflections, provide feedback on each other's work and find appropriate people with whom to collaborate and form working groups.

Creating and Shaping the Curriculum World

In this section of the chapter, we describe the ways in which the teachers set up the unit. While we are not presenting this work as a 'cookie cutter' type of curriculum that can be easily transplanted, we endeavour in our description to provide enough detail for others to develop curriculum, building on our experience, as well as showing the ways in which the unit was shaped to enable collective learning and self-organisation.

Designing the Ark

Students were given the task of designing an 'ark' to transport the group and their supplies to Aurora56z. They had to submit a design of the ark that included a complete Google SketchUp drawing (with the option of including accompanying drawings or models), details about the materials used (and justification of these) as well as a list of supplies that would be carried on board and appropriate spacesuits needed for the trip. The teachers incorporated this preparatory task so that students would think through the possibilities of and restrictions on leaving Earth

– and investigate the fact that large-scale migration to another planet, even if there was a close, compatible one, is not possible. Students had to complete a form for 'NASA', which required further details about the spacecraft, including name, dimensions, number of passengers, cargo, landing system, materials used for the main body and the heat shield of the craft. Students researched rockets and space stations and designed their own. While these craft were imagined, students read widely about aspects of design that were important to enable the spacecraft to travel safely. Students were given the following fact file about Aurora56z, in order to design a craft that could make it all the way from Earth to Aurora56z.

AURORA56Z FACT FILE

Distance from Earth: 6,905,326,156 km

Average distance from Sun: 149,553,698 km

Revolution period (length of year in Earth days): 365 days

Rotation period (length of day in Earth days): 24 hours

Diameter (km): 37,387

Mean maximum surface temperature (K): 308

Mean minimum surface temperature (K): 257

Moons: Serenity and Reverie

Highest point on surface: Mt Renaissance

Atmospheric components: 78% nitrogen, 21% oxygen, 1% argon

Geographic regions: Salt water oceans, fresh water lakes and rivers, desert, rainforests, grasslands, pastoral land, forests, mountainous regions, rocky regions, polar ice caps.

Compatible with Earth flora and fauna: Yes

New mineral element: Aurotonium

Figure 8.1 provides an example of one of the arks created by a student, in this case, a shuttle named *Prometheus*. This particular ark was accompanied by the text of a speech to be presented to NASA. The text was a sales pitch, trying to convince NASA that this would be the best ark to build, because 'this ship has more than enough space and power to get to Aurora56z, with the living space equal to a four star hotel, not only will the journey be fast it will also be enjoyable'. Additionally, the student noted that:

Once the PROMETHEUS has served its purpose of getting us to Aurora, it can also be reused as a new version of the HUBBLE or VOYAGER, exploring the galaxy, photographing it with its cameras and sending back the information using the aerials on the wings and main tail.

This student also discussed the naming of the ship:

The PROMETHEUS is named after the Greek titan, Prometheus, who is the benefactor of humans. He saved us many times – so will the shuttle. It will save the human race too, by taking us from this dying planet and helping us reach our new home.

He then presented the rest of the design features. The students researched and designed many different types of spacecraft from both fictional worlds and actual crafts, and their work covered aspects of design that needed to be taken into consideration when building a craft, including how it might be fuelled.

Once the designs had all been completed, the teachers and students role-played a trip to the new planet. Everyone set up a chair into a configuration to represent the ark. Together, they counted down to lift-off, and imagined the trip to the new planet. When they 'arrived', they entered the *Minecraft* server. The use of drama here enabled the students to enter the virtual world, through enacting the shift between the world of the classroom and the digital virtual world. Drama was chosen as it was a way for the students to work together, to build an ark and to think about the space they would have on the journey, and what they would feel like leaving Earth behind. This act of imagination through drama added realism to the establishment of the *Minecraft* world.

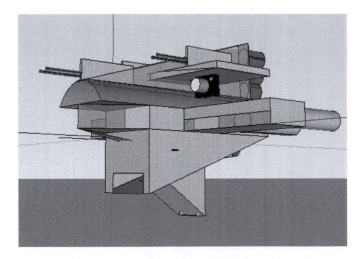

FIGURE 8.1 The space shuttle *Prometheus*, created on Google SketchUp.

Terraforming Aurora56z: 'The Districts'

Finally we have landed on our new planet and are ready to begin terraforming our new home. Remember to learn from the mistakes of the past and also to respect the ideas of your fellow council members …

(Opening lines of the Wiki)

The students then began the work on terraforming Aurora56z and they were given the task of working out a strategy to do this. After discussion with all participants, the students decided as a group to divide the planet into districts, with each district being assigned an overarching research task that would then lead into decisions on what was to be built within the world. The teachers supported this decision, and worked with the students to develop 'The Districts'. The districts were named according to specific areas of responsibility: Industry; Agriculture; City and Culture; Discovery and Education; and Recreation. The teachers then devised tasks for each district to complete. The complete instructions given to the Industry District are shown below.

INSTRUCTIONS FROM THE SUPREME COUNCIL TO THE INDUSTRIAL DISTRICT

As members of the Industrial District you are responsible for researching, selecting and building sustainable energy sources on our new home Aurora 56z that will keep our new planet safe and environmentally friendly while also supplying our population, businesses and industry with sufficient energy.

You must research every available energy source, and find the pros and cons of each one.

You must work as a group to decide what recommendations to make regarding energies we must use and how to best use them.

With knowledge of the features and properties of each energy source, you must work as a group and with other districts to decide where to best build and use each energy source and complete these building tasks on *Minecraft*.

Explore possible new energies on Aurora56z, including the use of newly found element Aurotonium.

Conduct conferences with a range of Districts in regards to your screen shot or recommendations through the Wikispace.

Video record lectures and information in regards to particular topics.

In researching energy sources for the Industry District, the students were asked to compare the environmental costs of different ways of generating energy for industry; decide on what energy sources would be best; and then argue for them. The Industry District quickly got to work, researching energy types, and finding out what the other students wanted. They produced an online survey using digital survey software, seeking feedback from the students in the other districts about the usage of renewable and non-renewable resources and their preferences. This information was used to help the group argue for their preferred energy types. They made a giant **I**, the symbol of the Industry District (see Figure 8.2) and began production of solar panels and wind turbines (see Figure 8.3).

FIGURE 8.2 The Industry District sign.

FIGURE 8.3 Piles of solar panels ready for installation (note the giant wind turbine in the background).

Other districts had similar tasks related to their themes. The Agriculture District was required to research and present findings about what quarantine rules and procedures needed to be in place to ensure the survival of the flora and fauna that were brought to Aurora56z. This group was also responsible for researching significant sustainable practices that the citizens of Aurora56z might undertake to preserve and protect the flora and fauna. They considered the impacts of deforestation, and the seed vaults and quarantine rules so that diseases did not spread, as well as building gardens and farms.

The City and Culture District team was set a series of questions to guide its research:

- What problems did we have to deal with on Earth in regard to waste management? What can we learn from this?
- What alternatives can we suggest?
- How much waste will we produce?
- What sorts of waste do we need to deal with and dispose of?
- How will we dispose of waste in an environmentally friendly manner?
- How can we minimise the effects of waste on Aurora56z?

They were tasked with researching the significant sustainable practices that the citizens of Aurora56z could undertake to preserve and protect the planet, and 'not make the same errors we did on planet Earth'. They were the ones who built waste-disposal units and worked out the logistics for transporting the waste. The students in this district did a great deal of work on achieving 'public buy in' for their recycling stations and waste-management systems, including designing advertisements that encouraged the citizens to reduce, reuse and recycle.

The Discovery and Education District team were charged with researching what the population needed to do to 'keep our new planet safe and environmentally friendly'. The main task given to this group was to build research laboratories that would help to educate the new civilisation about the latest scientific discoveries that would sustain them. They were asked to conduct conferences, inviting other districts to attend, and to create video lectures about their research. As with all districts, what was inside and outside their brief was constantly negotiated as part of the learning framework. For instance, when the Discovery and Education District team was also asked to explore recycling, future conservation and energy, some members of the district argued that this was outside their brief. Members' comments included points such as, 'I think that energy is something that Industry is supposed to do and that we should work with them but I believe it is their responsibility and not ours'. Negotiating the roles and responsibilities of each group throughout the unit proved to be an ongoing area where the teachers worked with the students to enable them to understand aspects of civics and citizenship, and how responsibilities were negotiated in society.

The District of Recreation was responsible for the establishment of parks and gardens across Aurora56z. This included ensuring an environmentally sound balance between the natural environment and the needs of humanity. They were briefed that 'Aurora56z is naturally abundant in the element Aurotonium. Whilst the element has many uses, it is, unfortunately, highly soluble. As such, all the naturally occurring water on Aurora56z is salt water'. This introduced a problem that this district had to solve – how to provide fresh water for the population. The district conducted research about salt levels and the effects of high salinity in soil, and briefed the District of Agriculture. They built parks and gardens and provided an engineered solution to meet irrigation needs. They surveyed the other districts about how everyone wanted to spend their leisure time, and built a range of facilities for the rest of the population. They wrote that one of their 'main priorities is parkland as that is a good place to exercise and stay healthy'. They also built gyms and aquatic centres and sporting facilities for both children and adults.

'All Citizens' Meetings

Every week, a one-hour 'all citizens' meeting was held in the school hall. These were significant meetings for the students, as it gave them the opportunity to organise themselves, and voice issues that potentially needed to reach the entire group. For the first two weeks, the meeting was done as a collective of all the students. By the third week of the project, the students worked in their districts, discussing matters relating to their district. At some point in the meeting, a chosen representative reported back to the entire group. As the work progressed, the students took more and more responsibility for organising these meetings, and the time was divided between districts reporting and talking amongst themselves, dealing with the weekly issues of their districts and also reporting what needed to happen on a systemic level.

In the final week of the *Minecraft* unit, a summit was held. All of the students attended, and presented their learning to a panel of real-world experts. This panel consisted of the head of the Australian Broadcasting Commission's Education Department, a science teacher from the local secondary school, their own school's principal and a representative from the Department of Education. Each district nominated members to present their work, through oral presentations and playing the videocasts they had produced of their district's collective work. These were usually in the form of filmed walkthroughs of the *Minecraft* world.

Classroom Engagement With the Aurora56z Project

The data collected from students and teachers showed high levels of engagement with this project-based unit. In our classroom observations, we observed that the young people were real stakeholders in this world. Kynan wrote about this in his novel, bringing together his observation notes, extracts from students' blogs and interviews. In working through the data later, Kynan was struck by the stillness and desolation compared to the liveliness when the world was being created and the server was a hive of activity. The extract below from Kynan's novel captures the energy of the *Minecraft* classroom, the language of the enterprise and the stillness of the empty server – with the world constructed by the students still there to be examined, but it is lonely, as all life and movement are absent.

> There were agents on Aurora56z. They were buzzing with participation, they were buzzing like fireflies excited by the others' lights. Divulging a collective morphing. The agents were all children from the original class of the Unmoulded, and they were growing vigorously and amongst an emerging labyrinth of layers, spreading in all directions.
>
> There was chatter everywhere, on all channels. This chatter created new fragments, new sounds; unfamiliar melodic echoes, whisperings of chaos, of intertwining roots and layers. Pulsed by the chatter, the system burgeoned forth with a sense of urgency.
>
> Aurora and her system breathed more life into herself. She sat like a wide-eyed child on an abandoned seesaw. Sawing up into the ordered clear sky, then seeing down into the unkempt grass below, never still for more than a fleeting breath. In moments resembling Icarus, flying too close to the sun of chaos, only to be just swept back to the right balance. And at other times, reaching a state of near equilibrium ...
>
> Does this explain her now eerie silence? Aurora56Z, do you speak no more? Now she is a place where only spirits and energies float amongst the corridors of infrastructure. Where one can still feel the dark shadow of a former child like an impression left upon a sheet, but one's eyes can never see these children anymore. Are they still here or have the system's lungs drawn its last breath?

We include this extract from the novel to demonstrate how we, as researchers, felt when we explored what the students had created. Inhabiting this world, tracing and tracking the students' creations and approaches to the curriculum tasks led Kynan, in particular, to discoveries like those described in the next section. Such feelings were not noticed or found in the classroom moment, but discovered in the silence and loneliness of what the students had created earlier.

Mining the Data: Escape to Club Med

The project documented many examples of young people playing with the resources and openness of *Minecraft*, making new games and exploring ways to play inside the environments that *Minecraft* provides. The young people played within the classroom environment – often as an aside to the world of the classroom project, but sometimes within it. As the full project was accessible through the server (the *Minecraft* world, the blogs, Wiki and chats), there was a large amount of data, which revealed more and more surprises from the young people. Close investigation and follow-up interviews with young people revealed the ways in which they had played, subverting the curriculum as they made their own games within the game world. Kynan traced the trajectories of a group of students who, unbeknownst to the teachers or many of the other students, had 'escaped' from Aurora56z. Through interviews and by tracking through their work and the world, he found their builds and notes and asked them about it, reconstructing and imagining their escape. Here is a section of Kynan's novel, where these pieces of data have come together to illustrate the escape.

ESCAPE TO THE ISLAND

Once the Supreme Council's presence floated above and throughout all parts of Aurora56z. But that was 'once' and no longer. Aurora56z had found a way to open cracks and crevices where the Supreme Council's spirit couldn't enter. Far away spots.

A group of eight agents built an island, far away. A hidden spot where no one could find them.

They escaped – they fled across the vast waters. Their floating bodies travelling at great speeds. They pushed on as far as they could go. As they flew the water looked like shards of sparkling blue ice underneath their bodies. As they flew the green disappeared, replaced by two shades of blue, the blue of the sky above them and the blue of the liquid mass underneath them. It was like a blue desert – flat, without the sand dunes. Eight boys – ambitioned to disappear.

The further they went, the less their flight path became one of singular purpose. The further they went, the freer they felt and ambition was replaced with happiness and the exhilaration of dissent. The boys now started to frolic in their flight paths, diving down into the water, down deep, turning when breath had almost escaped their lungs and racing to air again. Bursting free of water with a huge splash, shouting as they went up, soared into the sky. From blue to blue. They continued on until land was not visible anymore and then they stopped. Only ocean.

'What shall we do?', asked Red.

'Let's build – what else are we going to do?'

Using their new-found 'creative' skills, unique to this planet, they laid a bed of fresh grass directly on top of the ocean bed. From one block of grass sprung another, then another, then another.

The boys laughed as they laid down their own private island, one block at a time. It was the kind of laughter that simultaneously poured from the back of the throat and the wells of the eyes at the same time.

In no time at all they had a land mass and then a purpose. This could be our own private hideaway, a place we come to get away from the rest of them. A place where no one will find us, our own Contiki Island.

The boys roared with laughter again. This time it sprang out from their whole body.

A feeling of camaraderie flooded through the boys. A shared project, their own, with no implications or direct reporting back into the system required. An island separated not only from the Supreme Council, but also cleaved away from the system. Their responsibilities were their own on their island.

They helped each other with building houses, to live in on their holiday resort. Some houses were for a residency of one, others were lived in communally. They collectively built a restaurant, supposedly to be staffed and frequented by only themselves. They built resort-styled entertainment areas, the kind you would find on any sundrenched beach paradise back on Earth. They lazed around and idly chatted. On a planet a million miles from any other human contact, these boys had decided to hide.

To hide in their own version of paradise – without the lessons, without the structures.

But is it untrue that they completely deserted the remaining 136 Unmoulded?

'We need to go back from time to time', said Red while slowly swinging in his hammock.

'Why?' replied Angus.

'Well, it will lower suspicion if we are seen intermittently back with the others, and I quite liked some of the things I was working on.'

'Do you think we will get in trouble if the others find out we are not there?'

'I don't know.'

While this has been represented in a creative text, written to give the feeling of freedom the boys wrote about as they zoomed around the *Minecraft* server, it is based very closely on the data, and re-presents the boys' creation of their hideaway place. As researchers, we are extremely interested in the ways in which the students owned and worked the server. The enormous scale of what the students created meant that the teachers and ourselves, with our less developed skills, did not see much of what was happening on the server (none of us had spent as much time on the server as the students had). Instead, teachers relied on students to take them to places and show them, to make videos of short fly-throughs and to write about the world with screen shots. It was only later, during Kynan's deeper exploratory work, after the unit had finished, that he discovered these surprises.

Working the Ruins: the Server as Panopticon

We are interested in the ways in which the permanence of the server data as a complete data set makes it in some ways the ultimate panopticon (Foucault 1977), where we and the 'Supreme Council' (or teachers) can conduct surveillance on the movements and thoughts of the students, without them knowing when or where they are being watched. At the time of the world's creation, the young people also inhabited the world and could see what we are now only just finding out. Their ability to 'make their escape' so seamlessly, with time enough to build a fully equipped island, full of everything they wanted and needed, was possible because we weren't watching – there was too much to watch, too much to see, and no way for us to fast-track our searching of the world through a 'search function'; it had to be done through exploration, flight or on foot. When we see the island now, we are filled with delight at the daring of it and the identities the students created for themselves as escapees, while at the same time completing their assigned tasks and cooperating with others in the creation of Aurora56z.

In this chapter we have tried to show the affordances and possibilities that *Minecraft* offers educational settings, by detailing aspects of the Aurora56z curriculum and its enactment. The teachers worked towards being open in the administration of the unit, working to enable the students to have leadership of some sections of the curriculum, and to support them in the development of negotiation skills. In doing so, they opened up possibilities for themselves as teachers, and over subsequent years of running the *Minecraft* server to support their curriculum work, they have become more confident and less apprehensive about what might happen. Inside the virtual world, the students developed their own ways of being there, their own ways of working through the activities and crafting their landscape.

As well as highlighting some of the tensions inherent in bringing open gaming curriculum into the classroom, we have also discussed some of the challenges for us as researchers. While we used the traditional data-generation methods of a case study – interviews, observations and work samples – the addition of the server, student blogs and Wiki meant that the volume of data generated in a short period of time was magnified beyond what is usually possible to collect in classroom research. We began to think of the server as the 'ruins' of Aurora56z, an uninhabited world, which to us felt lonely at times. We have highlighted working the ruins (St Pierre and Pillow 2000) and the ways in which these ruins show more than was visible at the time, as it was hidden by the sheer volume of material and interactions that were occurring in this curriculum unit. In doing all this, we encourage teachers and researchers to take similar journeys of new discovery, to draw on the affordances of digital games such as *Minecraft* to engage their students and to enable them the possibility of imagining their worlds – our worlds – to be otherwise.

References

Beavis, C, Dezuanni, M, O'Mara, J, Prestridge, S, Rowan, L, Zagami, J and Chee, Y S (2011–2015), *Serious Play: Using digital games in school to promote literacy and learning in the twenty first century*, Canberra, ACT: Australian Research Council.

Consalvo, M (2007), *Cheating: Gaining advantage in videogames*, Cambridge, MA: The MIT Press.

Davis, B, Sumara, D J and Luce-Kapler, R (2000), *Engaging minds: Learning and teaching in a complex world*, Mahwah, NJ: Lawrence Erlbaum Associates.

Doll, W E, Flenner, M J, Trueit, D and St John, J (2005), *Chaos, complexity, curriculum and culture: A conversation*, New York, NY: Peter Lang.

Foucault, M (1977), *Discipline and punish: The birth of the prison*, New York, NY: Vintage Books.

Genette, G (1997), *Paratexts: Thresholds of interpretation*, New York, NY: Cambridge University Press.

Holmes, D (2014), '"Cli-fi": Could a literary genre help save the planet?', *The Conversation*. Available from: http://theconversation.com/cli-fi-could-a-literary-genre-help-save-the-planet-23478 (Accessed 28 July 2016).

Johnson, S (2002), *Emergence: The connected lives of ants, brains, cities, and software*, New York, NY: Scribner.

Laidlaw, L and So-Har Wong, S (2016), 'Literacy and complexity: On using technology within emergent learning structures with young learners', *Complicity: An International Journal of Complexity and Education*, vol. 13, no. 1, pp. 30–42.

McCarthy, C (2006), *The road*, New York, NY: Vintage Books.

Mason, M. (ed.) (2008), *Complexity theory and the philosophy of education*, Bognor Regis, UK: Wiley–Blackwell.

Meier S (1999), *Alpha Centauri*, Redwood City, CA: Firaxis Games/Electronic Arts.

Meier S (2014), *Civilization: Beyond Earth*, Austin, TX: Firaxis Games/Aspyr Media Inc. Available from: http://franchise.civilization.com/en/games/civilization-beyond-earth/ (Accessed 10 August 2016).

Mojang (2011), *Minecraft*. Available from: https://minecraft.net/en/ (Accessed 8 August 2016).

Moll, L C, Amanti, C, Neff, D and Gonzalez, N (1992), 'Funds of knowledge for teaching: Using a qualitative approach to connect homes and classrooms', *Theory Into Practice*, vol. 31, no. 2, pp. 132–141.

Morgan, N and Saxton, J (1989), *Teaching drama: A mind of many wonders*, Cheltenham, UK: Stanley Thornes Publishers.

Robinson, K (2017), 'Enabling a culture of creativity in schools', unpublished PhD Thesis, Faculty of Arts and Education, Deakin University, Australia.

Sierra Entertainment (2015), *Homeworld Remastered*, Rennes, France: Ubisoft.

Somerville, M (2007), 'Postmodern emergence', *International Journal of Qualitative Studies in Education*, vol. 20, no. 2, pp. 225–243.

St Pierre, E and Pillow, W S (2000), *Working the ruins: Feminist poststructural theory and methods in education*, New York, NY: Routledge.

Waldrop, M M (1992), *Complexity: The emerging science at the edge of order and chaos*, New York, NY: Simon & Schuster.

Digital Literacies in the Wild – Multimodality, Materiality and Embodiment

THEME PREFACE

As texts and textual practices are rapidly changing with new ways of mediation, teachers and schools are rethinking what constitutes a text for study in school, how these texts might be studied, and what is lost and gained by doing this. These questions are particularly pertinent when digital games are introduced into the school curriculum for textual analysis and for learning, as they are interactive texts, created in the process of play and centrally driven by action. When students play and create games, they draw upon a range of textual practices beyond what is typically described as literacy.

The tensions between understanding games as play (ludology) and as story (narratology) play out in the games-studies literature as well as in the curriculum work of teachers. Throughout the project, we worked intensely with the teachers, sharing our understandings of practice and theory with each other. The Games as Text, Games as Action Model was developed by Beavis and Apperley in a previous project through a similar process of collaboration with teachers. In the Serious Play project, this model was one of the theoretical approaches that we worked with, and Beavis, Prestridge and O'Mara apply this model to teachers' work in Chapter 9. The three examples used in the chapter illustrate the different ways and extents to which teachers in different schooling contexts enabled elements of the text and action of gameplay to come to the fore as the focus of their work with students. The use of the model worked as a framework to help in understanding how digital games can be used to enhance language, literacy and literary learning, and to work with games in these areas of the curriculum.

Gameplay and the worlds around games also exist within a series of material and non-material, embodied and disembodied relationships. In this project, part of our work was in exploring the ways and extents to which the real and virtual came together in the game worlds, and how teachers might make use of the affordances of games for curriculum purposes. As has been seen in other chapters, *Minecraft* was one of the most popular games used in schools in the project. In Chapter 10, Dezuanni draws upon Actor–Network Theory (ANT) to position *Minecraft* play as a process of co-authored assemblage. He examines one example of how *Minecraft* was used in our project, when a Year 3 class at a private girls' school built models of their school in *Minecraft* and *Lego*. In this project, students could choose the medium to replicate the school as assemblage; and building through creating in *Minecraft* can be understood as actual building and creating rather than a representation of building in creating. He describes how the Year 3 students in the project became designers/makers/architects through discursive and material assemblage.

9

GAMES AS TEXT AND GAMES AS ACTION

English, Literacy and Digital Games

Catherine Beavis, Sarah Prestridge and Joanne O'Mara

Introduction

Chapters to date have discussed numerous ways in which teachers and students worked with games to build knowledge in disciplinary areas; the ways in which they made and played games; opportunities for creativity in and around games; and the role of games in the everyday business of young people's lives. In this chapter, we discuss a third area of focus – the role of games as distinctive forms incorporating both text and action, within a context where attention to both print and multimodal literacies are a crucial but contentious area of English and Literacy education.

Through the work of scholars such as Gee (2007), Steinkuehler (2006, 2007), Marsh (2010) and others, we have a wealth of studies showing the depth and scope of young people's literacy practices within and around games in their leisure-time play; the textual complexity of games as multimodal forms and the embodiment of multiliteracies together with interrelationships between games, gameplay and the business of living. Research has explored links between games, gameplay and identity (Taylor 2006; Corneliussen and Rettberg 2008; Jenson and de Castell 2010; Chee 2015); and issues of investment, performance, status and community, and the development and role of affinity groups (Steinkuehler 2006; Chee 2011; Gee and Hayes 2011). With respect to language, literacy, learning and cognition, studies such as Steinkuehler's (2008) have mapped discourses generated through and apparent in games, particularly online multiplayer games. Much has been made also of games' capacity to generate deep understandings and high levels of cognition, foster collaborative learning practices and promote a range of new and traditional literacy practices.

In an expanded view of literacy, where multiliteracies and multimodal texts are recognised as a central part of young people's textual worlds, the incorporation and study of digital texts within the English and Language Arts areas have become an important priority at both policy and professional levels (International Reading Association 2012; Australian Curriculum Assessment and Reporting Authority 2016). Exploring what it looks like in practice to work with digital texts, however, and which cultural forms should be prioritised, is less clear. When it comes to bringing videogames into the English and Literacy classroom, conceiving of games in purely textual terms is challenging, even where there is an expanded view of texts to include audio, visual and moving texts. While narratively oriented digital games in some respects resemble other multimodal forms, such as television and film (Bolter and Grusin 2000), there are also significant differences to these forms, with activity and interaction at the heart of what constitutes games. The construction of games as text alone, however multimodal, raises major questions. As Apperley noted:

> [O]ne of the key difficulties facing teaching practitioners using interactive media, such as video games in the English and Literacy classroom, is identifying, describing and conceptualising the role that 'interactivity' has in the process of consuming the media, while still remaining relevant to the more literary concerns of the curriculum.
>
> *(Apperley 2010, p. 12)*

He called on core concepts from games studies – ergodicity (the 'actual effort or work' that goes into playing games); encoding/decoding ('how the ergodic process intersects with students' imagination and interpretation of games'); and ludology (the study or science of play) as helpful in allowing games 'to be understood in their own right both as a unique form of "interactive" entertainment media, and as a part of contemporary audio, visual and narrative cultures' (Apperley 2010, p. 13).

Games come into existence only when played, and are centrally driven by action. Tensions between views of games understood primarily as play – 'ludology' – and games understood primarily as forms of story – 'narratology' – run through games-studies literature, with positions strongly held on both sides, although something of a rapprochement has been reached in recent years. The key point, for literacy educators, is how to think about and understand games as both; and to recognise and respond to the specificities of the form, which encompass both. This requires stretching and reconceptualising constructions of texts and literacy, and a preparedness to engage with forms that cannot totally be contained, with attendant challenges for how curriculum subjects such as English are understood. Reconceptualising what counts as literacy and text similarly has implications for how games are utilised within existing subject parameters and assessment regimes.

Questions about the nature of games as text, the degree to which they could be conceived as such, and the challenges posed to traditional print-based literacies by games as multimodal forms – together with case-based studies of what might be gained through working with games – were a central focus in the antecedent project to Serious Play which was called *Literacy in the Digital World of the Twenty-First Century: Learning from Computer Games* (Beavis *et al.* 2007–2010). The Games as Text, Games as Action Model (Apperley and Beavis 2013) was developed as part of this three-year study, undertaken with Australian secondary school teachers working in the areas of English, Media Studies, Drama, Information Technology, and Literacy. In that project, working on a case-study basis in conjunction with members of the research team, participating teachers in five schools developed and taught a diverse range of curriculum units with and about digital games, primarily video and computer games. Students were engaged in activities that variously included playing, researching and analysing games; creating and presenting games; discussing, reflecting on and writing about games across these subject areas. Drawing on literature from the fields of games studies, literacy, literature and Language Arts education, together with observations of the teachers' curriculum planning and pedagogy, the Games as Text, Games as Action Model was developed as a tool that would work both as a heuristic for the observation and analysis of games and gameplay, and as a guide for planning classroom curriculum and pedagogy. Intended to highlight the double-sided nature of games as both text and action, the model was envisaged as two overlapping layers with much in common, but separated out to make the respective elements of each layer readily visible (see Figure 9.1).

Borders between layers, and between elements in each layer, were envisaged as porous and blurred, so that situatedness and design, for example, are present in both layers in overlapping ways. More than one element from each layer at any given time is likely to be in play, with both layers simultaneously in operation. The concept of gaming literacy as we constructed it drew on two bodies of understandings and related literature:

1. 'Textual literacy' – the 'new literacies' associated with digital iterations of 'reading' (or playing) and 'writing' (or producing) in combination and in multimodal forms (e.g. New London Group 1996; Street *et al.* 2009); and classroom-oriented iterations of literary theory (MacLachlan and Reid 1994; Mellor and Patterson 1996; Misson and Morgan 2006).
2. 'Literacies' specifically linked to the action-based processes of digital gameplay (e.g. Galloway 2006).

Running across both layers is the unifying notion of Design. The New London Group's (1996) model of multiliteracies reconceptualised literacy as 'Design', where 'the design notion emphasizes the productive and innovative potential of language as a meaning making system' (p. 79). In Design, 'we are both inheritors of patterns and conventions of meaning, and at the same time active designers of meaning' (p. 65). The term works as both noun and verb – a design as something to be recognised and made, and also, something you do. For Gee (2007), design and the capacity to recognise and work with/across multiple semiotic systems came right at the top of the 36 Learning Principles he observed in gameplay:

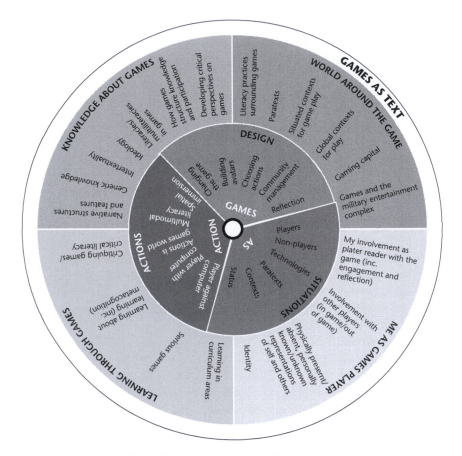

FIGURE 9.1 Games as Text, Games as Action Model.
Source: Apperley and Beavis (2013).

Principle 2: Learning about and coming to appreciate design and design principles is core to the learning experience.

Principle 3: Learning about and coming to appreciate interrelations within and across multiple sign systems (images, words, actions, symbols, artifacts etc.) as a complex system is core to the learning experience.

(Gee 2007, p. 207)

In the model, 'Design' is explicitly named as one of the three elements of the Games as Action layer. In the Games as Text layer, it is not singled out, but rather, runs across all four quadrants, requiring just those understandings and learning practices that Gee (2007) identified in Principles 2 and 3. At the heart of the model is enactment – with games 'enacted and instantiated through action' (Apperley and Beavis 2013, p. 2).

The model was introduced to the teachers at the start of the Serious Play project, to support the conceptualisation of games, and curriculum planning around games, with games presented as both text and action. Teachers were given copies of the book of case studies from the previous project as exemplars (Beavis *et al.* 2012), but were encouraged to develop their own units, according to their subject areas, student needs and their own and students' preferences and priorities. In the second year, after teachers had undertaken initial explorations with games in whatever ways they chose, the model was introduced again and teachers were asked to use it in their planning, or to reflect on how the work they had done previously mapped against conceiving of games as text and action.

The approach taken to games by teachers in the project, and the degree to which they saw games with respect to Action, Text and Design varied considerably. In conceptualising their teaching in these terms, their starting points were different, both with respect to what they saw as superordinate, and in the degree to which they saw games within these terms. Both their views about games conceived primarily as Text, Action or Design, and the curriculum and activities they developed, were reflective also of their prior experience of games. In all three instances given here, the teachers extended their teaching through the ways in which they worked with games. In the remainder of this chapter, we describe the approach they took in relation to this model, and this way of thinking about games. We foreground, respectively, games conceptualised primarily as Text (Jacinta), as Action (Janet) and as Design (Nick). Two of these teachers have been introduced already – Nick and his students 'bringing narratives to life' in Chapter 7; and Janet, teaching with Xbox Kinect, in Chapter 6, who worked with games in a surprisingly physical way. We meet Jacinta for the first time as she uses the game *Ratchet & Clank* (Insomniac Games 2002) with her Year 2 students, treating the game primarily as text.

Jacinta: Games as Text

While many of the teachers in Serious Play had had long-term involvement in teaching with games, for others, it was quite new. Jacinta's challenge, and achievement, was to think of games as text. Jacinta was a Year 2 teacher in a private primary school. She had no experience with computer games, doubts about their value as educational tools, and a pattern of restricting her own children's access to technology at home.

For Jacinta, as for a number of teachers, the main contribution of the model was the way it enabled her to conceive of games as text, and hence introduce them into her literacy work in the classroom. Early in the project, with her Year 2 class, she and the students played with *Ratchet & Clank* on a PlayStation, initially to support students' narrative writing, including structure, sequence and the organisation of ideas. To do so, Jacinta brought in the PlayStation from her home, where it was never used. In class, the children passed around the one controller, taking turns amongst the 28 members of the group. Working in ways analogous to how she might work with books, particularly the teacher-led 'Big Book' approach, both in teaching style and in learning outcome, Jacinta saw the game as a way to address a problem – boys' difficulty with writing narrative – and as an inspiration for writing and a source for language work and grammar.

Jacinta explained:

> We were doing narrative writing – we'd done a lot of structure in the way that a narrative should actually be structured. But I had a lot of kids who just – it was just too much. They couldn't come up with ideas, and when they did, they got jumbled everywhere because they couldn't sequence their actual ideas. So we would play the game and then we would use the game as a text and as a story, and then we'd duplicate that story and write it. We did a lot of character descriptions, we also used it as a text in the sense that we pulled it apart for grammar, we found verbs and nouns and thought of adverbs et cetera.

At this point, effectively, Jacinta had replaced the Big Book with the game, incorporating the game using her existing pedagogy, rather than changing her approach, in a way characteristic of how new technologies are often integrated into existing practices (Prestridge 2012; Prestridge and de Aldama 2016). Jacinta would stop the play and stimulate the children's thinking about game strategy, character, setting and narrative elements, in a classically teacher-centred approach: 'As soon as we identified the bomb, we would stop the game and go, "Right, so what's the problem in this story, where's it set, who's the character, now let's see how he's going to solve the problem."'

The class would brainstorm and she would write vocabulary lists on butcher's paper and draw story sequences developed by the class. She was excited by the degree to which the game lent itself to narrative:

> It was great, it was wonderful because it was so clearly – every time we played – sometimes it would take us a few days to get through because we had to get from a beginning to an end … except sometimes if we found that we couldn't get to the end, we would finish our stories by 'to be continued …'.

Consistent with school expectations more generally about using texts as a basis for language work, she used the game 'as a book, as a text, and … as an inspiration or something for writing, but also just for grammar, general grammar rules and stuff like that, and we used it that way'.

Jacinta was very proud of this use of a digital game. She felt herself 'lucky' to have found a game that exactly matched curriculum requirements, with the game working for her as a 'legitimate' multi-mediated text. She saw the game as providing models of narrative structure and sequence, motivation and powerful imagery for those students who seemed to lack interest or ability in story writing. Her experience had been that most narratives didn't engage her students, the children found them boring, whereas the digital game seemed to completely engage them and provide levels of success for all learners. She believed that this was particularly the case for boys, whom she believed were the ones most likely to be interested in games outside school. As she said, the students 'could have just kept going [playing and writing] and it was a great base'. The use of *Ratchet & Clank* provided the scaffolding needed, 'the images in their minds' that helped them to write so much more (Figure 9.2).

Jacinta's use of a digital game as a stimulus to writing and a source of knowledge about language within the English curriculum area was very successful with the younger students. It supported her rationale for curriculum alignment and student learning outcomes. Her conceptualisation of games as text was firmly strengthened over the course of implementation. The excitement and energy she believed it gave her students, especially the boys, led her to new understandings about how her students learnt with multimodal texts, and their understanding of narrative dimensions in their creation of stories around the game.

Mapping Jacinta's work against the model, she calls particularly on the Games as Text layer – narrative structures and features and literacies/multiliteracies in games – used as a springboard back to the development of print-based literacies and language as the curriculum required. The Games as Action dimensions are not focal areas of attention, but in the background, it is the actions, situations and designs that engage the students with the game and provide the 'glue' that allows them to see the structure, logic and drama of the narratives as they unfold. It is this that, in turn, informs their own writing and ideas.

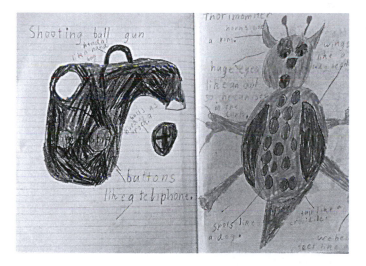

FIGURE 9.2 Characters inspired by Ratchet & Clank.

Janet: Games as Action

Janet was a teacher librarian in a private girls' school. In Chapter 6 we discussed Janet's use of the Xbox and digital games in exploring the ways in which, over the course of the project, teachers' practices and beliefs changed. In this chapter, we focus on the ways in which Janet came to think about Xbox-based games, and her shift to thinking about the games she introduced as forms of text – information texts – in which action and physical gameplay was the key.

Janet initially 'got involved with this thing [the Serious Play project] by accident' and she was somewhat sceptical. She bought an Xbox Kinect because she wanted to do something different from others in the project, something that no one else was doing. This dramatic choice, however, was also somewhat confronting. As she put it, 'I thought to myself, my God, what have I done! I've got the school to spend the money on this, how can I justify this?'

Initially, she saw the 'action' entailed in playing games as part of the lure, or motivation, that would ensure girls wanted to play, and hence come into the library. She thought the Xbox would provide 'another activity for the girls to do at lunch time'. Once they were in the library, she could encourage girls to borrow books.

Once the Xbox arrived, however, things took off. She started with *Kinectimals* (Frontier Developments 2011), 'the little animal one', but thought it was too young for her Year 5 students. Following research over the holidays, she bought *National Geographic*'s *America the Wild* (Relentless Software 2012) (regretfully noting that there was not a similar game about Australian animals). Watching students play, she became 'quite excited' and, in her words, 'when I get excited, things happen!' As Janet watched and listened to the chatter amongst the girls, her sense of what games had to offer grew, with an expanded understanding of the potential of games and learning. She was struck by the ways they saw the game, effectively, as a non-fiction text, as they moved through the game in various pathways, in an approach analogous to the use of information books, where the book is not read right through, but readers select what they need.

> It's suddenly clicked on me, oh my gosh, this is an information book really, that we're doing with action, and they're getting the avatars, getting the features of the wolf or the bird and using their bodies, and they've loved that … the discussion of a particular animal will be selected and learned about.

The realisation that the Xbox Kinect game *America the Wild* could be understood as an information text was very powerful for Janet. But what struck her most forcefully was the centrality of embodied, physical action in the way the game was played – the major impact on what the girls were learning, she believed, came from the actions they employed as they played the game. She saw their actions and the embodied nature of their play as not just engagement, but as actively shaping the learning and understandings they gained. The girls '*became* the animal', following tracks to find prey or shelter. Through their actions, they were analysing, evaluating and applying their knowledge to survive in the wild: 'it's that step closer to actually interacting, being with them, which you don't get in a physical book, and you don't get in the zoo'. She saw them as almost literally '*being* the animal and taking the façade of the animal into that and being part of – it's really good'.

Reminiscent of Bruner's (1966) notion of the enactive knowing mode, Janet saw learning through action and embodiment as an effective means to acquire knowledge and understanding. She noted learning process and higher-order thinking skills in describing the girls' interaction with the Xbox game. She spoke of students 'actioning' the content, in a process that made the subject come alive. Feeding patterns and features of habitats impacted on actions, producing knowledge of habitats first-hand, rather than at a distance – knowledge *of*, rather than knowledge *about*: the *application* of geographical concepts in understanding new landscapes or environments, rather than merely the acquisition of facts.

Learning processes such as analysis, evaluation and application of content represent higher levels of learning cognition (Jonassen *et al.* 2003). The affordances of the technology, and the ways in which students merged their bodies with the animals they played, Janet believed, allowed a form of understanding that was configured significantly differently from one arising from just words. Her perception of the intricate integration between action and learning is consistent with arguments advanced by Chee (2015) and others about the centrality of role and performance to learning in games – in this case, performance literally undertaken by bodies in physical space, as students took over paws, claws and actions to 'become' the animals on the screen. They were supported in this by other students in this community of players, co-constructing their knowledge and providing social negotiation and collaboration in learning (Jonassen 1999) that was focused on actions for learning. As Janet said:

> they're interacting with the story or the information they're getting about the animal. They have to either use their arms or their legs. It was interesting to hear the other girls supporting them, saying, 'Oh no, you get more if you do this, or if you use your head, or if you use your left arm, use your right arm' … it's physically the best movement to get the best results.

Janet set out to take a different approach from one narrowly framed by existing curriculum frameworks, with an exact match with concepts needing to be 'covered' (Ertmer *et al.* 2012). She viewed the game as more of an 'experiment'. As play progressed, however, she saw evidence of the development of complex learnings, with 'critical literacy, problem solving, interpreting, analysing' – important unanticipated outcomes. She felt very satisfied that without exactly looking to 'match' curriculum content, and make explicit links to content descriptors' specific content domains, the girls were nonetheless developing these twenty-first century skills and competencies. She summed up: 'investigating and discovering the game has been our goal ... as the teacher I can see different skills being acquired, interaction, understanding, interpreting information and visual literacy ... including the competition and pure fun the girls are having'.

With respect to the model, Action dominates, with the girls deeply immersed in all three sectors. Players were vividly situated as animals, with all elements of the environment and context shaping their actions and the necessity for play, in a design that demanded first-person participation through the physical merging of players' bodies and animals. In the Games as Text layer, they are learning through games, about animals and geography, and calling on their knowledge about games as they do so in order to play.

Nick: Games as Design

The work of Nick and his students in designing and making games has been discussed in Chapter 7, 'Narratives Come to Life ...'. In that chapter, the focus is strongly on the ways in which Nick conceptualised and built his games-making curriculum, and on the children's work on creativity and games design. In this chapter, we explore the ways in which Nick's work with games exemplified 'design'. For Nick, Text and Action were closely interlinked, unified by the notion of Design, with 'making' the organisational driver. Nick was not a fan of deconstructing games – 'we don't use games that way', but rather, he used deconstruction and analysis to help students arrive at the understandings they needed about how games work in order to create their own games.

In the first year of the project, Nick described his work in terms of what he called 'story elements', and the use of these elements in designing interactive games:

> In terms of deconstructing games, we just looked at the broad categories of visuals – design – as in, like, levels, and how levels work, characters, the narrative in games. So, you know, what sort of story elements are implemented in games, and looking at those four separate areas together, we then put them together to come up with and design our own interactive games.

The following year, 2013, students made a 'game pack'. Understandings were needed of narrative structures and organisation and of the affordances and requirements of games, in ways that were intrinsically operational – students needed to be able to actually make workable games, manage the technology, move from verbal to visual to technological forms, and anticipate players' experience and the needs of play. As Nick explained:

> Within that game pack, they need to have put everything in there. To show the journey, beginning with nothing, and then to the end product. So they have to have in there a story, that they have all come up with together, that is driving their game. Then a graphic novel that replicates the story from text to images and texts. And then a manual that explains how to play the game to the person that will play the game. And then the character profiles.

The game pack, however, was only part of the story. Students went on to make the game, and to work through the anticipated and unanticipated challenges entailed in doing so. As Nick explained:

> And then there's the actual game itself. And we will assess if there are glitches. Does the game run smoothly? And the visuals, did they create them themselves, or did they import jpegs? Is there a start menu? That's something new … Last year, you just pressed a button and it started, and this year, we've talked about having a title screen where you press start to play. And it says, 'So and so welcomes you to whatever the game is, and it will start in five seconds'. And in five seconds, it starts. We've told them also to have an ending. With last year's games, there really wasn't an ending. You just kept playing until you lost. So this year, we want them to have a screen that says, 'Congratulations! You have completed such and such'.

Nick's focus on design unified the game-making process. By the third year of the project, Nick's class was engaged in deconstructing games as text, and also some game paratexts – the texts around games. In their study of games, they analysed all the marketing around the games – both seeing how it was working on them and investigating this so that they could market their own games. As part of the classroom work, to create the game pack, the students analysed existing games, and considered how these games were designed, including attention to how the game makers had designed packaging to make the game more appealing and easily marketable. This deconstruction was important for students to understand more deeply the designing process, and the ways in which these design aspects influenced the consumer. Students had to design a logo for their company, and this logo appeared on their game box. Unlike the kind of text deconstruction that Nick had criticised early in the project, this activity was different, with an authentic purpose related to the critical task.

In his final interview for the project, Nick described the unit as having been extensively developed over the intervening years:

> The first year was [about] building an interactive game. Because that was the first year, it was more about getting games working and having sort of a rough story. And the second year was more consolidating, that and getting all that literacy stuff like character design and character profiles and

stories and trying to get it together. And then this year, actually, we have been getting it all together. So this year, they were able to build a game, build a game booklet, and then like a DVD case that went with it. So they have actually produced a product like you would buy in the shop. So, we finally got it to where we wanted it. So it feels like we have accomplished more this year than ever before.

Nick's focus on design through the Building Games unit of inquiry was satisfying for him as well as the students. The focus on the game design led to a range of other aspects of curriculum being covered, including literacy, critical literacy and art skills as well as critical mathematics and science skills. In taking the unit forward, Nick has renamed it 'Coding Games', emphasising the coding aspects, as he was disappointed that some parents did not recognise the complexity of the coding design work their children had achieved. Not only had they planned and developed narratives for their games, storyboarding them as a sequence of drawn snapshots where both words and images were involved, with core elements of narrative – actions, characters, motivations, scenery and the like – entailed, but they had also created persuasive texts, again of a multimodal kind, in the packaging they created for their games. More than this, they were involved in actual programming; they were actively working with the technology, and learning and using game-making programs to create something new.

As Gee (2007) noted, 'learning about and coming to appreciate design and design principles is core to the learning experience' (Learning Principle 2: Design Principle, p. 207). In the unit that Nick developed for his students, as it evolved over time, 'design' encompassed both literacy and the coding dimensions as students planned, created and played their games. 'Text' and 'action' were combined, in the conceptualisation and development of real games that others could play. In this third version, Nick covered many of the aspects integral to the Games as Text, Games as Action Model. The young people developed their understandings and skills in developing games, in designing and making their games, and in thinking through both the textual and the action aspects of the game. For Nick, this third version of the unit (described in Chapter 7) was the most satisfying. In his final interview, he discussed how the Serious Play project gave him 'permission' to develop and refine this curriculum work. Nick's approach drew effectively on the affordances of game making to enable students to engage deeply with games as both texts and action.

Conclusions

In all three teachers' work, games as text and games as action are present in the ways they think about games, but are configured differently. The teachers incorporate games into their existing teaching practices and approaches, or use them as springboards into new pedagogies, or change the ways they think about literacy in the context of games. For Nick, text and action are integrated almost seamlessly, under the unifying organiser of design. For Jacinta, one of the main effects of learning about the model, and being in the project, was to convince her that games could be thought about as texts, and used to foster both print and multimodal literacy development. Games as text is her dominant concern, and games waver on the edge of being seen as legitimate in this way, in a context trending always towards print and traditional literacies.

Janet was perhaps the most dubious of all the teachers at the start of the project about thinking about literacy and games. She was also the one who most seriously studied the book of case studies from the previous project and thought about the model explicitly, and spoke about her work spontaneously in these terms. When Sarah, who worked with Janet, asked her what had made a difference, it boiled down to three things: in Sarah's words, 'a substantive period of time (to get used to things), engagement with the literature, and the refocusing of ideas to look and see the opportunity or relevance to it'. For Janet, action is the entry point and is most interesting. Through the girls' physical engagement with the game, she comes to think differently about engagement and interaction. While recognising a raft of formal literacy and learning skills and behaviours in girls' activities with and around the text, she sees the games in terms of both text and action, with games seen as specific cultural forms in their own right with embodied knowledge and transformation driving exploration and play.

The main use of the model across the group appeared to be its value in shaping teachers' thinking about games, with respect to literacy, text and learning; and in providing a framework and language with which to identify and think separately and together about these core dimensions. While the concept of games as text and action at the macro level was very useful, at the micro level, it was rarely used for planning. It was taken up according to context and need, and served different purposes. For Nick, it merely affirmed what he was doing already, and like others in the group who were making games, he was wary of losing a strong sense of what games actually were if they were seen too narrowly in textual terms. For Jacinta, the model and the talk around it strengthened her preparedness to explore games in the English classroom. For Janet, the model led her to an unexpected but highly productive set of insights, actively linking text and action, when she observed her students and what they learnt from play.

The multimodal nature of meaning making and the representation of knowledge exemplified by videogames have implications for all areas of schooling. If teachers are to fully utilise digital games, practice and planning need to call on understandings of games as both text and action, while addressing curriculum priorities consistent with existing discipline-specific subject areas. At its deepest level, this requires a profound reconceptualisation of the nature of literacy. In this study, teachers took up this challenge to varying degrees, with curriculum planning and classroom practice shaped by an imaginative sense of possibility and openness to the literacy and/or learning experiences enabled through working with games.

References

Apperley, T (2010), 'What games studies can teach us about videogames in the English and Literacy classroom', *Australian Journal of Language and Literacy*, vol. 33, no. 1, pp. 12–23.

Apperley, T and Beavis C (2013), 'A model for critical games literacy', *E-Learning and Digital Media*, vol. 10, no. 1, pp. 1–11.

Australian Curriculum Assessment and Reporting Authority (2016), *The Australian Curriculum English*. Available from: www.australiancurriculum.edu.au/english/rationale (Accessed 15 July 2016).

Beavis, C, Bradford, C, O'Mara, J and Walsh, C (2007–2010), *Literacy in the digital world of the twenty-first century: Learning from computer games*, ARC Grant No. LP0775072, Canberra, ACT, Australia: Australian Research Council.

Beavis, C, O'Mara, J and McNeice, L (2012), *Digital games: Literacy in action*, Adelaide, South Australia: Wakefield Press.

Bolter, J D and Grusin, R (2000), *Remediation: Understanding new media*, Cambridge, MA: The MIT Press.

Bruner, J (1996), *Toward a theory of instruction*, Cambridge, MA: Harvard University Press.

Chee, Y S (2011), 'Learning as becoming through performance, play and dialogue: A model of games-based learning with the game *Legends of Alkhimia*', *Digital Culture and Education*, vol. 3, no. 3, pp. 98–122.

Chee, Y S (2015), *Games-to-teach or games-to-learn: Unlocking the power of digital games-based learning through performance*, Singapore: Springer.

Corneliussen, H G and Rettberg, J W (2008), *Digital culture, play, and identity: A World of Warcraft® reader*, Cambridge, MA: The MIT Press.

Ertmer, P A, Ottenbreit-Leftwich, A T, Sadik, O, Sendurur, E and Sendurur P (2012), 'Teacher beliefs and technology integration practices: A critical relationship', *Computers & Education*, vol. 59, no. 2, pp. 423–435.

Frontier Developments (2011), *Kinectimals* (Kinect Xbox), Redmond, WA: Microsoft Studios.

Galloway, A (2006), *Gaming: Essays in algorithmic culture*, Minneapolis, MN: University of Minnesota Press.

Gee, J P (2007), *What videogames have to teach us about learning and literacy* (2nd ed.), New York, NY: Palgrave McMillan.

Gee, J P and Hayes, E (2011), 'Nurturing affinity spaces and games-based learning', *Cadernos de Letras* (UFRJ), no. 28, pp. 19–38. Available from: www.letras.ufrj.br/anglo_germanicas/cadernos/numeros/072011/textos/cl2831072011gee.pdf (Accessed 11 July 2016).

Insomniac Games (2002), *Ratchet & Clank* (PlayStation 2), Sony Computer Entertainment. Available from: www.insomniacgames.com/games/ratchet-clank-ps4/ (Accessed 17 November 2016).

International Reading Association (2012), *Adolescent literacy: A position statement of the International Reading Association*. Available from: www.literacyworldwide.org/docs/default-source/where-we-stand/adolescent-literacy-position-statement.pdf?sfvrsn=8 (Accessed 15 July 2016).

Jenson, J and de Castell, S (2010), 'Gender, simulation and gaming: Research review and redirections', *Simulation and Gaming*, vol. 41, no. 1, pp. 51–71.

Jonassen, D H (1999), 'Designing constructivist learning environments', in C M Reigeluth (ed.), *Instructional-design theories and models: A new paradigm of instructional theory* (vol. II), Mahwah, NJ: Lawrence Erlbaum Associates, pp. 215–239.

Jonassen, D H, Howland, J, Moore, J and Marra, R M (2003), *Learning to solve problems with technology: A constructivist perspective* (2nd ed.), Upper Saddle River, NJ: Prentice Hall.

MacLachlan, M and Reid, I (1994), *Framing and interpretation*, Carlton, Victoria, Australia: Melbourne University Press.

Marsh, J (2010), 'Young children's play in virtual online worlds', *Journal of Early Childhood Research*, vol. 8, no. 1, pp. 23–39.

Mellor, B and Patterson, A (1996), *Investigating texts*, Cottesloe, Western Australia: Chalkface Press.

Misson, R and Morgan, W (2006), *Critical literacy and the aesthetic: Transforming the English classroom*, Urbana, IL: NCTE.

New London Group (1996), 'A pedagogy of multiliteracies: Designing social futures', *Harvard Educational Review*, vol. 66, no. 1, pp. 60–92.

Prestridge, S (2012), 'The beliefs behind the teacher that influences their ICT practices', *Computers and Education*, vol. 58, no. 1, pp. 449–458.

Prestridge, S and de Aldama, C (2016), 'A classification framework for exploring Technology Enabled Practice – FrameTEP', *Journal of Educational Computing Research*, pp. 1–2. Available from: doi: 10.1177/0735633116636767 (Accessed 11 July 2016).

Relentless Software (2012), *National Geographic: America the Wild* (Kinect Xbox), Redmond, WA: Microsoft Studios.

Steinkuehler, C A (2006), 'Massively multiplayer online video gaming as participation in a discourse', *Mind, Culture, and Activity*, vol. 13, no. 1, pp. 38–52.

Steinkuehler, C A (2007), 'Massively multiplayer online games as a constellation of literacy practices', *E-Learning and Digital Media*, vol. 4, no. 3, pp. 297–318.

Steinkuehler, C A (2008), 'Cognition and literacy in massively multiplayer online games', in J Corio, M Knobel, C Lankshear and D J Leu (eds), *Handbook of research on new literacies*, New York, NY: Lawrence Erlbaum Associates, pp. 611–634.

Street, B, Pahl, K and Rowsell, J (2009), 'Multimodality and new literacy studies', in C Jewitt (ed.), *The Routledge book of multimodal analysis*, London: Routledge.

Taylor, T L (2006), *Play between worlds: Exploring online game culture*, Cambridge, MA: The MIT Press.

10

MATERIAL AND DISCURSIVE LEARNING WITH *MINECRAFT* AND *LEGO*

Michael Dezuanni

Introduction

This chapter argues that it is necessary to expand beyond socio-cultural and 'multimodal' approaches to literacy when aiming to understand how digital literacies are produced through *Minecraft* (Mojang 2011) play. The chapter argues that *Minecraft* players assemble literacies as they interact with materials and conceptual understandings through processes of embodied media production and social interaction (Dezuanni 2015). This socio-material framework is used to explain how designing and building in *Minecraft* extend beyond inscription (making meaning through symbolic representation) to incorporation through embodied practice (Hayles 1999, 2003). Through this lens, playing a digital game like *Minecraft* can be understood as actual building and creating, not merely a representation of building, and this has significance for how we conceptualise digital literacy, meaning making and material practice. These concepts are explored by drawing on data from a class involved in the Serious Play project in which *Lego* (The Lego Group 2016) and *Minecraft* were used to undertake design thinking, collaboration and problem solving. The project occurred in a Year 3 class in which students were required to redesign their school in either *Lego* or *Minecraft*. The project demonstrates the social and material aspects of *Minecraft* play that became integral to the students' learning and development of socio-material literacies. The chapter draws on observational data, interviews with students and teachers and student work samples, and provides insight into the production of digital media literacies by comparing *Minecraft* digital making with building in *Lego*.

Moving Beyond Socio-Cultural Literacy Frameworks for Understanding Gameplay

Socio-cultural literacy frameworks, while providing essential elements for describing gameplay practices, do not adequately account for the meaning-making practices individuals experience when they interact with digital materials in a game like *Minecraft*. These limitations are recognised by previous research (discussed in Chapter 9) about the challenge of describing literacy in gaming contexts, which makes a significant distinction between games as text and games as action (see also Beavis *et al.* 2009; Beavis and Apperley 2012; O'Mara 2012). In this approach, the bodily and material aspects of digital gameplay are distinguished from the representational elements of games as textual entities. As Beavis and Apperley noted:

> The notion of action marks a key difference between digital games and other media forms. Actions define both the characters – in terms of the type and variety of actions that the avatar can perform – and the virtual spaces of the digital games, because actions define *how* the space(s), and the objects in it, will be used by the players.
>
> *(Beavis and Apperley 2012, p. 14, original emphasis)*

This chapter seeks to build on this distinction between text and action to identify some of the ways in which games players produce meaning and potentially learn while socially and materially interacting with and through games. Gameplay might be understood not merely as 'textual' experience, but as an embodied practice that breaks down the distinction between the so-called 'real world' and virtual environments. Playing a digital game requires direct bodily interaction with a technological system such as a computer keyboard and mouse, a videogame system controller or a touch screen on a tablet computer. Furthermore, digital games might be considered 'material', despite some theorists' claims that digital things have an empirically different status to non-digital materials (Belk 2013, pp. 478–481). From a materialist perspective, the status of the 'text' comes under question as a useful unit of analysis and therefore the limits of socio-cultural literacy frameworks must also be acknowledged.

Hayles (2003, p. 279) deployed aspects of Actor–Network Theory (ANT) to argue not for 'text', but 'Work as Assemblage' (WaA) as the most useful unit for analysis. In comparing printed books with electronic books available on computers, she argues that both are material because while print and electronic books' materiality may differ, electronic books require material interaction to be read, just as print books do; neither analogue or electronic 'texts' can be adequately understood unless we recognise the materiality of both. She further suggested that the '*materiality of an embodied text is the interaction of its physical characteristics with its signifying strategies*' (p. 277, original emphasis). That is, the 'text' cannot be assembled without bodily interaction of a reader and co-authorship with the technology. Hayles argued that 'with an electronic text, the computer is also a writer, and the software programs it runs to produce texts as process and display also have complex and multiple authorship' (p. 280). Therefore, digital assemblages are authored not only by the individuals interacting with them, but also through interaction and negotiation with the hardware and software required to display and manipulate objects on the screen. From this perspective, *Minecraft* play involves a complex process of co-authored assemblage, where the player, the technological device and the game software combine to actively assemble the experience.

Material/Discursive Assemblages in (Game)play

It is tempting when considering digital play to think of digital experience as inauthentic in comparison to the 'real' experience of bodily interactions with material things. *Minecraft* play occurs on a screen in a constructed environment composed of digital materials (which can be further broken down into code), whereas a play system like *Lego* involves 'actual' blocks that can be physically picked up and manipulated. *Minecraft* is 'just a game' and is not part of the 'real world', might be the claim. Indeed, Belk (2013) argued that digital texts are dematerialised and cannot be real things (pp. 478–481). But Belk's claim was made within the confines of 'representationalism', in which a digital game can only ever aim to discursively approximate 'reality'. Belk did not recognise that digital play matters in the world. In contrast, Barad (2007) built on Foucault's theory of discursive practice and Butler's theory of performativity to argue that 'the move toward performative alternatives to representationalism shifts the focus from questions of correspondence between descriptions of reality (e.g., do they mirror the nature of culture) to matters of practices, doings, and actions' (p. 135). Barad's 'agential realism' suggested that '*the material and the discursive are mutually implicated in the dynamics of intra-activity*' (p. 152, original emphasis) and that the material and discursive exist in a non-privileged relation to one another. The implication is that it is as important to account for materiality and bodily practice as it is to understand the representational aspects of a digital game such as *Minecraft*. Gameplay is an ongoing socio-material assemblage and this has implications for learning with games.

Minecraft is particularly interesting to consider as a performative system for producing authentic 'works as assemblage' because a significant objective of the game is precisely to construct new things to share with others. The game requires players to attain digital materials to create structures block by block. These materials are digital instances of the physical world – dirt (earth), wood, stone, steel, sand, glass, wool and precious gems, to name a few. The 'crafting' of items and then the combination of these items to construct recognisable structures involve simultaneous material and discursive practices. Hayles (1999) made an important distinction between writing (inscription) and bodies' disciplined capacities (incorporated habits). She said, 'I mean by an incorporating practice an action that is encoded into bodily memory by repeated performances until it becomes habitual' (p. 199). She contrasted incorporating practices with inscription practices, which she defined as 'systems of signs operating independently of any particular manifestation' (p. 198). Through deploying Hayles's theory, *Minecraft* gameplay might be understood as socio-material interaction involving inscription and incorporation. 'Work as Assemblage' seems particularly pertinent to making sense of the structures that players build in *Minecraft*, literally assembling artefacts block by block as an aspect of 'inter-action' within the game. The mediations that occur between the individual playing *Minecraft*, the computer, device or system on which the game is being played and the digital 'stuff' within a *Minecraft* play experience provide considerable insights into the practices of digital culture. Taking account of the processes of inscription and incorporation involved in *Minecraft* play and thinking about it as a performative process of intra-active becoming can illustrate the ways in which players dynamically assemble new knowledge and co-create the world around them.

The Building Blocks of Digital Media Literacy

To apply these theories to understanding how students assemble knowledge with *Minecraft* in a school setting, I employ a generative model (Figure 10.1) for understanding digital media literacies in school settings (Dezuanni 2015). The purpose of introducing this framework is to provide a mechanism for identifying practices assembled around nodes that may be useful for producing knowledge about the learning which takes place when individuals combine digital materials through gameplay for a purpose. In the case of *Minecraft*, digital materials include the blocks that players gather to assemble structures; production is the process of interacting with the machine and software to 'co-author' the gameplay experience. The machine and software have significant power in this relationship to cause the player to undertake particular kinds of practices (to the exclusion of others). Conceptual resources are the socio-culturally produced ideas and knowledge deployed during gameplay – narrative, structure, symbolic systems, categories, formulas, audience, design features, representational choices and so on. Analysis is an ongoing practice of assembling conceptual resources to produce reflection and dialogue.

The model's nodes enable investigation of how building systems were used to assemble knowledge in the project considered in this chapter; redesigning the Junior School in *Minecraft* and *Lego* in a Year 3 class. The nodes are used to tease out aspects of the assemblages that form in order to gain insight into the specific socio-material learning practices experienced by students in a specific context.

For instance, *Minecraft* allows building with digital materials that both simulates and defies the properties of objects existing in the physical world – in the 'survival' gameplay mode, a player can fall off a high structure and 'die'. But at the same time, blocks of dirt can float in mid-air if they are placed in a

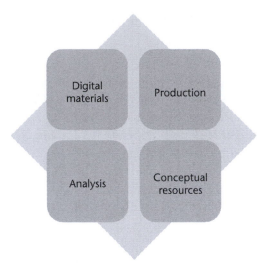

FIGURE 10.1 The building blocks for assembling digital media literacies.

certain way. Furthermore, all blocks are one standard-sized cubes and cannot be split or changed. The game's internal logics and affordances therefore allow and disallow particular types of block construction. Like all communicational systems, the *Minecraft* production process is both restrictive and generative, and specific processes must be followed in order to gather and use blocks; but the game allows a great deal more flexibility than most digital games. *Minecraft* has been used by literally millions of builders of all ages around the world to make a vast range of incredibly complex structures and builds, many of which are available on YouTube. *Minecraft* design genres have emerged and some young people spend a great deal of time both casually and intentionally analysing other Minecrafters' builds. The conceptual materials available for *Minecraft* construction are vast and ever-expanding. The remainder of the chapter focuses on a project that involved students designing and building with *Lego* and *Minecraft*. It is useful to consider some of the similarities and differences of building with these two block play systems and how they provide opportunities to assemble knowledge.

Recreating the Junior School in *Minecraft* and *Lego*

As outlined in Chapter 3, *Minecraft* was introduced into a Year 3 classroom in a private girls' school as part of the Serious Play project. Initially, the teacher chose to introduce the game as a way to engage students with writing for English curriculum, and she later went on to use the game as an aspect of Design and Mathematics curricula experiences through a project in which the students recreated their school using either *Lego* or *Minecraft*. About one-quarter of the students chose to work in *Lego* and about half of them in *Minecraft*. Another group of students worked with 3D printing. In this section of the chapter, I discuss how the students worked with *Minecraft* and *Lego* in material and discursive ways to assemble new knowledge. Both building systems were available to the Year 3 class throughout the year, and the students regularly used both before school and during class time. The students each had access to a laptop computer that they could use at any time, and the teacher had set up a dedicated '*Lego* Land' room for the students to play in (Figure 10.2). She explained that the students liked to 'touch and create' with the coloured blocks and her *Lego* Land was a popular space used by the girls on a regular basis.

Designing and Building With Lego

The teacher believed *Lego* was an appropriate system for encouraging creativity and problem solving, and she had maintained a *Lego* space for her students for several years, regardless of her students' ages. At the start of the Serious Play project, the teacher's Year 6 class was using a *Lego* space; and by the end of the project, her Year 2 class was using one. The teacher's commitment to *Lego* was exemplified by her decision to dedicate a room to the activity that might have been used for other activities, or as her office space. The teacher also believed it was important for the students to experience building and designing in both digital and non-digital environments. To this end, when she decided to design a project around design thinking and mathematics in which the students would

FIGURE 10.2 Students playing in *Lego* Land.

recreate their school, she gave them the choice to build in either *Lego* or *Minecraft*. She also explicitly drew attention to the difference between the two systems by asking the students to reflect on what they liked about each, which led to some revealing responses. The students were asked to complete a 'T-Chart' graphic organiser, explaining 'What I like about "building" games', under the headings '*Lego*' and '*Minecraft*'. Most of the students wrote positively about using their hands to manipulate the *Lego* blocks; for instance, one student wrote, 'I get to build it in person' and 'I can do it with my hands'. Another wrote, 'Hands on – don't have to go on a computer'. The students also wrote positively about the lack of technical and in-game interference: one wrote, 'Can't go offline', and 'Control over everything – teacher doesn't have control over you' and 'Monsters can't destroy anything'. Another said, 'Don't have to worry about running out of battery'. These kinds of statements were repeated across the class.

The responses are interesting because writing positively about *Lego*, the students have tended to compare their experience to their digital experiences in *Minecraft*, encouraged by the T-Chart structure. As indicated below, most students also outline positives for *Minecraft* in contrast with *Lego*. The main differences the students identify are about the materiality of the two systems, including the ability to directly pick up blocks and feel them in your hand, in contrast to working with the computer apparatus to assist with picking up blocks. The students' focus on the control they have, provided by the simplicity of *Lego* as a non-electronic system is informative, because it points to the frustrations children sometimes have with digital technologies. *Lego* does not run out of power or go offline, and while playing the game, there are no non-player characters like monsters to interfere with the game experience. In addition, from the students' perspective, there is less possibility of the teacher controlling their play. Because the game is not digital, the teacher cannot 'freeze' the students in the space, as she can with the modified education version of *Minecraft* used in this class. It is interesting that the students do not mention that the teacher does, of course, have control over their temporal and physical access to *Lego* Land.

The affordances of *Lego* bricks and the physicality of *Lego* as a play system were also preferable for some students in contrast to *Minecraft*. For instance, one student said in a written reflection, 'The bricks in *Lego* have lots of different shapes, colours and size but in *Minecraft* they only have different materials and some coloured blocks'. This focus on the material affordances of *Lego* draws attention to the production processes involved in each system. The student seems to prefer making with blocks of different shapes and colours and is frustrated by the affordances of the uniform-sized *Minecraft* blocks. Another student said:

> I like *Lego*. Here's why. *Minecraft* is confusing in so many ways where you have to move. I like *Lego* because it is not online. *Minecraft* is online which means that you have to use the keyboard to move around. Obviously that gets frustrating.

This student's ability to undertake production with *Minecraft* is inhibited by her lack of experience with the 'mouselook/keymove' controls required to operate the game on her school laptop. The specific material practice of using the mouse or trackpad to see the game from the avatar's first-person perspective, and the use of keys to move forwards, backwards, to jump and to place blocks is difficult for novice players. Many of the students had only played *Minecraft Pocket Edition* on a touchscreen prior to using the game at school, which involves an entirely different material experience. Making something with *Lego* blocks was a much more straightforward construction process, which this particular student preferred.

The students who chose to build the school in *Lego* spoke positively about what *Lego* allowed them to do. The students created a two-storey version of the school (Figure 10.3) where the roof is missing from the upper layer to allow 'visitors' to see inside the classrooms. The main conceptual resources the students worked with were mathematical and design concepts related to scale, measurement, distance, space, volume and colour. The students measured up the school and made decisions about which blocks to use to recreate different buildings according to the size and shape of the available blocks. They were required to physically experience familiar spaces in new ways, to measure the spaces and gain a sense of the relationship between buildings and the overall school landscape. This also required collaboration and problem solving as the students took on different tasks in the build, which eventually had to be combined as a single build.

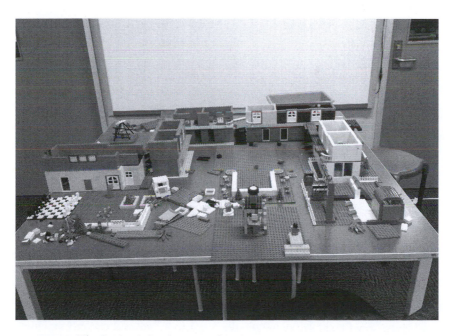

FIGURE 10.3 The Junior School recreated in *Lego*.

The Junior School build allowed the students to use *Lego* in a way that went beyond casual or individually purposeful play. They used the materiality of the blocks and the affordances of the interlocking system (different shapes, colours and connections) to make something new, in the process drawing more on architectural practices than is generally invited within casual *Lego* play. This led to a satisfying learning experience, as the following student reflected:

> Now that the *Lego* Junior School is finished, I am extremely proud with what it turned out like. It looks great and the comments that visitors gave were fantastic. I think all the time and effort was totally worth it! I know how not everything can be perfect in *Lego*, but we tried our best, and that is what makes it special. I've seen some models of massive buildings done by Uni-students [in *Lego*] and they were great. Ours is one of them!

The connection this student makes to the conceptual and analytical by locating her work within a field of practice generally undertaken by more experienced builders points to the identity work being assembled alongside the material build. In discussing their observations of two young boys' *Lego* play and its connections to global media myth making, Carrington and Dowdall argued that *Lego* was central to the boys' constructions of literate identities in everyday practice:

> The object ethnography reminds us that the material matters. In fact, it matters a lot. Children live and learn in spaces made possible and populated by artifacts … artifacts work to co-construct our perception and experience of the worlds around us. For young children, those worlds are constructed out of the artifacts of the home.
>
> *(Carrington and Dowdall 2013, p. 105)*

The everyday availability of *Lego* blocks is material, but also discursive, and presents opportunities to assemble stories in part made available by global media franchises. In this sense, *Lego* play often includes the representation of conceptual resources made available by popular media, deeply connected to children's popular cultural experiences. It is likely that the girls often played in the *Lego* Land space before school in just this way. The Junior School project, though, provided an opportunity to use *Lego* differently, drawing on different material and conceptual resources, including the girls' personal experience of their school spaces and their knowledge of *Lego* construction play.

Designing and Building With Minecraft

The teacher introduced *Minecraft* into her Year 3 class because, like *Lego*, it was a popular cultural phenomenon enjoyed by many of her students and she identified an opportunity to repurpose the game for educational outcomes. Fanning and

Mir (2014) have suggested that *Minecraft* extends a history of progressive pedagogy through construction play, which emerged in the nineteenth and early twentieth centuries through the work of educationalists such as Johann Heinrich Pestalozzi, Friedrich Froebel and Maria Montessori. Fanning and Mir (2014) argued that the construction toy genre exemplified and commercialised by *Lego* encourages 'players to build, tinker, and create new objects or structures from modular units' and educational benefit is assumed to derive from the positive consequences of children playing, building and undertaking architectural practice' (pp. 38–40). In addition, Fanning and Mir drew on Kozlovsky's (2008) work to suggest that *Minecraft* may be considered a version of the 'adventure playgrounds' developed by philanthropists and designers in war-torn European cities in the 1940s and 1950s, which repurposed rubble and building materials to foster 'an active, messy process of creativity and self-determination through play for urban children' (p. 40). The Year 3 students' perspectives on the advantages of *Minecraft* over *Lego* support the concept of *Minecraft* as adventure play. In the T-Chart graphic organiser activity described above, the students said that *Minecraft* allowed them to 'explore caves', 'go hunting', 'tame animals and eat', 'fight monsters' and 'have your own pet'. They wrote statements like, 'In Creative [mode] you get to fly and in *Lego* you can't', 'I like going to all the different environments (desert, snow, planes etc)' and 'I like how you start with nothing but you find things to use'. One student said, 'you also don't know what is going to happen next like exploring caves'; and another reflected, 'I think *Minecraft* is WAY better than *Lego* and I'm going to tell you why. In *Minecraft* you can tame animals and make them yours. I just love the wolves'.

The pleasures these students derive from *Minecraft* include the freedom the game provides to explore new worlds and spaces; to fight and hunt; to experience the fantastical by moving beyond the human body's constraints to fly and to interact with exotic animals in otherwise impossible ways. For these children, at least, the game seems to provide ways to be adventurous that are otherwise unavailable to suburban children attending a conventional academically oriented school in the 2010s. While the school's *Lego* Land may offer a place of retreat from regimentation and an opportunity for imaginative and sometimes narrative play through construction, the affordances of a virtual environment like *Minecraft* significantly expand what some students are able to experience discursively and materially. This extends to *Minecraft*'s materiality as a construction play system. One student suggested that 'the blocks are more realistic than *Lego*', and another argued, '*Minecraft* is much better than *Lego* because the blocks have more detail'. Yet another explained that in the game's creative mode, 'you never run out of blocks but in *Lego* you only have the blocks that came with the packet'. The digital materials available to students for construction in the game are limitless, but they also presented a challenge in a classroom setting, particularly as the students worked in a large group in multiplayer mode. About ten students often worked simultaneously on the Junior School build in *Minecraft*.

As a formal production platform, *Minecraft* emerged in the class as a complicated system for designing and building, with varying levels of student knowledge about how to use the game for construction. One or two students became the class construction experts whom the other students turned to for advice, which was important because the teacher chose not to play alongside the students. Some students became frustrated with this approach. The teacher's decision to have the students use *Minecraft* to recreate the Junior School was a fundamental challenge to how most students had previously played the game. Student interviews suggested that only two or three of them had previously built complex structures in the game, and most class members had generally played the 'pocket edition' version of the game to explore, fight and tame pets. In addition, building in a large group required planning and advanced design work, which didn't always occur. In reflection, one student wrote:

> It is very hard work. First we had to dig so that we had enough room to do the Junior School. When we had enough space to build it got all confusing because I did not know when to put rock on the top, so I decided to put it on anyway, but people kept breaking it.

Observations of the students in multiplayer mode in *Minecraft* revealed that there was a lot of very excited in-game and offline talk (the students often called out to each other from across the room as they played on their individual laptops), but this sometimes led to confusion when more formal outcomes were required. Despite these challenges, the students engaged with conceptual curriculum knowledge in ways that the teacher appreciated as rich learning opportunities. For instance, she noted how the students experienced mathematical concepts as they aimed to recreate the school:

> Somebody noticed at one stage that the tiles on the carpet looked like *Minecraft* squares, so to work out the size, to build our very first room – we decided we would build one room first, and see what it looked like, and make adjustments based on ratio, proportion, in a beginning way, so we counted the number of squares long that our classroom was, and the width, and the girls created a basic room like that. And then somebody decided it was way too tall for the width and the length of the room, so they decided then we would halve the proportions. So, you know, all that mathematical work came into it as well.

For the teacher, the *Minecraft* build became a process of collaborative problem solving that lent an authenticity to learning that her students did not always have an opportunity to experience. For the Junior School build, the game was redeployed away from being the adventure and exploration game played by the students for fun to becoming a reconstruction tool not dissimilar to a computer-assisted design (CAD) package. This redeployment required student interaction with the physical environment and application of conceptual and curriculum-aligned knowledge. The teacher noted that the students were required to analyse their school environment in a very physical way to understand how to best recreate it in the digital environment.

> While the girls were building the Junior School, it was interesting to see that they would actually physically go outside and look at something and work out, oh, that's left or that's on the right, and then go back to their computers.

The process of physically analysing the immediate built environment was also the focus of several of the students' reflections following the completion of the build, along with their judgments about how accurately they believed they had recreated the school (see Figure 10.4).

Several students wrote that despite the short time available to them, they were happy with their build. One said, 'I think it looks GREAT! That's because I never knew it would turn out like that'. Another said, 'I didn't expect it to look real but it actually does look real. There's art in the Art room, Signs on the doors, soft beds in the sickbay and desks in the classrooms'. Where the students identified opportunities for improvement, they often mentioned a need to look more closely at the original rooms to get a better understanding of how to recreate them. For instance, one student said, 'If I had a chance to do it again I would … get to look in all the classrooms not guessing what's in there, and maybe check 2

FIGURE 10.4 The Junior School recreated in *Minecraft*.

or 3 times in each classroom'. These judgments about accuracy are revealing, because despite most of the students' previous lack of experience with complex *Minecraft* builds, they seem to have embraced the opportunity to assemble knowledge that closely aligns to the teacher's curriculum objectives. They have accepted a new way to play the game that assembles discursive and material knowledge in ways that have not previously been part of their *Minecraft* play.

Conclusions: Socio-Material Gameplay Practices

This chapter has argued that both the *Lego* and the *Minecraft* block construction systems provide opportunities for learning through discursive and material practices, and that both systems were successfully redeployed by the Year 3 teacher to develop curriculum-aligned knowledge. As we argued in Chapter 5, there is a danger, when using digital games in the classroom, that the passion and enthusiasm children and young people bring to gameplay may be undermined when games are used in the classroom. The case of the Junior School build seems to provide an example of a successful use of a game, and one reason for this is likely to be the teacher's willingness to account for both the discursive and the material implications of using *Minecraft* in her class. By providing students with a choice of using either *Lego* or *Minecraft*, the teacher recognised that her students often felt more comfortable building in one system or the other, and this choice enabled the students to pursue their passions accordingly. The students' written reflections suggest that their choices were as much material as discursive. Some students preferred the touch and feel of the plastic *Lego* blocks, the range of block sizes and colours and the simplicity of the interlocking system. Other students liked the endless digital blocks available to them in *Minecraft* and the fact that the blocks aimed to represent real-world blocks (a dirt block looks somewhat like a dirt block, for instance). More than one student noted that the different materials available in *Minecraft* allowed them to make the school look 'realistic'. As noted, one student preferred the *Lego* system because she had not yet mastered the physicality of the *Minecraft* 'mouselook/keymove' controls; and another student stated that she liked the relative quiet of the *Lego* Land room because *Minecraft* play was noisy as the other students yelled out to each other in the classroom as they played. It was also notable that the students involved in both the *Lego* and the *Minecraft* builds were happy with their achievements, and the students in each group seemed to learn a lot. This seems to support Hayles's (1999) argument that inscription may operate independently of a material form (a similar meaning can be assembled using different materials), but incorporation requires bodily and sensory familiarity.

In the case of the Junior School build, exploring the use of the digital game *Minecraft* also draws attention to the performative dimension of digital making. As Barad (2007) has suggested, the performative is a fundamental challenge to representational accounts of human action. From this perspective, digital making is actual making, not a digital representation of making, and not an inferior practice or less meaningful than, for example, the *Lego* build. The Year 3 students assembled knowledge within *Minecraft* as they brought themselves into being as designers/makers/architects through discursive and material assemblage. The digital literacies assembled through *Minecraft* making, both for fun and for more formally recognised learning, provided these Year 3 students with a unique opportunity to co-construct the world around them.

References

Barad, K (2007), *Meeting the universe halfway: Quantum physics and the entanglement of matter and meaning*, Durham, NC and London: Duke University Press.

Beavis, C and Apperley, T (2012), 'A model for games and literacy', in C Beavis, J O'Mara and L McNeice (eds), *Digital games: Literacy in action*, Adelaide, South Australia: Wakefield Press, pp. 12–22.

Beavis, C, Apperley, T, Bradford, C, O'Mara, J and Walsh, C (2009), 'Literacy in the digital age: Learning from computer games', *English in Education*, vol. 43, no. 2, pp. 162–175.

Belk, R (2013), 'Extended self in a digital world', *Journal of Consumer Research*, vol. 40, no. 3, pp. 477–500.

Carrington, V and Dowdall, C (2013), '"This is a job for hazmat guy!": Global media cultures and children's everyday lives', in K Hall, T Cremin, B Comber and L C Moll (eds), *International handbook of research on children's literacy, learning, and culture*, Chichester, UK: Wiley, pp. 96–107.

Dezuanni, M (2015), 'The building blocks of digital media literacy: Socio-material participation and the production of media knowledge', *Journal of Curriculum Studies*, vol. 47, no. 3, pp. 416–439. Available at: doi: 10.1080/00220272.2014.966152 (Accessed 29 July 2016).

Fanning, C and Mir R (2014), 'Teaching tools: Progressive pedagogy and the history of construction play', in N Garrelts (ed.), *Understanding Minecraft: Essays on play, community and possibilities*, Jefferson, NC: McFarland and Company.

Hayles, N K (1999), *How we became posthuman: Virtual bodies in cybernetics, literature, and informatics*, Chicago, IL: University of Chicago Press.

Hayles, N K (2003), 'Translating media: Why we should rethink textuality', *The Yale Journal of Criticism*, vol. 16, no. 2, pp. 263–290.

Kozlovsky, R (2008), 'Adventure playgrounds and postwar reconstruction', in M Gutman and N de Coninck-Smith (eds), *Designing modern childhoods*, New Brunswick, NJ: Rutgers University Press, pp. 171–190.

The Lego Group (2016), *Lego*. Available from: www.lego.com (Accessed 10 August 2016).

Mojang (2011), *Minecraft*. Available from: https://minecraft.net/en/ (Accessed 8 August 2016).

O'Mara, J (2012), 'Process drama and digital games as text and action in virtual worlds: Developing new literacies in school', *Research in Drama Education: The Journal of Applied Theatre and Performance*, vol. 17, no. 4, pp. 517–534.

Assessment, Digital Games and Teachers as Creative Professionals

THEME PREFACE

The Serious Play project would not have existed were it not for the enthusiasm, creativity, intelligence and grit of the teachers with whom we worked. In this final section of the book, the vital role of teachers in the success of games-based pedagogy, learning and curriculum is examined more closely as we consider their approaches, beliefs and the outcomes they observed.

Teachers and schools do not work in isolation – their approaches to teaching, learning and assessment are influenced by and answerable to systemic, state and national policies and requirements. Throughout the Serious Play project, we were aware of the need for the teachers, who were frequently innovating/making/creating curriculum, to have ways of assessing and reporting that aligned with current approaches in their school systems. In doing this, we considered the informal and formal assessments, formative and summative assessment tasks. We also recognised the professionalism of teachers in making judgments about learning, and the unique insights and depth of knowledge that they brought into the project of their own classroom situation, the students they were working with, and the ways in which the work with digital games was positioned within the curriculum.

In Chapter 11, Rowan and Beavis report on teachers' beliefs about the use of digital games in the classroom from their examination of the interview data from the teachers involved in the project, and their views about how this work can or should be assessed in diverse educational contexts. They describe the teachers' beliefs about the benefits of games-based learning and the close relationship between many of these outcomes and formal curriculum requirements. The chapter also outlines other valuable outcomes that teachers attributed to their games projects, which may or may not be mapped onto existing curriculum frameworks.

Rowan examines the role of the teacher more broadly in Chapter 12, and argues that it is the teacher who is 'best placed to identify how a particular example of digital play might impact upon a specific group of students: be it academically, socially or emotionally'. She describes how teachers involved in the Serious Play project found multiple links between games-based activities and both formal and informal assessment, as well as formative and summative assessment.

In Chapter 13, Rowan and Prestridge consider the teachers' views about the extent to which the potential benefits often linked to digital games are actually experienced by diverse learners. They draw upon the gaming metaphor of 'levelling up' to consider how students who may have been on the margins of mainstream schooling were given opportunities to be successful – to star – in the games-based curriculum. Through their analysis of the examples provided by the teachers, Rowan and Prestridge demonstrate that

> the time, effort and a leap of faith that may be required to start on the kinds of journeys undertaken by our project teachers can generate multiple, positive, unexpected outcomes for very different students: including those who may otherwise not have experienced what it means to be successful, a winner or a star.

11

SERIOUS OUTCOMES FROM SERIOUS PLAY

Teachers' Beliefs About Assessment of Games-Based Learning in Schools

Leonie Rowan and Catherine Beavis

Introduction

As digital games move from the margins to the mainstream of increasing numbers of school classrooms, questions invariably arise about how working with games articulates with teachers' broader teaching and learning plans; and, also, with policies and practices relating to the assessment of student learning. Drawing upon the Serious Play research conducted with teachers in diverse primary and secondary schools in Victoria and Queensland, Australia, this chapter reports on teachers' beliefs about how working with games can or should be assessed in diverse educational contexts, and how this influences the way they work with games.

More specifically, the chapter outlines the beliefs of teachers in the project about the various kinds of outcomes that they believe can be traced to games; the ways in which these outcomes do (or do not) articulate with existing and dominant curriculum and reporting frameworks; and the potential of games to generate valuable outcomes that may or may not be mapped onto existing curriculum frameworks. From this basis, it outlines their beliefs about whether they have a need or a desire to assess (and report on) all of the diverse and multiple outcomes that they attribute to gameplay in their specific context; and, finally, the factors which they believed would help them combine their games-based activities with their responsibilities regarding assessment and reporting. In addressing each of these issues and questions, we are conscious of growing attention within games-based literature to the challenges that the 'not-school' nature of many digital games might pose for those who work in formal education. We therefore begin this chapter with a brief review of some key issues raised within recent games-and-assessment literature, and then draw upon project data to discuss related questions in more detail. The chapter then concludes with implications for those interested in working further with games-based learning in school settings.

Background and Literature

While digital games have long been an important part of Media and Technology areas focused specifically on coding, game making and design in other areas, the past ten years have seen what Tobias and Fletcher (2011) described as an 'explosion of publications and research studies dealing with the value and effects of games' (p. 4) in various educational contexts. Jenson *et al.* made the point that:

> Claims about the educational value of digital gameplay and immersive, playful virtual worlds are by now widely rehearsed, with proponents arguing for games as designed learning environments that can offer their players experiences different from, contextually richer than, and more engaging than those available in traditional schooling models.
>
> *(Jenson et al. 2016, p. 22)*

Claims about the potential for games to enhance students' motivation and engagement, and improve achievement as well, have increasingly prompted questions about the extent to which this apparent potential has (or can) actually be realised.

This has fostered two strands of inquiry connected to the broad theme of assessment. The first is concerned with the extent to which games have been proven (through research) to improve student performance in school-based assessments. Growing interest in this question has produced multiple, single-site research projects and, more recently, a number of useful meta-analyses of related literature. Young and several colleagues (Young *et al.* 2012; Young, Slota and Lai 2012), for example, conducted an analysis of 39 studies that explored the relationship between educational uses of videogames and academic achievement gains. Focusing on 'the educational affordances of video games in the content areas of mathematics, science, language learning, physical education, and history' (Young *et al.* 2012, p. 66), they identified a range of individual studies that *did* link gameplay to increased achievement within standardised tests, particularly in the areas of physical education and languages. However, the authors also report on other studies which did *not* produce evidence of gains in achievement that could be attributed to students' gameplay. As a result, they ultimately concluded that 'there is limited evidence to suggest how educational games can be used to solve the problems inherent in the structure of traditional K–12 schooling and academia' (Young *et al.* 2012, p. 62); but Young, Slota and Lai (2012) argued in a follow-up paper that there is, nevertheless, 'reason to be optimistic about the educational impact of video games despite a shortage of definitive evidence to that effect' (p. 296).

It is worth noting, however, that the bulk of the literature here and elsewhere, concerned with 'measuring' the educational 'usefulness' of games commonly refers to a specific subset of games – 'serious' or 'educational' games, and their capacity to enhance understandings of core curriculum concepts and content, or to build, for example, mathematical or literacy capabilities. However, the kinds of games used in educational settings and the ways in which games are used are significantly broader than this. Thus, the slippage between discussion of games, in general, and 'educational games', more narrowly, is risky. Focusing discussion of the outcomes from games-based learning to specific measures of purpose-built 'educational games' overlooks the wider set of outcomes that a more diverse range of games and games-based work in schools might strive to achieve, and reflects a limited conception of the relationships between games, learning and curriculum.

The equivocal nature of their findings led Young and co-authors (Young *et al.* 2012; Young, Slota and Lai 2012) to join a widespread call for further research into the uses and outcomes of games in educational settings. They advocated, in particular, for:

- More 'up close' studies of teachers who are currently working with games: a focus which they argue 'would go far in furthering the total sum of how video games affect student performance in school achievement, engagement, behaviour motivation, and other areas of interest' (Young *et al.* 2012, pp. 81–82).
- Longitudinal studies that explore schools' uses of educational videogames over periods longer than those commonly reported on in literature; that is, studies that run longer than the common ten-week period (Young *et al.* 2012, p. 82).
- The development of assessments and assessment frameworks that are purpose-built for games-based teaching and learning, and focus on multiple outcomes including 'relationships among players, their social interactions with one another, their games, and their metacognitive reflections' (Young *et al.* 2012, p. 83).

As the previous chapters have helped to illustrate, the great strength of the Serious Play project was that it allowed us to explore these very issues, in individual classes and over time; to see long-term changes as teachers became more experienced and adventurous; and to observe teaching and learning opportunities and practices across a wide variety of curriculum areas and games. This longitudinal analysis has also provided sustained opportunities to explore teachers' beliefs about the need for assessment frameworks that are purpose-built for games. Our interest in the pragmatic concerns of teachers and schools regarding *how* to link games to assessment reflects a second strand of literature that has informed the writing of this chapter. This strand (which is, of course, closely related to the first) also considers whether assessment frameworks need to be purpose-built for gaming projects, in order to ensure that teachers can appropriately justify their decisions to work with games and, in this process, report appropriately on the full range of outcomes that might flow from using non-traditional learning resources.

These two strands in the literature (one asking what games can achieve in supporting learning in curriculum areas; the other asking how work with games can be assessed) overlap and interconnect: a relationship which reflects the context within which teachers now work, and the potential for particular beliefs about assessment to limit if and how schools make use of games-based learning. Jenson *et al.* (2016, p. 21) suggested that 'near-universal mandates promulgating standardized assessment models continue to work, antagonistically, to undercut the very potential of these novel educational models'. Where the logic of arguments such as these point to the flattening effect of standardised assessment models on the use of games, and the invisibility of much of what games might achieve under current mandates, an alternate approach argues that (serious) games themselves need to demonstrate their worth within these terms. Bellotti *et al.* (2013) argued that better assessment mechanisms need to be built into the design of serious games, providing player feedback en route, to support learner progress, and better integration of assessment in games:

> For serious games to be considered a viable educational tool, they must provide some means of testing and progress tracking and the testing must be recognizable within the context of the education or training they are attempting to impart.
>
> *(Bellotti et al. 2013, p. 3)*

Such an approach, however, while actively utilising the potential and affordances of games, in other ways flies in the face of the nature and experience of gameplay; and is, for many, consistent with a larger concern over the domestication of games.

Consistent with the position argued by Jenson *et al.* (2016), print-dominated assessment frameworks, rooted in conventional constructions of school subjects and discipline knowledge, correspondingly struggle to map the kinds of multimodal understandings made possible through learning in and with digital environments, literacies and technologies. From this basis, suggestions have been made that teachers might benefit from access to 'practical instruments that enable us to rethink and reassess the outcomes – and the creative expressions – of student learning that emerge through deep engagement in dynamic game-based, socially-networked learning environments' (Jenson *et al.* 2016, p. 21): a claim which they illustrated through the application of Green's 3D Model of L(IT)eracy (1988), and its later use by Beavis (2004), to the analysis of students' work. Jenson *et al.* (2016) analysed student performance in terms of their operational, cultural and critical literacies. They argued that their use of this model opened up a different assessment lens capable of evaluating a wider range of symbolic-semiotic action and meaning-making than had the conventional pre-post-tests, enabling us to seek out and take account of student learning that was not discernible with, nor measurable by, traditional assessment instruments.

(Jenson et al. 2016, p. 33)

Jenson *et al.* (2016) further suggested that 'standard assessment models prefigure and routinize a systemic myopia with regard to the forms of learning transpiring in multimodal and ludic contexts and sites' (p. 36) and endorsed Yancey's 2004 (p. 90) warning against using the assessment frameworks of one medium to assign value and interpret work in a different medium.

The picture that emerges within discussions such as this is one of a potential incompatibility between what might be thought of as 'mainstream' assessment practices within 'typical' schools conducted by 'typical teachers' and serious involvement with games-based learning: an incompatibility which can leave teachers vulnerable to claims of inappropriate use of time, and unable to defend the legitimacy of their actions. Put more bluntly, these concerns raise questions about the ability of teachers to bring together serious play and serious assessment without domesticating games to the demands of schooling and losing, in the process, the very features of gaming that appear to offer so much to schools in the first place.

The wider literature relating to games-based learning has highlighted the importance of ensuring that questions such as these are considered, not only by academics or researchers, but also by teachers themselves. In the Serious Play project, we were keen to explore the way teachers in the project schools perceived the relationship between games-based learning and school-based assessment (and any incompatibilities that may exist). Drawing upon data collected from teachers across the whole length of the Serious Play project, in this chapter, we focus specifically on two key questions:

1. How did teachers describe the relationship between games-based learning and school-based assessment?
2. What are the implications of these teachers' beliefs for future research in this field?

Data Collection

In the Serious Play project, teachers and students worked with digital games in three ways – *using* or playing games, to promote learning in content areas, *analysing* popular commercial games, and *making* games through either free-to-download or commercially available game-making software. Purpose-built commercial educational and free-to-download games were used in a number of classrooms where the focus was on using games to learn in curriculum areas: for example, *Statecraft X* (Chee 2010), *National Geographic's America the Wild* (Relentless Software 2012), but others were also used (many of which are also discussed in the following chapter). A number of teachers and schools worked with *Minecraft* (Mojang 2011); other popular 'non-educational' games included *Assassin's Creed II* (Ubisoft Entertainment 2009), *Myst* (Cyan 1993), *Zork* (Infocom 1980), *Secret Agent: Mission One* (Kolbe 1988) and *Ratchet & Clank* (Insomniac Games 2002). Teachers' comments, therefore, include their evaluations of the use of 'serious' or formally constituted 'educational' games, but also reflect their experience of the use of a wider range of games, and wide-ranging purposes.

Discussions relating to assessment were woven across the length of the project, but were a particular focus across 2013 and 2014. The detailed exploration of teachers' beliefs about the relationship between games and assessment involved several phases. First, during a professional development day conducted in June 2013, the research team foreshadowed the particular focus on assessment that was planned for 2014. As part of this discussion, we returned to one of the project's initial aims, namely: 'Consider [options for] an assessment framework which can identify and support the multimodal literacies and e-learning capabilities made possible through the use, analysis and creation of digital games (Aim vi).'

As a starting point, we showed the teachers an assessment framework previously developed in Australia to support teachers in the sharing, analysis and creation of online/digital materials: Kimber and Wyatt-Smith (2010). We asked them to consider whether or not their work with games would be enriched by access to a model such as this, and if such a model might help educators more broadly when it came to the work of assessing the full range of skills or capabilities that students might develop or display in a games-based learning environment.

Late in 2013, and again in 2014, this initial discussion was revisited multiple times, initially with a view to exploring the application of this model to their own games' work, or the development of one that was similar. During professional development days, focus-group discussions and interviews conducted during researchers' visits to the various schools, we asked teachers to:

- Reflect upon the various outcomes which they believe could be tied to their specific use of games (and how these outcomes were experienced by the full range of students in a cohort).
- Identify links that might exist between these outcomes and the Australian Curriculum with particular reference to subject-area content descriptors and general capabilities.
- Identify if/how they were able to assess and report upon these outcomes and the extent to which learning with games requires new/different or purpose-built assessment tasks.

Additionally, we asked teachers to:

•   Outline factors they believe impacted upon their ability to successfully combine working with games and assessment.
•   Make recommendations concerning future directions for research/practice relating to games-based learning and assessment.

Their reflections on these issues are outlined in the remainder of this chapter.

Games, Curriculum and Assessment

Reflecting upon the various outcomes that they believe could be tied to their specific use of games (and how these outcomes were experienced by the full range of students in a cohort), teachers made the following comments.

First, teachers reinforced a common theme in games-based literature, arguing that games had a valuable role to play in terms of engaging and motivating students, and thus ensuring they were in the best position to learn core material and, by extension, improve performance. One teacher captured this sentiment well when noting:

> a game can provide that sort of – the dynamics, or the excitement, or the wonderment, or – to that degree so that when you're doing the history and the maths, that's all lost because we're playing the game. So it becomes a platform that, as you were saying, it's much more than the movie or the book that you're reading. It's like when you get a book and the book comes alive.

Second, teachers also argued that these sorts of benefits flowed to a wide range of learners, including those who were often positioned as marginal to classroom activities, and who might not routinely experience academic success. This was illustrated in diverse contexts and in multiple year levels. One teacher noted:

> I think that the increments would have been across the board for everybody … academically. Having said that, there were big gains, I think, socially and – for all children – and, in particular, those who were highly academic, with not very good social skills, and for those who were very weak academically with not sensational social skills either. So I think the benefit there was the biggest increment that I saw.

The capacity of benefits from gaming experienced by all students was also noted in the following comment:

> Those kids that would never have made a start were able to have a start, and those kids who would have done little or who would have shown little

interest showed a lot more interest and a lot more enthusiasm and therefore got more out of it.

With this acknowledgement that games have multiple benefits and can create pathways to new educational and social experiences as a starting point, teachers were asked to discuss whether or not they were able to link their work with games directly to the Australian Curriculum and, in particular, to subject-area content descriptors and general capabilities. Across Queensland and Victoria, and in quite different schools and subject areas, teachers agreed that games-based activities could be directly linked to large sections of the Australian Curriculum and its many and varied content descriptors.

The ability to make these links was regarded as important for the legitimacy of games-based learning. One teacher summarised the perspectives of her group's discussion, and the needs of other stakeholders by citing the importance of 'justifying to the parent body what you're doing and how that applies to learning and, more importantly, how that applies to the different subject areas and how you're going to assess it'.

This same conversation also acknowledged 'the challenge of initially making it fit. Teachers are time-poor. The notion of making it fit into an already busy day, week, year, and you've just got to be a little bit smart about how you implement these games.'

With constraints of time noted and acknowledged, teachers were consistent in arguing that, given the opportunity, they were able to link their gaming work not only to an overarching curriculum, but also to assessment practices that can appropriately recognise most and major learning outcomes associated with games-based learning. When asked how well the assessment requirements of Australian Curriculum, Assessment and Reporting Authority (ACARA) or state-backed curriculum guidelines support or recognise these things, one teacher, Ang, responded simply: 'Well, brilliantly'.

Another noted:

> [it's just] a matter of simply a matter of looking at curriculum documents and making curriculum connections, [we] felt it was quite possible to align your game plan to many of them. It's just a bit of planning and preparation required to make it worthwhile and to align closely with requirements.

Similar claims were made by teachers in regard to diverse curriculum subjects, ranging from English and Mathematics through to Chinese, IT and Media Studies. Ingrid made these comments:

> Because I'm an IT specialist, so I don't see the other curriculum areas, only the IT. So using the digital technology draft, I've just put together a rubric so that when the students do their work, I've got some way of assessing

them that's up to date. Yeah, so I just – it's quite easy; I'm looking for skills that are actually part of the Digital Technologies curriculum and it's very similar to the old curriculum in a lot of ways, I suppose.

The two areas, the knowledge and understanding, [are] just how they're handling the skills that we've actually put together, whether they can apply it to old situations or new situations. Then the second part, the production, is how well they can actually synthesise the information and put it together in a new situation, their evaluation of their work, whether they're testing debugging and things like that comes into the second part. So it's quite easy to map against.

This is not to say that teachers believed that assessment of games-based learning was always straightforward. Some noted that the alignment between curriculum and a particular gaming activity was sometimes more implicit than explicit. As Janet said:

I went into all the content descriptors of English and I couldn't see anything explicitly referring to gaming; however, there are certain elements that do support the outcomes I've witnessed, the girls playing the games, okay, with both the games we've been doing. For example, they're interpreting what they're seeing, they're analysing, they're evaluating and the girls are certainly engaging with the text. Now a lot of those are in the content descriptors, but I couldn't actually see anything that was explicit to what I've been doing.

At the same time, however, teachers agreed that, in their experience, games could be woven into a broad teaching, learning and assessment plan for most subject areas in ways that would also engage and motivate their students:

So you can be assessing the science and the maths and the English, but the game is just sitting underneath all that. It provides a more dynamic way to bring it all together. So that, as you move through, the children are engaged so much more by playing with the game. But you can still assess the persuasive texts that they might have produced or the – or doing the mathematics that they were doing, maths in action. So it just provides that level, that platform.

The idea that games function as a platform, or vehicle, for learning and thus assessment, is captured in another interview.

Researcher: So how would you assess whether students' work with games has been successful? So how do you assess what they're doing with their games, what [are] you doing?

Ang: Well, we're going to assess a number of things. We're going to assess their understanding of the history elements, geography elements, English and the final assessment is an English thing, the CTJ. So they're going to be persuading people like [Paul] and like [Pat] [other teachers] that they would want to live in their community. So I've actually done a – a bit like an [word unclear] below and above, based on the content descriptives. So we'll highlight and do what they most like at – what they most like about for that subject, but the game itself is the tool.

This brings us to a *third* point. Teachers also argued that some games-based work, although not directly linked to an assessment task, facilitated the development of various skills and abilities which would subsequently be assessed in other ways. This included, for example, the development of knowledge of vocabulary that would help students complete a formal assessment task conducted at a different time. Zhi, for example, made a connection between a game played in Chinese and a forthcoming Chinese assessment task:

> The other game [we used] is called Language Learning Space (Education Services Australia 2015), but this one is just a game about itself; it's not really related to what I am teaching, like particularly what I'm teaching. But still, because language is such a broad area, it's not like – it's a continual thing. Anything they do on the game will benefit them while they're doing their assignment and stuff, especially in term four [when] our assessment is [to] design an itinerary. So you design a five-day itinerary to go to China and they can draw all the bits and pieces that they learned from the game and put it into the assessment.

In another example, Diane, a teacher who had worked extensively with *Minecraft*, noted that the discussions produced during the *Minecraft* project appeared to impact positively upon students' later assessment tasks and, in particular, their ability to express and defend an opinion:

> A lot of the girls who in the beginning – and I don't know how much this relates directly to Minecraft or what – it's been something I've been trying to achieve with them all year, but certainly I've seen the results come through in their last lot of assessment, is those girls who in the beginning wanted to give only the answer they knew was correct, that now they're much – because I say to them, I don't care what answer you give me, but justify it. Like this – I'm asking your opinion.

FIGURE 11.1 Making connections between a game played in Chinese and a forth-coming Chinese assessment piece.

> So I don't care if I agree with your opinion, but if you can justify your opinion then you'll get the marks, kind of thing. So they've learnt to do that through all the open-ended discussion that's come through Minecraft. So a lot of them have improved in that area. As a result their overall marks have gone up because they now can justify their thinking.

Fourth, teachers were consistent in linking game-based projects to the development of a wide range of generic skills and general capabilities which, they argued, shaped students' ability to work effectively at school, and with their peers even if they were not directly assessed. For example, Janet noted that:

> the girls have learned from scratch how to even load up the machine to get it working. So there's a lot of learning going on there. Then after just watching their collaboration and their communication between each other, they assist each other, all of those things that you'd normally do in a normal classroom with any subject that you're teaching.

To summarise, despite an awareness of the scrutinised nature of their work, and time constraints associated with teaching, the teachers in this project expressed relatively little difficulty in linking their games-based projects to their overarching

FIGURE 11.2 The girls interpreting, analysing, evaluating and collaborating through Xbox Kinect games.

assessment frameworks. They were well able to draw links between games and content descriptors in the Australian Curriculum; between games and the general capabilities in the curriculum; and between games and students' sense of belonging and security in educational contexts. The relationship between these various dimensions is captured in one further comment from Janet:

> First of all there's knowledge, there's information being delivered; there's the fact that they are motivated from it to go and research and find out more, which they have been doing; it's also got the – actually playing the game, the girls are having fun, they're enjoying it, they're also talking, they're communicating; there's all of that social interaction going on. There's a collaboration because if things don't happen, they'll help each other, direct each other so [words unclear]. So there's an awful lot going [on].

Summary and Discussion

Literature has suggested that, if games are to be given a routine or credible place within formal schooling – and the domestication of technologies that has been so consistently documented in the past 20 years is to be avoided – then teachers may need access to new ways to assess the learning that flows from games. This reflects beliefs about the particular affordances that can be linked to games, and also, the highly scrutinised context within which teachers work.

Accordingly, teachers in the Serious Play project were asked to consider whether or not their (already evidenced) ability to work with games would be enhanced, or made easier, if they had access to, or were able to develop, a particular 'formal' framework or model for assessing games-based learning. Across two years, and in multiple contexts, the answer to this question was consistently 'no'.

Teachers did acknowledge the pressure they sometimes felt to be able to justify their use of games internally and externally. In discussion with Sarah, Janet commented:

Janet: I get a bit stressed with so much assessment. It takes a lot of the actual learning enjoyment out of it, and from the teacher's point of view.
Sarah: But really, from what you assess …
Janet: But I feel that we need to justify it …
Sarah: Well that's it. So what …
Janet: … and I feel I can justify what I'm doing now. This time last year, when I first got this Xbox, I was putting my – I actually thought to myself, my God, what have I done, I've got the school to spend the money on this, how can I justify this? – I can justify this now; I am so sure I can justify what I'm doing and what we've been doing. I feel good.

Another teacher noted that she felt more confident with her gaming work when she could 'defend' it through reference to curriculum objectives. In her words:

[I]f somebody wants to question what I'm doing in class, I need to have it aligned. The way I feel, we don't have freedom just to do it because it's a really positive interesting thing for the kids to do. Yes, it is all of that.
But if I can't validate the purpose of it, then there's no point me doing it.

Despite these kinds of comments, however, teachers argued that there was no need for (or benefit to be had from) development of a 'special' or modified approach to assessment in order to respond to, justify or assess the use of games. They were, in fact, quite emphatic about their belief that a purpose-built framework for assessing learning from or through games was *not* needed and would *not* support their work in this field. The following conversation captures much of the mood of a professional development day focused on assessment:

Teacher: [I]f we gave a child or a student a board game to do, why wouldn't we assess it in the same manner if they were just doing it in a game style? So provided they are following or ticking off the content or what's required for their assessment piece, that should really be assessed in a similar way.
Researcher 1: By which you mean that you don't have to create a fake assessment task.

Teacher: No.

Researcher 1: So you don't do this game activity and then go and [words unclear].

Teacher: Is it right, yeah.

Researcher 1: You can actually be – use the skills that you've already got in assessing different types of …

Researcher 2: … content and knowledge. Yeah.

Researcher 1: Everybody here was really positive … just matter of fact about that and to [not] try and assess it in some artificial way.

At the same time, however, teachers were equally insistent that not everything that flowed from games *needed* to be assessed. Across 12 months of discussion about the relationship between their games work and their assessment practices, teachers defended the need for schools to encourage the development of students' confidence, personality and character, and to foster engagement and enthusiasm – regardless of whether or not these outcomes can or should be formally assessed, as shown in the following comments: 'How do we assess enthusiasm and interest and that being able to go and spontaneously – go out and find out more about it. Like the girl that went off to read to the class.' And:

> Because – well, when I reflected on it because I think about what the girls have been doing. I think about the way they – there's all the other social side of it too. Just things of manners, all the things we try to teach to our children; the holistic child, on interacting with each other, socialising, helping, support. All those things and the way they talk, it's just fantastic in that, because I've watched that happening in the group, and the support.

They explicitly valued the potential of games for: 'educating the whole child, so manners, just trying to find it – socialising, all those things that you would hope children are learning through school and home life but aren't necessarily part of the curriculum'. And therefore they argued that 'assess-ability' is not the only justification for the use of games:

> Why do we always have to have a rubric or assess these things when really I would like to see children come out the end of their education being able to think on the fly, being able to problem solve, being thrown a curved ball and know what to do with it. It doesn't always come down to pen and paper and that sort of traditional way that we think.

Taken together, these kinds of comments provide powerful evidence that teachers are not controlled by assessment, but rather, they are creative professionals able to work within existing frameworks to achieve multiple goals. This is not to suggest that teachers did not believe they needed any form of support in regard to their work with games. Rather, the support they valued did not take the form of purpose-built assessment rubrics, frameworks or principles. Instead, they spoke positively about the benefits of having:

- Access to the experiences of peers and colleagues who have also worked with games (a key feature in teachers' positive evaluations of participation in the Serious Play project).
- Time to invest in thinking about the relationship between curriculum and diverse games and using this to inform planning. One participant commented:

> I think that's where your planning is really important and the writing of your assessment task. It is based heavily around your game. It's not an add-on. So, if you're still assessing similar outcomes and criteria and whatever, learnings from a well-planned game project, there's no difference to that to giving a written assignment or a test or another assessment instrument.

- Freedom and flexibility to follow the various learning outcomes that can appear through sustained engagement with a game-based project: as illustrated in the following observation:

> I guess looking at the comments from Victoria and then the comments from Queensland, the underlying theme was around that notion [of] flexibility. So realising that yes, there is a[n] ACARA [the Australian Curriculum] or is it AusVEL[s] [the Victorian Government's resource relating to the Australian Curriculum] that people need to work off and according to, but you can still bring a certain amount of flexibility to your daily classroom life so that games-based play can happen and other things can happen as well.

Conclusion

Literature that explores what happens when digital games are brought into classrooms has increasingly emphasised the pivotal role that teachers play in regard to what games 'become' in a particular context. Games do not automatically transform learning environments or generate quality outcomes. Nor do they automatically disrupt or transform any other aspects of education such as assessment and reporting. But the decisions taken by individual teachers help to determine whether games allow students to experience *multiple* forms of educational, social and emotional success. Teachers participating in the Serious Play project expressed a clear belief in the potential of games to help students achieve both formal and informal outcomes, some of which could and would be assessed by teachers where it was appropriate for the students. These beliefs are paralleled by faith in their own ability to work creatively and flexibly within an existing curriculum, and inside the boundaries provided by different states, individual schools and specific students' needs.

Research cited above suggests that this work would perhaps be facilitated by access to 'close-up' studies of teachers who are currently working with games; and, in particular, studies that run for longer than ten weeks, and assessments and frameworks purpose-built for games-based teaching and learning. While the teachers in the project rejected the need for purpose-built assessments, they strongly endorsed the value of hearing from others working with games, and learning through shared conversations and sustained opportunities to work on games-based projects. Building upon these insights, the following chapter provides some further detail about a number of the 'small affordable experiments' conducted by teachers within the Serious Play project, and focuses on providing examples of how various teachers selected, worked with and connected assessment to diverse curriculum areas and different teaching levels and age groups.

References

Beavis, C (2004), 'Critical perspectives on curriculum and ICTs: The 3D model, literacy and computer games', *Interactive Educational Multimedia*, vol. 9, November, pp. 77–88. Available from: www.raco.cat/index.php/iem/article/viewFile/204567/273101 (Accessed 22 November 2016).

Bellotti, F, Kapralos, B, Lee, K, Moreno-Ger, P and Berta, R (2013), 'Assessment in and of serious games: An overview', *Advances in Human–Computer Interaction*, vol. 2013, pp. 1–11. Available from: doi: http://dx.doi.org/10.1155/2013/136864 (Accessed 5 August 2016).

Chee, Y S (2010), *Statecraft X*. Available from: http://cheeyamsan.info/NIEprojects/SCX/SCX2.htm (Accessed 8 August 2016).

Cyan (1993), *Myst*. Available from: http://cyan.com/games/myst/ (Accessed 8 August 2016).

Education Services Australia (2015), *Language Learning Space*. Available from: www.lls.edu.au/home (Accessed 10 August 2016).

Green, B (1988), 'Subject-specific literacy and school learning: A focus on writing', *Australian Journal of Education*, vol. 32, no. 2, pp. 156–179. Available from: doi: 10.1177/000494418803200203 (Accessed 5 August 2016).

Infocom (1980), *Zork*, personal software. Available from: https://archive.org/details/a2_Zork_I_The_Great_Underground_Empire_1980_Infocom (Accessed 8 August 2016).

Insomniac Games (2002), *Ratchet & Clank* (PlayStation 2), Sony Computer Entertainment. Available from: www.insomniacgames.com/games/ratchet-clank-ps4/ (Accessed 17 November 2016).

Jenson, J, de Castell, S, Thumlert, K and Muehrer, R (2016), 'Deep assessment: An exploratory study of game-based, multimodal learning in *Epidemic*', *Digital Culture and Education*, vol. 8, no. 1, pp. 21–40. Available from: www.digitalcultureandeducation.com/cms/wp-content/uploads/2016/03/jenson.pdf (Accessed 5 August 2016).

Kimber, K and Wyatt-Smith, C (2010), 'Secondary students' online use and creation of knowledge: Refocusing priorities for quality assessment and learning', *Australasian Journal of Educational Technology*, vol. 26, no. 5, pp. 607–625. Available from: doi: http://dx.doi.org/10.14742/ajet.1054 (Accessed 5 August 2016).

Kolbe, B (1988), *Secret Agent: Mission One*. Available from: www.gameswin.org/gameen. php?id=1142 (Accessed 14 July 2016).

Mojang (2011), *Minecraft*. Available from: https://minecraft.net/en/ (Accessed 8 August 2016).

Relentless Software (2012), *National Geographic: America the Wild* (Kinect Xbox), Redmond, WA: Microsoft Studios.

Tobias, S and Fletcher, J D (2011), 'Introduction', in S Tobias and J D Fletcher (eds), *Computer games and instruction*, Charlotte, NC: Information Age, pp. 3–15.

Ubisoft Entertainment (2009), *Assassin's Creed II*. Available from: http://assassinscreed. ubi.com/en-au/games/assassins-creed-2.aspx (Accessed 10 August 2016).

Yancey, K (2004), 'Looking for sources of coherence in a fragmented world: Notes toward a new assessment design', *Computers and Composition*, vol. 21, no. 1, pp. 89–102. Available from: doi:10.1016/j.compcom.2003.08.024 (Accessed 5 August 2016).

Young, M, Slota, S, Cutter, A, Jalette, G, Mullin, G, Lai, B, Simeoni, Z, Tran, M and Yukhymenko, M (2012), 'Our princess is in another castle: A review of trends in serious gaming', *Review of Educational Research*, vol. 82, no. 1, pp. 61–89. Available from: doi: 10.3102/0034654312436980 (Accessed 5 August 2016).

Young, M, Slota, S and Lai, B (2012), 'Comments on "reflections on 'a review of trends in serious gaming'"', *Review of Educational Research*, vol. 82, no. 3, pp. 296–299.

12

PLAYING, MAKING AND ANALYSING GAMES

Cases of Assessment and Serious Play

Leonie Rowan

Introduction

Chapter 11 outlined diverse teachers' beliefs about the relationship between serious play and various dimensions of assessment and reporting. It explored the benefits that teachers believe can flow from games-based learning and the close relationship between many of these outcomes and formal curriculum requirements. This exploration of teachers' beliefs about games and assessment emphasised, as well, a view expressed quite firmly by many teachers in our project: that not every benefit associated with games-based learning actually *needs* to be formally assessed and/or reported upon in order to be considered legitimate.

Underpinning many of these arguments is an understanding of the importance of teachers having the opportunity to make site-based professional judgments about when/how to work with digital games; and whether the assessment is formal, informal, overt or by 'stealth' (Shute and Fengfeng 2012). These judgments, moreover, must reflect the needs of each *specific* cohort of students rather than a generalised or idealised version of the 'contemporary learner' or a 'digital native' (Rowan 2012). In other words, it is the teacher who is best placed to identify how a particular example of digital play might impact upon a specific group of students, be it academically, socially or emotionally.

The previous chapter also argued that in making these decisions, teachers do not want access to a purpose-built, formal or artificial model to guide their assessment of digital play. Rather, they function as informed professionals who make judgments appropriate to their own context about how and when to engage in assessment. Nevertheless, participants in the research agreed that opportunities for teachers – not just students – to play, experiment with and talk about games impact directly upon their confidence in this emerging area of educational innovation. Indeed, the Serious Play project has demonstrated that teachers' capacity to exercise professional judgment about games-based learning and assessment is maximised when they are given regular and sustained opportunities to experiment with various forms of digital games, and to share their experiences with others who are working in similar *and* different contexts. This project therefore endorses the recommendations of Young *et al.* (2012) who advocated for both longitudinal and 'up close' studies of teachers who are currently working with games in order to move understanding of the relationship between games and student performance forward.

Recognising the value of sharing real-world stories and practical examples for shaping teacher practice and confidence regarding games-based learning – and thus for informing future and ongoing work in this area – this chapter provides brief descriptions of some of the specific ways in which teachers integrated games into their teaching and assessment and reporting practices. Drawing upon examples from different year levels and across various areas of the school curriculum, the chapter provides examples of the ways in which teachers were able to create spaces within which student experiences – be they academic, social or emotional – were enhanced, and how this supported learning and informed assessment. The examples are organised into three sections. The first section offers examples where games were linked directly to assessment: thus assessment was conducted in or through games in some way. The second section explores uses of games that helped students develop what might be thought of as complementary skills and/or knowledge that ultimately supported their work on other (generally non-game) assessment tasks. The third section has a slightly different focus. It explores instances where teachers in the project believe that games helped students to develop what might be described as general capabilities and life/learning skills.

It is increasingly argued that there are various foundational or meta-skills (such as communication, collaboration, persistence and problem solving) which increase students' ability to experience educational and social success (including achievement within assessment tasks). Literature has also consistently shown that students are more likely to engage with, and succeed within, educational challenges (games-based or otherwise) if they believe that their classroom provides opportunities for them to be seen, valued and successful. Thus, the third set of examples explored in this chapter is not directly and immediately connected to the formal processes of (or outcomes from) assessment tasks. Rather, the examples report on how students developed skills or displayed abilities that position them well for both educational and social achievement or success. They are included here to acknowledge (and celebrate) the multiple skills displayed by the students across the length of the Serious Play project; and also to respect the project teachers' unanimous insistence (discussed in Chapter 11) that not everything that counts in school needs to be measured … and that the benefits which flow from games are valuable even if they are not directly assessed.

The overarching goal in the sections that follow is not to provide ethnographic accounts of how and what the teachers did. Rather it is my intention to demonstrate the multiple possibilities that teachers explored through their Serious Play activities as an invitation to other teachers to engage in their own forms of serious play and learning from and with their colleagues.

Assessment With/Through/in Games

As noted in the previous chapter, not all teachers believed that games needed to be directly connected to assessment. Nevertheless, there *were* several cases where teachers used games to assess student knowledge and understanding. The emphasis, in these instances, was generally on identifying the various forms of disciplinary knowledge demonstrated through playing, making or analysing games; and not on the 'quality' of any game-related product that may have been involved (although some ICT-related courses are an exception to this scenario). Some brief examples illustrate this approach.

Making Games: Scratch

Perhaps not surprisingly, one of the first areas where teachers linked gaming projects with the formal curriculum and planned assessment was in subject areas relating to information technology (IT). One teacher, Ingrid, described the clear links between the Digital Technology curriculum and her work in developing and assessing a unit of work with Year 6 students during which they made games with *Scratch* (Lifelong Kindergarten Group 2003).

> So using the digital technology draft, I've just put together a rubric so that when the students do their work, I've got some way of assessing them that's up to date. Yeah, so I just – it's quite easy; I'm looking for skills that are actually part of the Digital Technologies curriculum and it's very similar to the old curriculum in a lot of ways, I suppose.

She went on to note:

> The two areas, the knowledge and understanding, is just how they're handling the skills that we've actually put together, whether they can apply it to old situations or new situations. Then the second part, the production, is how well they can actually synthesise the information and put it together in a new situation, their evaluation of their work, whether they're testing debugging and things like that comes into the second part. So it's quite easy to map against.

A less direct approach, but a similar ease in alignment, was demonstrated in the work of a teacher at a Queensland private secondary school.

Making Games: Studies in Religious Education

In this second example, the teacher involved students in the creation of a game designed to illustrate (and assess) their understanding of topics previously studied in a Religious Education (RE) class: the seven deadly sins, the seven heavenly virtues, the Beatitudes and the Ten Commandments. To demonstrate their knowledge of one of these topics, students created a game focused on the overarching theme: 'making good moral choices'. In this case study, the teacher allowed students the freedom to work with any sort of digital platform they wished (PowerPoint and specialised game-making software such as *GoAnimate* [GoAnimate Inc. 2011] and *GameMaker* [YoYogames 2016] were some examples). This freedom was facilitated by an assessment focus on content knowledge, not game-making ability:

> [T]here wasn't any specific software that they had to use as such. But having said that, I guess because of that, and because it wasn't really a game-making unit that we were doing, it was more focusing on the RE moral aspects. I'd say the quality of the games weren't tremendous, but I was still very happy with the outcomes of the unit.

The teacher of this class also noted that his students expressed a strong preference for this assessment, rather than the 'assessment task the other RE classes were doing, which wasn't quite so engaging. They were very keen to give this a bit of a go'.

Playing Games: Language Learning

Language learning was another area identified as a space within which it was relatively straightforward to link assessment directly to games. While the language teacher working across the length of the Serious Play project primarily used games to develop students' overall language familiarity and complementary skills (as discussed further below), there were instances where she spoke about the benefits of purpose-built 'educational' games that were explicitly tied to, for example, the Year 8 Chinese Language curriculum and assessment. The teacher acknowledged that purpose-built educational games could play a valuable role in language assessment:

> [L]ast year – the year before when I had the first year summit class, academic class, I actually played a game which was developed by [Language Learning Space] centre in Queensland; they said they'd put a lot of funding into that.

The ultimate goal was using all these online games, it's like a big massive program called New Land New Language, has got five or six languages there and Chinese was one of them. To enrol kids into the program, it's a bit of work; you have to get all the IDs and everything and send them through and sometimes you've got new kids coming and somebody's pulled out. It's just this updating the data makes it hard for us. But the program itself was pretty good. All my Year 8s loved it because they were the academic class. The game has got all assessment and is all curriculum-related. So they're writing the program according to the curriculum, attaching it with assessment and ticking all the boxes.

Playing Games: Cross-Curriculum Opportunities

One of the most powerful discussions about the learning that was linked to and assessed through games related to teachers' uses of *Minecraft* (Mojang 2011). This has been discussed earlier (see particularly, Chapters 3, 5, 6, 8 and 10), but in this chapter, with its focus on assessment, it is necessary to note that some of the project teachers were able to link their *Minecraft* experiments to a wide range of curriculum areas. The primary school teacher quoted below (and in previous chapters), for example, paints a picture of how things develop when teachers have the opportunity to experiment, rather than being constrained by a lock-step curriculum: 'I started off with *Minecraft* as a literacy unit and then saw the possibilities as we went along to make it into a science–engineering design-type project'.

The key point made in this quote – and consistently echoed by teachers throughout the project – was that even if gameplay begins with one particular assessment focus in mind, it is possible for further opportunities to develop as the project unfolds.

To summarise, therefore, across the length of the Serious Play project, teachers found a number of ways to assess student learning *directly* through games-related activities. This assessment was both formative and summative and involved feedback from teachers, peers and other student groups. For students who were engaged in *making* games, this kind of peer review was regarded by teachers as particularly important, because it provides a level of authenticity to assessment that is often missing in school contexts. One participant described this as 'assessment through use rather than assessment through comparison against a set of criteria'. This prompted the following comments from the teacher who had worked with primary school students to build games in *Scratch*:

[T]his is part of normal testing that actually goes on game production. So in a way, it's like a real … assessment. It's like when you are doing English, you end up having [a] story and you feed it to an audience for feedback, it's the same kind of level of working that is an authentic-type practice within the game, I think.

These brief examples illustrate teachers' beliefs that games could be used as a vehicle for formal assessment. As outlined in Chapter 11, they also believed that, in cases such as this, there was no difficulty to be found in terms of assessing learning achieved in a games-based project. The next section of this chapter explores a different role for games in assessment: the development of what might be thought of as complementary skills and knowledge.

'Supporting' Assessment With/Through/in Games

The majority of the teachers who took part in the Serious Play project linked students' engagement with games to development of knowledge and skill sets that ultimately improved their ability to undertake (and experience success within) formal assessment tasks, regardless of whether these tasks also had a games-related component. This was again illustrated in very different subject areas.

Supporting Assessment in English

One teacher involved in the project, Kathy, explored the potential of video clips taken from game trailers to support the development of Year 9 students' verbal and written English skills. Kathy works in a Queensland public secondary school. To try and develop increased vocabulary and greater variety in descriptive texts, Kathy played students in her English classes a trailer to the videogame *Assassin's Creed Unity* (Ubisoft Entertainment 2014). Although not willing to suggest that this impacted directly upon their assessment results, she noted that the discussion prompted students to contribute more to discussions, and gave them an opportunity to demonstrate (and develop) skills in analysis:

> [W]hen I used the Assassin's Creed Unity YouTube clip or the trailer, they enjoyed that lesson. They really liked the brainstorming of the vocabulary, talking about the history of the period that the game was set in. It just – because it was a visual, they could understand and relate, because they all played it. So yeah, definitely, it was productive in terms of engagement.
>
> *(Kathy, Interview 2)*

> Even just breaking down, there was a scene where he was walking through the town, and then all of a sudden he's up on top of a building, and just talking about how would he get to the top of the building and talking about Parkour [current outdoor phenomenon related to moving rapidly through a physical environment] and things like that, that kids these days are far more interested in, and they can talk about it, and how else could you describe it and what, you know.
>
> *(Kathy, Interview 1)*

She went on to say:

> I think some students just need that visual, particularly when it comes to
> writing about figurative language – like using figurative language. It just –
> it helps them then visualise what could – what – how dirty the area was, or
> what the buildings looked like, and what the sounds were like and smells
> and whatnot. So it just really helps them.
>
> *(Kathy, Interview 2)*

This same teacher also used games to engage students in the development of
knowledge about *Romeo and Juliet*. After watching Baz Luhrmann's movie, she
felt that student understanding of the play was unclear. Students were then asked
to create a game based upon a *Who Wants to Be a Millionaire* (PDST n. d.)
template. Kathy argued that the students demonstrated much greater knowledge
of the original text in the gameplay than they had been able to do in their written
essays. She noted:

> The general interest, enthusiasm and engagement of the whole class
> increased incredibly which was a great outcome. It was enjoyable to find
> that these students had learnt to identify the literary techniques and could
> showcase their knowledge in a format other than an essay. I also believe
> there was a sense of pride within the class as they could see their work
> being used in the game.

FIGURE 12.1 Playing *Who Wants to be a Millionaire* in a lesson on Romeo and Juliet.
Source: http://pdst.ie/

Supporting Assessment in Languages

The secondary school Year 8 language teacher, Zhi, referred to above ('Playing Games: Language Learning') also provided her Chinese Language class with opportunities to play with games that she believed supported their completion of assessment tasks both directly and indirectly. Commenting on a range of (personal computer) games that she had used, this teacher noted:

> The games we play, it just ties nicely with the unit we're doing this term because we're travelling, so basically related to the Chinese [College and all those] attractions in Beijing, Shanghai, those major cities. The game we're playing is called China Game (Asia Society n.d.) so it's like a trivia sort of game, and at the end of the game, they'll be rewarded with wallpaper stuff, and when you look at the kids' computers, you can see half of them have already got that wallpaper, which is an achievement.

Zhi made similarly positive observations about other games:

> Anything they do on the game will benefit them while they're doing their assignment and stuff, especially in term four [when] our assessment is [to] design an itinerary. So you design a five-day itinerary to go to China and they can draw all the bits and pieces that they learned from the game and put it into the assessment. It doesn't matter if they do it in Chinese language or just in English; it more matters that they understand the culture and they know where to visit, why – the reason behind it.

Supporting Learning in Citizenship Through Statecraft X

As outlined previously (see particularly, Chapters 4 and 5), *Statecraft X* (Chee 2010) is purpose-built to support the development of students' understandings of issues relating to citizenship education. Through playing this purpose-built game, students studying Queensland's Year 8 Studies of Society and Environment curriculum demonstrated focused understanding of key aspects of the relevant curriculum. The game was loaded onto iPods, which students had access to for the course of the activity. Over a period of three weeks, teams played at home, over the internet, competing at first with each other, and then joining forces to fight an external threat. For Cole, one of the teachers involved, the game provided students with opportunities to develop the kind of higher-order skills that are necessary to achieve well in this subject area. As he noted:

> The big problem doing the civics component [of the Studies of Society and Environment curriculum] is trying to get the kids to think at a higher level. 'We should just build the hospital and we should build the roads and

everybody should have access to computers and all those types of things' –
it's really hard for them to understand it's a resource-driven model. … I was
very impressed with the way that kids could draw upon in-game experiences
and compare and contrast them against systems within state, systems within
countries et cetera. I thought that was a real strength of the game.

To summarise, therefore, teachers across the project spoke regularly about the
ways in which gameplay supported students' achievement in assessment, even if
the assessment was not linked directly to their activities.

A third, but slightly different, relationship between games and assessment
identified by the project teachers concerns the ways in which games-based
activities improved students' overall skill set and sense of self. This is the focus of
the next section of the chapter.

Supporting Learners With/Through/in Games That Develop Personal Skills and General Capabilities

Literature exploring game use in educational contexts has consistently highlighted
the potential of games to help students develop what can be variously described as
twenty-first-century skills, general competencies or practical life lessons – outcomes
that might be described as 'tangential learning in games' (Floyd and Portnow
2008). Similarly, teachers within the Serious Play project consistently and
emphatically argued that some of the most powerful outcomes that emerged from
students' engagement with games related to this broader set of outcomes, rather
than specific assessment tasks. While achievements in these areas (such as teamwork
or problem solving) do not have the same official status as performance in subject
areas – and may or may not be reported upon – teachers nevertheless argued the
relevance of these areas to their assessment conversations and assessment practices.

In this section of the chapter, therefore, we explore teachers' beliefs about how
their gaming activities developed what the Australian Curriculum describes as
'general capabilities': a set of knowledge, skills, behaviours and dispositions that,
together with curriculum content in each learning area and the cross-curriculum
priorities, will assist students to live and work successfully in the twenty-first century
(Australian Curriculum Assessment and Reporting Authority [ACARA] 2016).

The specific general capabilities outlined in the Australian Curriculum are:

- literacy;
- numeracy;
- information and communication technology (ICT) capability;
- critical and creative thinking;
- personal and social capability;
- ethical understanding;
- intercultural understanding.

Links were made between games and each of these areas – individually and in combination – and were repeatedly identified by the project participants. We provide brief examples of these links here.

Literacy

First, teachers were consistent in noting a link between gameplay and the development of literacy skills. For example, as outlined in Chapter 9, Janet, a teacher librarian, worked first with a *National Geographic* Xbox Kinect game, *America the Wild* (Relentless Software 2012), to support the development of students' understanding of information books. This same teacher also made use of *Edmodo* (Edmodo 2016) (a web-based collaboration platform – with echoes of Facebook – designed specifically for educators, students and parents) to encourage students to write about their Xbox Kinect experiences. Combining their gaming with another platform, students were able to demonstrate interaction, communication and verbal and written literacies:

> So we used Edmodo, so the girls treat that a little bit like Facebook; they wrote comments to each other, 'Oh, I've just learned all about the owl and the owl can do this, and with its prey it did this, and I was able to do this action which worked out better than that action'. So there was a lot of interaction going on, verbal interaction and literacy with the Edmodo.

Another example is provided by Kate's work with primary school children:

> [With] Minecraft – kids create entire stories where they've written, you know it's sort of digital literacy stuff … they have written scenarios where, you know, a team of fairies have to flee home, and they are being chased by witches, and the witches have all these powers, so they have to build this fairy village in Minecraft with all these specifications and stuff, and they have to have escape tunnels and all sorts of cool things.

Information and Computer Technologies (ICT)

Perhaps not surprisingly, teachers in the project saw clear parallels between their work with games and students' development of new or enhanced skills and dispositions in regard to ICT. For some teachers, the fundamental relationship between game work and the ICT curriculum was self-evident: 'So, for example, with the digital technology spectrum, games are mentioned 31 times in terms of different learning outcomes and places where they can be used.'

In this same conversation, another teacher commented:

> We ticked all of them when we wrote our programs because, you know, we put all our programs on one school, and at the beginning you have to

tick the boxes, and we should just tick all the ICT because we use a lot – we use them a lot. They [games and ICT] are closely related.

It is important to recognise that students were not just given opportunities to display skills they already possessed, but also to develop new skills. The project participants were consistent in demonstrating that – despite common stereotypes – the students involved were not all 'digital natives' and, in many cases, needed explicit opportunities to develop new skills. That said, several of the teachers also emphasised the power of letting students problem solve when confronted with a new technology/platform/interface/game; and the power of the learning that resulted.

While literacy, numeracy and ICT underpinned many of the teachers' comments, it is reasonable to say that the greatest number of teacher comments relating to general capabilities referred to a combination of critical and creative thinking; personal and social capability; ethical understanding; and intercultural understanding. As many of these capabilities were discussed in combination, the following sub-sections provide brief snapshots of games-based initiatives that had various outcomes related to this broad set of capabilities.

Ethical and Intercultural Understanding

The relationship between games and the development of ethical and intercultural understanding was highlighted by teachers working on a number of projects, and particularly by teachers who worked within subjects linked to Studies of Society and Environment, History and Religious Education. For example, a cohort of Queensland Year 10 History students played the game *Ayiti: The Cost of Life* (Global Kids and Gamelab 2006). *Ayiti* is a web-based game (based on Haiti) that has been purposefully designed to introduce players to various social concepts including, specifically, the impact of poverty on educational opportunities. Within the game, players need to make decisions about how a family will spend their time and resources. The teacher leading this initiative noted that the gameplay may have helped students develop some important skills such as empathy and intercultural understanding:

Researcher: When you were talking a bit earlier, you said that part of the reason you wanted to work with games was to build empathy or help these kids' understanding through putting themselves in people's shoes.

Kathy: Yeah. Well I was just saying, I have one boy in my class who's very right wing and very 'they have a choice, they don't have to work on a farm, they don't have to work in a sweatshop'; it's – because the previous game we played, they just had to make shoes and they had to reach a certain quota to earn enough money to eat and drink, and if they couldn't afford to eat, their vision got blurry so they couldn't work out where to put the shoe parts. Then they eventually either died or lost their job or something like that. 'But they don't have to work in a sweatshop, they can quit if they want to.' I said, 'Are you sure about that, they have to feed children and they may not have an education to get a better job.' 'Oh that's not true, they can quit.'

So I think his perception on life in the developing world has changed a little bit, but I think he might be stubborn and I was saying you can't really gauge attitude to knowledge.

A further example of the development of intercultural understanding came from students playing the Chinese language games discussed above. As their teacher noted: 'It doesn't matter if they do it in Chinese language or just in English; it more matters that they understand the culture and they know where to visit, why – the reason behind it.'

Teachers across all subject areas identified links between game activities and the development of critical and creative thinking and problem solving, as well as personal and social capability. Comments relating to these strands were often woven together within the project data, as the following sections indicate.

Creativity, Collaboration, Critical Thinking

Early in the project, teachers were asked about their beliefs concerning outcomes that could flow from games. Creativity and problem solving were key themes in thes early data, with teachers noting: 'Gaming is one of those areas that does actually facilitate creativity and innovation.' And, 'it gives them the chance to really work their imagination and keep that stuff going, and from industry, from everywhere, there is that demand on education to produce creative and innovative thinkers, but hardly any education actually does that'.

Similar, but more elaborate, comments were made by participants at the end of the project. For example, when asked about the most productive feature of the project, Bill, a Victorian primary school teacher, commented:

> I think for the students, um, there have been a number of key things for them. Engagement … the opportunity, um, to achieve success and to be challenged in something that they hadn't really, I mean, some had experienced. But a lot of them took the opportunity to take something they were interested in and look at the mechanics behind it. And to express themselves creatively, thinking critically, working collaboratively to solve problems.

Another teacher at this school, Heather, made similar points:

> I agree with Bill. I think at the start, the creativity is amazing – I mean what the kids come up with. We have a topic and then they brainstorm all their ideas. In that they are working collaboratively, we have done groups of three

before in the past, but this year we worked in groups of two. So that seems to work really well. And they are learning sort of about teamwork and how to work together as well. And now that we are in more of the programming part, it is super challenging for them. Which I think is awesome. And every day, they write a new goal with something they have found challenging. And they persist. And they help each other which is awesome. And then they come back and they say, 'Oh, I was struggling with this and then I solved it,' and they are so happy when they have those achievements. So the fact that they are challenged and persisting, and overcoming, daily, is fantastic.

The emphasis on creativity was echoed by Benjamin:

Researcher: Have you seen, um, and created opportunities where games have supported student creativity?

Benjamin: Creativity? Yeah, absolutely. Certainly in the making of the games, and our blog, we have one kid that has produced a game that – it looks like it belongs to one of the games from an early 90s console. I mean, it's great. It's that slick and that well produced. And certainly in terms of creativity he has thought about the narrative, and the dialogue and the characters, um, and he's coded it all as well. It's absolutely brilliant. Other students take a much more rough-and-ready approach and they are using programs that allow them to do something quickly. And that's great for boosting their creativity as well because it's much more that kind of sandbox approach of putting something together, seeing how it goes, and quickly being able to change it or start again or move on.

Personal and Social Capacity: Relationships, Teamwork, Leadership

The Australian Curriculum describes personal and social capability in the following ways:

> [S]tudents develop personal and social capability as they learn to understand themselves and others, and manage their relationships, lives, work and learning more effectively. Personal and social capability involves students in a range of practices including recognising and regulating emotions, developing empathy for others and understanding relationships, establishing and building positive relationships, making responsible decisions, working effectively in teams, handling challenging situations constructively and developing leadership skills.
>
> *(Australian Curriculum Assessment and Reporting Authority*
> *[ACARA] 2016, 'Personal and social capability', para. 1)*

There were multiple examples across the project of students displaying these and related skills. Teachers commented on opportunities for effective collaboration, teamwork and communication, all of which feed into positive relationships. Commenting on her use of the Xbox Kinect with girls in a library setting, Janet (also featured in Chapters 6 and 9) said:

> [T]he girls are having fun, they're enjoying it, they're also talking, they're communicating; there's all of that social interaction going on. There's a collaboration, because if things don't happen, they'll help each other, direct each other so [word unclear]. So there's an awful lot going [on].

Other teachers commented on the skills that students acquired, not only in terms of working together on collaborative products, but also in asking questions and providing feedback:

> So the communication, it's not just about the numbers, it's about the communication, the social skills, the interaction. They are developing their social awareness. How do I ask someone? How do I not offend someone by giving them an answer or helping them out? So it's just a broad spectrum, I'm finding, of opportunities.

Kate and Pat, teachers in Victoria, noted that the use of games also fostered students' independence, and reduced reliance on teacher direction:

Pat: I think what Kate said before is becoming more and more. I mean, through gaming, that we are, um, I mean, we are initiating instead of leading?
Kate: I said facilitating instead of dictating ...
Pat: [Y]eah, facilitating ... that's it. The gaming and all that sort of, you know, it encourages that idea. Because half the time you are not standing there teaching them something rote-learning-wise, you're having them explore on their own through gaming. So they are learning through their own initiatives and learning and collaboration and stuff like that. So, yeah.

Final Points

The brief examples provided above are not intended to overstate the outcomes relating to games. Rather, our goal is to demonstrate that teachers involved in the Serious Play project found multiple links between games-based activities – be it making, playing or analysing games – and formal and informal assessment as well as formative and summative assessment. As noted in the introduction to this chapter, providing these examples is intended to give others working within the field some examples of how the participants experimented, and the various outcomes they achieved in their particular contexts.

There are a number of final points to be made, each one of which relates to the importance of considering the role that *teachers* and *context* play in shaping what actually happens when games-based learning is introduced into schools.

It is important to acknowledge that assessable and broader outcomes attributed by teachers to their work with games didn't just magically happen. Although the teachers cited above all indicated that they had few difficulties in assessing students against a national curriculum while using games in various ways, this was not the result of chance, but rather a product of deliberate and careful decision making, ongoing reflection and a willingness to adapt games and game platforms to their specific contexts.

For example, the participating teacher who integrated tablet-based games such as *Sonic and Friends* (SonicGames.cc 2015) and *Mario Kart* (Bumario.com 2011) into numeracy lessons, emphasised the need to take the time to choose games that support the acquisition of specific skills. This, it was argued, makes assessment more straightforward and eliminates the sense that games are just random inclusions:

> I think key to that whole concept is very clearly to find a starting point. So we certainly [focused on] games just this semester and tying it through to numeracy. We'd look at what we wanted to cover in numeracy first, think about how we use a … game to do that, and then choose a game that would satisfy … so we already knew what we were assessing at the very starting point and it was very, very focused. It meant that when you get to the end of it, you know, through the successful gameplay you have … kids work whether or not they [get] those concepts.
>
> In that way, it also makes use of the games, no different from any other kind of media or any other kind of strategy you would use in [word unclear]. You could set it up by knowing exactly what your outcomes are going to be in the first place, and then you can see exactly where it would go.

The importance of teacher planning, ongoing reflection and close attention to what actually *happens* when games are used by students was also emphasised by Kate, a Victorian primary school teacher working with prep students (age 4 to 5):

> Yeah, I use – when I'm looking at choosing suitability of apps for iPads and looking for a couple of things, something that I really like is when kids are able to establish an ongoing profile in a game or an app; this also gives me feedback and data on how the kids are going.
>
> So, for example, when I'm working with preps in the morning, I will have five groups, each group will be level-based on their reading group. So even when they're not working with me doing reading, when they're on the

iPads, they might be doing a specific app at a specific level that's at their point of need.

So at the end of each session, where the kids have had a turn on the iPad, I've been looking around and gathering the data that that app has given me so that I can work out what that group needs to be doing next week.

These brief examples remind us of the role that teachers play in designing, implementing, monitoring and evaluating what actually happens when they work with games. They do not, in other words, devolve responsibility for student learning to the games that they work with, but continue to be active in the analysis of student needs and student outcomes. It is worth mentioning that teachers made use of diverse forms of data in their analysis of their games activities including their own observations (and those of other teachers), student journals (in various forms), students' self-reflections and evaluations of their learning:

[O]ur kids do write reflections at [the] end of each term about what progress they have made throughout the term, and they will be writing something about using the games and playing the games and [whether] they found it interesting or beneficial or not.

Review of student work by teachers and peers was also a feature of the project. Teachers in both Queensland and Victoria noted the benefits to student learning *and* confidence that came from access to peer feedback. The Religious Education project described above produced the following comment:

I said, 'Okay, well, we're going to have to wrap this up. We've got to do an awful lot more the following term. Pop out of your seat, go round to somebody else and sit down and play their game and offer a bit of positive criticism; even if it's negative criticism, couch it in a positive framework'. So that was good, but noisy. Certainly others – that was quite beneficial. Getting up and that's all they wanted to do towards the end, they just wanted to see what other people's games were like and what they'd created.

This point was expanded through discussion of the way one project involved Year 9 students providing feedback on games developed by Year 3 students:

Nick: [W]hen we ended the unit, we ran like a gaming expo, and we were lucky enough that [the] research team was able to create a partnership with [a] High School, and Year 9 students came into our classroom. They got to play Year 3, our Year 3 students [word unclear] and they got to, like, fill in some pro forma and give them verbal feedback and give them written feedback. It was quite – it was just an experience.

Facilitator: Yeah. So what did the students – so the students who made the games, how did they respond to the feedback?

Nick: Oh yeah, they really – they took more of the feedback more – they took it on board more than the feedback I gave them. When I was telling them their games were good, they weren't that sure, always questioning themselves. But when the Year 9 students came in and said, 'Oh wow, I tried to make a game from Scratch and could get this far, can't believe you got this far', they were getting nine out of tens. The Year 3 students were like, 'Oh, man, we are good at making games'. So that was really nice.

This teacher comments that his students were 'lucky enough' to have opportunities to have feedback from secondary school students about the games they built. In actual fact, of course, this 'luck' was the result of the teacher's decision making, and commitment to experimentation and risk taking.

At various times throughout the project, teachers expressed both frustration and appreciation regarding the lack of specific instructions they were given by the project team in terms of what game to use and how to work with games. Some believed it would have been easier to get started if they had been given a specific game to work with, or task to try. Nevertheless, teacher interviews and classroom observations showed that the teachers displayed an ability to work creatively with games, and that games often evolved into projects that were richer, more complex and more satisfying than the teachers originally imagined.

There is a final point that must be made. Assessment with or through games in schools depends upon teachers' ability to act as informed professionals who make day-to-day (even minute-by-minute) modifications to their teaching as a result of their analysis of students' achievements, needs and experiences. Games provided students with opportunities to experience multiple forms of educational, social and personal success. But these opportunities were, in some cases, constrained by teachers' awareness of the emphasis that some contexts place on formal measurements of student achievement and formal measures of learning. This point was made powerfully by Shae. She noted the positive outcomes that came from gameplay for very different groups of children:

> Well, we do have games where almost all students experience success. I've got kids that can't quite read, and maybe don't understand what is happening, but they seem to be having a good time. They are having really great conversations with the people in their group, and it comes in with all the teamwork and those kinds of things that are really valuable, but aren't measured by most academic standards. So, teamwork, getting along, incorporation, communication, those things. It doesn't matter about a child's reading ability, but they can still achieve success in terms of communication and collaboration.

Poignantly, Shae concludes her comment by saying that these skills are the 'things that aren't measured'.

Other teachers throughout the project expressed a similar sense of frustration when an existing assessment model was used as the only means of assessing the multiple achievements to be displayed during a games-based initiative, particularly if the criteria focused only on mastery of content or specific literacies. Commenting on the need to assess one particular student's achievement in a *Minecraft* activity, Diane, a teacher with Year 3 students at a Queensland girls' school, made the following points:

> Yeah. I said that to you when you came to interview me that day. I thought what we've just done is an amazing unit of work; the kids have loved it; the parents [can] tell [through] this unit of work [how the kids are doing], but yes, this little girl who can't write still, can't spell, but she's keen to write now and she's – and she loved everything, she wanted to come to school and all that sort of thing. I thought, but still I'm going to have to give you a D for English and how does that make her feel, when she knows she's done really well on this unit of work, and was like, 'Why didn't we just read a book then, I could have got a D'.

And on another occasion, Diane went on to make further points linked to this issue:

> [I] don't have any trouble finding things to assess, that's not my issue. My issue is that there are some things that we don't get the chance to put as much value or weighting on in terms of what the school wants us to assess. I think the things that I – the greatest growth I've seen in some of these children has not come in those traditional areas that we assess, and they're the ones that get all the weighting. They're the ones that everyone, when it comes down to it, that's all anyone seems to care about. So yeah, my frustration just comes because I value the other stuff equally.

Conclusion

Since at least 1975, considerable effort has gone into describing, identifying, clarifying and expanding what is meant by terms such as 'serious games' and 'serious play'. Within the related literature, some authors have argued that to be taken seriously, 'serious games' must have 'explicit and carefully thought-out educational purpose and are not intended to be played primarily for amusement' (Abt 1975, p. 9). Thirty years later, Zyda (2005) picked up on this point to suggest that '[s]erious games have more than just story, art, and software, however … [t]hey involve pedagogy: activities that educate or instruct, thereby imparting knowledge or skill. This addition makes games serious' (p. 26).

In a similar manner, the data explored throughout the Serious Play research clearly demonstrated that games were not magical in their ability to 'guarantee' learning in 'teacher-proof' ways. Rather, all of the cases outlined briefly in this chapter (and across the book) illustrate the fundamental role that teachers play in what games *become*. There were no instances that we encountered where teachers introduced a game without at least some plan to explore how it would improve the learning of their students. Rather, teachers were explicit about their commitment to experiment, to develop, to collaborate and to play as they developed their own skill base and confidence. Summarising the outcomes which teachers linked to their involvement in the Serious Play project, Catherine Beavis noted:

> My very clear sense from hearing people's stories is that over the time they've been involved with games, whether it's in this project or even earlier, the more you do it, the more you get a sense of what's possible.

During their involvement in the Serious Play project, teacher participants have provided valuable examples of what became possible in their particular contexts. This work, we argue, has the value, not only to legitimate the role of games in schools, but also to reinforce the importance of acknowledging teachers as informed professionals, and to ensure that educational environments embrace what games may have to offer: including opportunities for students to develop skills that may never be formally assessed, but which are central to their educational, social and personal development. This point becomes the focus of Chapter 13.

References

Abt, C C (1975), *Serious games*, New York, NY: Viking Compass.

Asia Society (n.d.), *China Game*. Available from: http://asiasociety.org/china-game (Accessed 11 August 2016).

Australian Curriculum Assessment and Reporting Authority (ACARA) (2016), *The Australian Curriculum version 8.2. General capabilities: Overview and introduction*. Available from: www.australiancurriculum.edu.au/generalcapabilities/overview/introduction (Accessed 11 July 2016).

Bumario.com (2011), *Mario Kart*. Available from: www.bumario.com/category/Mario-Kart-Games (Accessed 12 August 2016).

Chee, Y S (2010), *Statecraft X*. Available from: http://cheeyamsan.info/NIEprojects/SCX/SCX2.htm (Accessed 8 August 2016).

Edmodo (2016), *Edmodo*. Available from: www.edmodo.com/ (Accessed 11 August 2016).

Floyd, D and Portnow, J (2008), *Brain training: Video games and tangential learning*, EDGE: Global Industry Games Network. Available from: www.youtube.com/watch?v=rN0qRKjfX3s%3E (Accessed 10 July 2016).

Global Kids and Gamelab (2006), *Ayiti: The Cost of Life*. Available from: www.gamesforchange.org/play/ayiti-the-cost-of-life/ (Accessed 11 August 2016).

GoAnimate Inc. (2011), *GoAnimate*. Available from: https://goanimate.com/ (Accessed 10 August 2016).

Lifelong Kindergarten Group (2003), *Scratch*, MIT Media Lab. Available from: https://scratch.mit.edu (Accessed 9 August 2016).

Mojang (2011), *Minecraft*. Available from: https://minecraft.net/en/ (Accessed 8 August 2016).

PDST (n. d.), *Who wants to be a millionaire PowerPoint template*. Available from: http://pdst.ie/sites/default/files/millionairetemplate_o.ppt (Accessed 11 August 2016).

Relentless Software (2012), *National Geographic: America the Wild* (Kinect Xbox), Redmond, WA: Microsoft Studios.

Rowan, L (2012), 'Educated hope, modest ambition and school-based equity reforms: Possibilities and perspectives for change', in L Rowan and C Bigum (eds), *Transformative approaches to new technologies and student diversity in futures oriented classrooms*, Dordrecht, The Netherlands: Springer, pp. 45–63.

Shute, V and Fengfeng, K (2012), 'Games, learning, and assessment', in D Ifenthaler, D Eseryel and X Ge (eds), *Assessment in game-based learning: Foundations, innovations, and perspectives*, New York, NY: Springer, pp. 43–58.

SonicGames.cc (2015), *Sonic and Friends*. Available from: www.sonicgames.cc/ (Accessed 12 August 2016).

Ubisoft Entertainment (2014), *Assassin's Creed Unity*. Available from: http://assassinscreed.ubi.com/en-au/games/assassins-creed-unity.aspx (Accessed 11 August 2016).

Young, M, Slota, S, Cutter, A, Jalette, G, Mullin, G, Lai, B, Simeoni, Z, Tran, M and Yukhymenko, M (2012), 'Our princess is in another castle: A review of trends in serious gaming', *Review of Educational Research*, vol. 82, no. 1, pp. 61–89. Available from: doi: 10.3102/0034654312436980 (Accessed 5 August 2016).

YoYogames (2016), *GameMaker*. Available from: www.yoyogames.com/gamemaker (Accessed 8 August 2016).

Zyda, M (2005), 'From visual simulation to virtual reality to games', *Computer*, vol. 38, no. 9, pp. 25–32.

13

QUESTS, ACHIEVEMENTS AND EXPERIENCE POINTS

Opportunities to Level Up Through School-Based Serious Play

Leonie Rowan and Sarah Prestridge

This book has explored the growing presence of digital games in formal schooling contexts and mapped the willingness of many teachers and students to explore the benefits that might possibly flow from the introduction of so-called 'serious play' (de Castell and Jensen 2003). Some of the initiatives the book has investigated were motivated (at least in part) by a representation of videogames as 'learning machines' (Gee 2004); possessed of an exceptional ability to improve student engagement and student achievement, while also fostering the development of new literacies and twenty-first-century skills such as teamwork, creativity and problem solving (New Media Consortium 2012). Previous chapters have provided compelling evidence of the impact of games upon each of these areas. At the same time, however, the examples explored within the book have also demonstrated that *what actually happens* when games are brought into classrooms can vary dramatically; and that contexts and teachers both have a major impact on what a games-based initiative does or does not enable (Mehrotra *et al.* 2012; Stevens *et al.* 2008).

Digital gameplay in schools shapes, and is shaped by, teacher beliefs (about games, learners, curriculum and assessment), student characteristics (such as gender, socio-economics, first language, prior achievements and cultural background) and the 'in and out' of school gaming experiences of all those involved (Stevens *et al.* 2008). Recognising the impact of teachers' beliefs on what various instances of serious play might ultimately look, sound and feel like, this chapter explores teachers' views about the extent to which the potential benefits often linked to digital games are actually experienced by diverse learners. It focuses particularly closely on students who maybe have been previously positioned on the margins of mainstream schooling, and the opportunities they experience to 'level up' within their classroom environments.

We pause here to acknowledge the influence of gaming metaphors on the focus and writing of this chapter. As researchers within the Serious Play project and as parents of children who have been playing digital games for many years, we have come to appreciate the commitment and resilience that games players often need to demonstrate in order to achieve various in-game goals, such as unlocking rewards ('Mum! I've got a new egg to hatch!'); opening up new game pathways or challenges ('Mum! I beat the Elite 4'); defeating a powerful opponent, or boss ('Mum! The blue team took over the railway gym!'). The excitement associated with these and seemingly endless other examples of in-game success echoes regularly through our homes. These successes come with effort and persistence. In digital games, this persistence is often charted via the allocation of 'experience points' (or XPs). These points reflect a player's in-game achievements (such as quests completed, opponents defeated, Pokémon captured and problems solved). Players generally start a new game with little in the way of 'strength' or 'power' or XPs. Increasing points is therefore vital and, as they rise higher, a player may be said to 'level up'. When this happens, a game can change and evolve, generally offering new quests or challenges, an increased set of powers, attributes or resources and, of course, more status as a player (Wikipedia 2016).

Previous chapters have provided accounts of how games enhanced students' engagement and motivation and supported, as a result, students' learning and achievement, providing them, in the language of games, with valued opportunities to gain experience points and, thus, to level up. Many of the students who participated in the Serious Play project experienced academic success relatively often, and enjoyed the kind of emotional security that comes from being a valued or accepted member of a classroom environment. For these students, being seen as a success or a higher achiever was not, in reality, anything particularly new. But these were not the only project participants. Across the three years of the research, teachers also worked with students who were positioned, for one reason or another, on the margins of their classrooms. Some were underperforming academically, and some saw themselves as educational failures. Other students lacked confidence to speak or be heard or join in a group. Some were socially isolated. Some were … just … average … unremarkable … easy-to-forget children who never attract much attention and seldom experience what it feels like to be seen as a success story, a leader or a star.

All of the teachers within the project were able to identify students of this kind: students who were in some way, or for some reason, or at some times, overlooked or forgotten by their peers, or by the 'system' of formal education.

It is these students who provide the focus for this, our final chapter.

For reasons relating to privacy, ethics and duty of care, these students could not, of course, be photographed, quoted or even referred to by their real names. Yet in preparing to write this final chapter, we wanted to ensure that their existence and their emotions were at the forefront of our mind. We therefore turned to drawings provided by the 14-year-old daughter of one of the project researchers (Leonie). We asked if she could illustrate what it might mean to be overlooked or forgotten within the formal schooling system. In response, she offered us two sketches which we include below. The first, *Rose Untitled*, in its image and title communicates a struggle to be seen and valued which characterises so many children's lives. It captures as well some of the emotion expressed by teachers when they spoke about the students in their care.

While the first image (Figure 13.1) communicates a sense of alienation associated (for many young people) with mainstream schooling, the second image (Figure 13.2) highlights the experience of fun, play and positive performance that can be sparked by creative, careful, genuinely student-centred teaching.

We begin the chapter with these images because together they remind us that the aims and outcomes from Serious Play can be diverse and impact upon students in ways that go well beyond issues of academic achievement or motivation. Through a range of short examples and vignettes, our goal in this chapter is to illustrate the possibilities associated with digital games in education *for diverse cohorts of students*, and the new or changed opportunities that games can provide

FIGURE 13.1 *Rose Untitled* stands in contrast to the second image *Mystic Unlocked.*
Source: by Sophie Bigum.

FIGURE 13.2 *Mystic Unlocked.*
Source: by Sophie Bigum.

for students who, for one reason or another, may be at risk of educational or social alienation, disengagement or underachievement.

With this focus, the chapter responds to two strands of literature. First: decades of research has taught us that factors such as gender, socio-economics, cultural background, first language as well as physical appearance, religion, family form, geographical location and dis/ability impact upon educational (and social) experiences, pathways and outcomes (Groundwater-Smith 2006; Holmes *et al.* 2011; Keddie 2012; Malin 1994; Martino and Pallotta-Chiarolli 2005; Nichol 2009; Niyozov and Pluim 2009; Teese *et al.* 2007). This extensive body of scholarship has also demonstrated the multiple ways in which young people who do not match up to the 'mythical norms' (Lorde 1990, p. 282) regarding what it means to be a good student or good learner in a particular context (i.e. a 'good literacy student' or a 'typical' physics student) can feel excluded and devalued in educational settings – feelings which can impact upon both sense of self and academic achievement (Rowan 2012). In addition to this, it has been clearly demonstrated that learning is enhanced when students feel included, safe and valued, and that the relationships which students develop with their peers, their teachers and *learning* more broadly can have a direct impact upon what they do, or do not believe, achieve and aspire towards. We proceed in this chapter from the belief that gameplay has a powerful role to play in this transformative agenda.

This brings us to the second strand of literature that provides the motivation for this chapter (for examples, see Connolly *et al.* 2012; Derryberry 2007; Francis 2006; McFarlane *et al.* 2002; Mehotra *et al.* 2012; Pelletier 2009; Perrotta *et al.* 2013). Much has been written (including the chapters in this book) about the potential of games to improve school environments, increase student motivation and foster the development of disciplinary knowledge, complementary skills and twenty-first-century skills. There is always a risk that, read uncritically, this literature could reproduce the long-standing tendency of educational innovations to position 'students' as a relatively homogeneous group who, it is often argued, encounter the world in similar ways (Rowan 2007). More nuanced readings of how educational innovations are *actually* experienced by the diverse students in various educational settings have shown that it is difficult work transforming long-standing patterns relating to how a student is positioned in/by school experiences. The persistence of patterns of success and failure makes it vital for all educators to remain open to the possibility that change *can* happen. Our goal in this chapter is therefore to capture small, everyday, almost ordinary examples of game use in school contexts which, nevertheless, have extraordinary impact tied to their ability to help students finish quests, collect achievements, gather experience points and, by extension, to level up in ways that allow them to be seen, heard and valued by their schools, teachers, peers and, of course, by themselves.

Quests, Achievements and Experience Points

We have noted above the ways in which games players commonly earn experience points by completing quests, overcoming obstacles and defeating opponents. Extending the metaphors provided by this aspect of gaming, our goal in the brief snapshots that follow is to illustrate various obstacles that were overcome, and quests that were completed. Our goal is to explain why, or in what ways, the student is in some way 'at risk', and then to explore how a gaming experience disrupted or challenged this position, and the obstacles that were overcome.

Overcoming Obstacles: New Skills

Educational success is closely tied to a student's ability to acquire and demonstrate the kinds of literacy skills valued in school systems. Many students start in the school system with limited understandings of key literacy conventions. Working with games has the potential to help children without these skills to navigate an unfamiliar territory in a comfortable way and learn, in the process, the operational skills necessary to succeed in areas such as literacy. Kate described this potential through reference to one young prep (kindergarten) student, Kimmy:

She came to school and I don't think she knew how to turn the pages on a story, she hadn't had any experience with books at all. So I don't think she had been read a story before she came to school, or had read a book. Because part of the English assessment online is to get the child to orient the book correctly, prior to reading. So they need to have an understanding of front cover, back cover, and how to turn pages. So it's not reading, it's just knowing how a book works. So ... and it was really lovely to do books with her where you have to turn the page. And Beatrix Potter has a lovely app where you have to turn the page, and it gives the kids a little instruction on turning the page and tracking the letters and words – that was fantastic for her. Because she just didn't know what to do with a book.

Kate also identified the ways in which games such as *Choiceworks* (Bee Visual LLC 2016) also helped students with autism spectrum disorders (ASD) learn to navigate the school environment:

It's fantastic to use with all children, but it is specifically designed for use with children with ASD. And what it does is it enables you to make a schedules board and a feelings board, where kids have interactive options for how they deal with their emotions – so I am going to sit down for five minutes if I am feeling angry – and if I do that, I can choose one of these two options. And often too, kids with ASD respond really well to ICT equipment.

Overcoming Obstacles: Being Heard

Acquiring practical skills and knowledge sets was not the only way in which games improved the learning of children who were sometimes seen but not heard in their classroom setting. Teachers also noted the ways in which games provided vehicles for students to communicate what they know, and to be valued for this demonstration.

Issues of personal literacy are illustrated by another primary school teacher, Monica, with reference to a different young learner whom we will call Josef:

Yeah, I had – particularly last year, with [The] Land of Um (Greygum Software n. d.) – I had one child who is extremely talented, quite, actually, verging on gifted, really, really clever, but very subdued and very – you couldn't see his abilities because he didn't give it to you. With [The] Land of Um he actually excelled. It actually enabled him to express himself in a thing that he loved. He really found it quite good. He was one of the only few children that could actually create their own game successfully.

The potential for games to give students new ways to communicate their knowledge – and thus to have this knowledge seen and valued, was also recognised by Beau, a teacher who commented on how avatars can help students with presentations:

> I saw something on the net the other day about – it's a website where you just create avatars. I can't remember what it's called now? – I had a look at it, someone sent me a link and I had a little play. That sort of thing they'll love. But then I sit and think, 'Okay, but how can I use this in an educational way?'

> But I think it's an avatar you can create and then you can record your voice and it'll speak. So they can use it as a presentation forum rather than them getting up. Some girls don't want to get up and do a presentation – not too many – but some of them. If I could give them that as an option, where they can have an avatar they've created. They do all the formal talking into the computer and then present it on the interactive whiteboard. Well, that's getting the same information out of them, but in a much more – for them – more comfortable way of doing it.

Developing Confidence

The impact of gaming experience on students' confidence is also a commonly cited outcome of the games-based projects. Many teachers noted that students who were socially isolated also developed more confidence through their use of digital games. For example, secondary school teacher Mark noted the positive impact of games on:

> the ones who socially in class seemed to be very quiet and reserved and just sort of tended to just sit in class in the past. Some of those got particularly enthused about their project that they were working on. So I certainly saw some boost in confidence and social interaction with some of those students because of the fact that they were involved in the game-making process.

He went on to say:

> What I did find with the game-making aspect, some kids obviously have more skills or a better idea or picked [up] concepts quicker. So those quieter or shy kids definitely gained with the status of the class. They'd go over and see Jerome, he was really good at working out how to solve that problem or [they'd say] 'Did you see what was happening with the way he integrated sound into his?'… From a teacher's perspective, it was great to be a guide and a mentor rather than an instructor. To let some of these other kids take on some of those leadership roles. So I guess in that sense, it was a benefit to some of the students, for sure.

Being an Expert, Becoming a Star

As Mark's comments indicate, running alongside teacher observations about the impact of games upon students' skills and confidence are many comments about the ways in which gaming provides opportunities for students to extend themselves, showcase their talents and be seen as experts. Peer recognition of skills associated with gameplay and game creation helped these students to level up. Primary school teacher, Ang, for example, noted the impact of being seen as the expert on a student with whom she worked:

> He was one of the 'go to' kids and he benefited greatly from being [that], having a better self-esteem, and so also because his behaviour improved with the bribe of being able to be that person or actually play the game, he felt better about himself, I believe, and so performed better in class and worked harder.

Another teacher noted that gameplay provided an opportunity for some easily overlooked students to be noticed by their peers, perhaps for the first time. Jacinta made the following comments about a student she worked with who had English as an additional language, and how she benefited from the games-based initiatives this student, Wren, was involved in:

> Her writing was always okay, but I certainly don't remember it made a particular impact in changing her writing. I think for her it was more like a social thing, that she was the girl that was good at playing the games. It gave her a way to stand out because she would not have stood out in many other ways in class. A lovely kid, but just didn't have anything that made her stand out amongst the other kids, so yeah, maybe her.

The link between being seen as a competent student – or, indeed, being seen at all – and opportunities for marginalised students to feel valued as learners, and as people, is a key theme in many of the teacher interviews.

For example, in discussing the case of Josef, referred to earlier, his teacher Monica went on to say that, through his experience in creating a successful game, Josef not only got to demonstrate skills that the teacher had rarely seen, but was also able to receive public praise for one of the first times in his schooling career:

> I was able to praise him and tell him how awesome it was, so that made a big difference to him. That piece of, what's the word? Perhaps his self-esteem or that self-efficacy, that belief in himself, certainly transferred across. I actually got more work out of him in that last term last year than I had all year, so it did make a big difference to him.

Another teacher commented on how the introduction of games re-motivated some low-achieving students:

> The kids who were my low achievers were deadset keen, because it's like they had nothing to lose. So they were happy to go with it. I saw the tables turn then. I saw those girls become the popular ones, the ones that were being called on to help.

Secondary school teacher Paul expanded on this point, noting that when students were motivated by the gaming activities (and thus school's connection to their outside lives), they were able to perform at a higher level:

> I think what struck me from early on was that the students who were disengaged in other areas of the curriculum would become more interested. And when you start tailoring content to their interests … it was good to see some students extending themselves in the unit. And I couldn't get them to extend themselves in other units … It's not a lot of them, but every kid deserves an opportunity to show their best.

These kinds of experiences also impacted upon the roles that students went on to play in their classrooms. For example, Beau noted how gameplay changed the roles that students would take up:

> I guess there were other students who just took a bit more of the leadership that don't normally take leadership roles and expressed themselves more confidently, and through that game I saw them do that. I think about Hannah in my class who – she's quite an enthusiastic student, but probably not as willing to take leadership roles, whereas she did and continued to after that day, with our *Edmodo* conversation she continued to add information and put forward her point of view.

More Skills, More Confidence, More Visibility, More Happiness: Levelling Up

The brief examples above illustrate the ways in which teachers believe students who were in some way underperforming, anxious, marginalised or overlooked were able to attract, and benefit from, positive peer and teacher attention. In this final section of this chapter, we want to illustrate this relationship between the development of new skills, increased confidence, visibility and happiness through a longer discussion of the experiences of a Year 3 student we call Tammy, and her teacher, Diane.

Diane is an experienced Year 3 teacher at an all-girls' college in Brisbane. She chose to use the sandbox game *Minecraft* (Mojang 2011) to directly support the learning opportunities for Tammy, a severely dyslexic girl in her Year 3 class. Tammy struggled with reading and writing, Diane noted: 'I was constantly trying to find ways to motivate and engage her [in *Minecraft*] so that she had a reason for writing'.

Knowing she had to do something with digital games as part of the Serious Play project and acknowledging Tammy's interest in *Minecraft*, Diane decided to experiment with this game that she was, in fact, entirely unfamiliar with. Diane's first thoughts were to use *Minecraft* purely to motivate Tammy and her peers. She saw it as: 'an inspirational device to build literacy tasks around, so let's write about it, let's reflect on it, let's compare it to other building games as we also have a big *Lego* room, so here is an opportunity to write'.

As Diane had never played *Minecraft* before, she literally said to her girls, 'you now have *Minecraft*', and then sat back and watched what they did. When she tried to join the game to be a 'participant' in the activities, she recalls 'dying' within the first three minutes and feeling a total sense of helplessness. This lack of ability to engage gave her some sense of what Tammy would be dealing with on a daily basis when she is being taught something new in the classroom. It also allowed her to see a very quick change in the way that Tammy was positioned:

> [Tammy] who was the real struggler, she'd always been the one who was always helped, became the expert. She was the *Minecraft* expert in the classroom. She was helping me. She was helping the really good English students to actually get a feel for the game.

It is important for us to note here that Diane had never used *Minecraft*, and did not have a clear picture of how it would be used in a classroom setting. As her first move (and in order to link the game to the curriculum), she asked the girls to do a writing task to tell her why they thought she had introduced *Minecraft* into their class. Some of the responses were: 'to help us with our imagination', 'to do problem solving' and 'I think we are going to do an engineering or a design task'. This gave Diane ideas on what she could do with *Minecraft*. Instead of staying with a writing focus, Diane quickly moved on to a design-based technology task. Through conversations during a period of experimentation with *Minecraft*, the girls soon came up with the idea of recreating the entire junior school in *Minecraft* for a School Science and Technology showcase (as explored in Chapter 10).

The girls worked out the sizes of classrooms by counting the squares of carpet in their own classroom, and then halving it for proportions in their *Minecraft* world. Once they had made one room, they went on to the next: ultimately recreating the whole school.

Diane reflected on the way both the use of *Minecraft* and the open-ended nature of her early planning allowed girls with different ways of learning or communicating to experience things differently. She noted that:

> The more traditional learners, those girls that liked to be told what to learn and then they just give it back to you in a nice neat form struggled with *Minecraft*. Whereas those girls who are the more out-of-the-box thinkers were the ones who got onto the whole *Minecraft* project faster.

She went on to observe:

> [It] was a really interesting dynamic to see … for the first time that they were on an even keel with the other girls, and those that were used to being the best and brightest in the class became the strugglers a little bit, but in the end, it all evened out. And that was the best bit, no one was better than anyone else, and the girls saw that too, and it was just different.

It would be possible for us to go on here, and recount the multiple learning outcomes that Diane saw linked to the game: outcomes relating to literacy and numeracy skills and the ability to work in 3D spaces, and an understanding of perspective which 'wasn't something that came easily to them'.

Our primary aim in this chapter, however, is to make a different point. For girls like Tammy, being on the edges of a classroom which values very specific kinds of skills, and dispositions, and equally specific ways of *demonstrating* these skills, the introduction of *Minecraft* gave genuine opportunities to overcome long-standing barriers: barriers relating not only to an ability to show what she knew, but also to be seen and valued by others. Like Josef and Kimmy and Jerome and Wren and Hannah, Tammy was able to experience what it was like to be seen as competent, successful and skilled and, by extension, to be noticed, valued and rewarded.

These outcomes were facilitated, not by an abandonment of formal curriculum goals or a lowering of expectations and standards, but rather by the use of innovative pedagogies and games-based programs that allowed students to work with the curriculum in different, empowering ways.

Unlocking the Adjacent Possible

Expanding on the work of Stuart Kauffman, Steven Johnson (2010) used the concept of the 'adjacent possible' to describe the ways in which ideas can develop and grow if we are open to the possibilities that come from linking where we are to new, adjacent ideas. He wrote:

> The strange and beautiful truth about the adjacent possible is that its boundaries grow as you explore those boundaries. Each new combination ushers new combinations into the adjacent possible. Think of it as a house that magically expands with each door you open. You begin in a room with four doors, each leading to a new room that you haven't visited yet.

These four rooms are the adjacent possible. But once you open one of those doors and stroll into that room, three new doors appear, each leading to a brand new room that you couldn't have reached from your original starting point.

(Johnson 2010, p. 31)

Throughout the length of the Serious Play project, teachers and students demonstrated a willingness to experiment with digital games: making, playing and analysing many different games, in many different curriculum areas, across many different platforms, devices and interfaces. This openness to experimentation, uncertainty and risk taking allowed students in our projects to access a whole range of adjacent possibles, many of which began with simple links built between students and their outside lives, and blossomed into links between students and each other. This interrelationship is noted by Paul:

I think it's, you know … it's likely to establish that connection in their personal lives, and a connection with social things. Those kids on the edge might have a lot of reasons why they can't connect academically, but gameplay might be one of the things that they do have in common.

The examples we provide in this chapter might seem small, but (as Paul noted above), each time a student overcame an obstacle, gained an experience point or levelled up, they had access to an adjacent possible: a space within which further doors can, in the future, be opened.

Our claims in this regard are deliberately humble, characterised by 'modest ambition' – ambition that is humble, but in no sense 'unexceptional' (Rowan 2012, p. 10) and 'educated hope' (Giroux 2003). We do not wish to represent games as having any 'magical' or innate capacity to enhance every student's sense of belonging, or to impact positively upon achievement and performance everywhere, and all the time. As in the context provided by games beyond schooling, completing a particular quest can take multiple efforts and considerable time. Nevertheless, the stories we have charted throughout the Serious Play project have demonstrated the value of these efforts, and the powerful impact of games-based learning on students in contemporary schools. Thus, our goal in this chapter has been to demonstrate that the time, effort and a leap of faith that may be required to start on the kinds of journeys undertaken by our project teachers can generate multiple, positive, unexpected outcomes for very different students – including those who may otherwise not have experienced what it means to be successful, a winner or a star.

In the complicated and uneven landscape of formal schooling, educators who are genuinely committed to the creation of learning environments characterised by the pursuit of excellence and equity must work constantly and actively to find ways to disrupt the 'default futures' that appear to exist for so many of our students.

By illustrating the *possibilities* that creative experimentation with digital games generated for heterogeneous students (and, of course, their teachers and the research team), we acknowledge the ever-present potential of the adjacent possible and celebrate the moments when students moved from one classroom position to another. The final word goes to one more project participant: a 13-year-old student who was part of the Serious Play research. Like many of his peers, the boy completed a survey about his gaming use and concluded his feedback in the following way:

All Id like to say is Thank you 😊 (Serious Play)

References

Bee Visual LLC (2016), *Choiceworks* (app). Available from: https://itunes.apple.com/au/app/choiceworks/id486210964?mt=8 (Accessed 11 August 2016).

Connolly, T M, Boyle, E A, MacArthur, E, Hainey, T and Boyle, J M (2012), 'A systematic literature review of empirical evidence on computer games and serious games', *Computers & Education*, vol. 59, pp. 661–686.

de Castell, S and Jensen, J (2003), 'Serious play', *Curriculum Studies*, vol. 35, no. 6, pp. 649–665.

Derryberry, A (2007), *Serious games: Online games for learning*, San Jose, CA: Adobe Systems Inc.

Francis, R (2006), 'Towards a theory of a games-based pedagogy', paper presented at the JISC Online Conference *Innovating e-Learning 2006: Transforming Learning Experiences*, 27–31 March. Available from: www.online-conference.net/jisc/content/Francis%20-%20games%20based%20pedagogy.pdf (Accessed 12 September 2013).

Gee, J (2004), 'Learning by design: Games as learning machines', *Interactive Educational Multimedia*, vol. 8, April, pp. 15–23.

Giroux, H A (2003), *Public time and educated hope: Educational leadership and the war against youth*. Available from: www.units.miamioh.edu/eduleadership/anthology/OA/OA03001.html (Accessed 23 November 2016).

Greygum Software (n. d.), *The Land of Um*. Available from: www.greygum.com.au/nebula/index.php/the-land-of-um (Accessed 11 August 2016).

Groundwater-Smith, S (2006), 'Understanding learner diversity', in S Groundwater-Smith, R Ewing and R LeCornu (eds), *Teaching: Challenges and dilemmas*, South Melbourne, Victoria, Australia: Thomson, pp. 51–74.

Holmes, D, Hughes, K P and Julian, R (2011), *Australian sociology: A changing society* (3rd ed.), Sydney, Australia: Pearson Education.

Johnson, S (2010), *Where good ideas come from: The natural history of innovation*, London: Allen Lane.

Keddie, A (2012), *Educating for diversity and social justice*, New York, NY: Routledge.

Lorde, A (1990), 'Age, race, class and sex: Women redefining difference', in R Ferguson, M Gever, T T Minh-ha and C West (eds), *Out there: Marginalization and contemporary cultures*, New York, NY: New Museum of Contemporary Art, pp. 281–288.

McFarlane, A, Sparrowhawk, A and Heald, Y (2002), *Report on the educational use of games*, TEEM: Teachers Evaluating Educational Media, London: Department for Education and Skills.

Malin, M (1994), 'Why is life so hard for Aboriginal students in urban classrooms?', *The Aboriginal Child at School*, vol. 22, no. 2, pp. 141–154.

Martino, W and Pallotta-Chiarolli, M (2005), *'Being normal is the only way to be': Boys and adolescent perspectives on gender and school*, Sydney, NSW, Australia: UNSW Press.

Mehrotra, S, Chee, Y S and Ong, J C (2012), 'Teachers' appropriation of game-based pedagogy: A comparative narrative analysis', in G Biswas, L-H Wong, T Hirashima and W Chen (eds), *20th International Conference on Computers in Education*, Singapore: National Institute of Education, Nanyang Technological University, pp. 467–474.

Mojang (2011), *Minecraft*. Available from: https://minecraft.net/en/ (Accessed 8 August 2016).

New Media Consortium (2012), *N.M.C. Horizon report 2012 K–12 edition*. Available from: www.nmc.org/pdf/2012-horizon-report-K12.pdf (Accessed 20 July 2016).

Nichol, R (2009), 'So, how and what do we teach? Indigenous pedagogy and perspectives in the curriculum', in *Dare to lead: Partnership builds success*, proceedings of the Principals Australia National Curriculum Perspectives Conference, Canberra: APAPD.

Niyozov, S and Pluim, G (2009), 'Teachers' perspectives on the education of Muslim students: A missing voice in Muslim education research', *Curriculum Inquiry*, vol. 39, no. 5, pp. 637–677.

Pelletier, C (2009) 'Games and learning: What's the connection?', *International Journal of Learning and Media,* vol. 1, no. 1, pp. 83–101.

Perrotta, C, Featherstone, G, Aston, H and Houghton, E (2013), *Games-based learning: Latest evidence and future directions*, Slough, UK: NFER.

Rowan, L (2007), 'Theorising innovation and knowledge creation in pursuit of educational justice', in B Somekh and T Schwandt (eds), *Knowledge production: Research work in interesting times*, London: Routledge, pp. 111–125.

Rowan, L (2012), 'Educated hope, modest ambition and school-based equity reforms: Possibilities and perspectives for change', in L Rowan and C Bigum (eds), *Transformative approaches to new technologies and student diversity in futures oriented classrooms*, Dordrecht, The Netherlands: Springer, pp. 45–63.

Stevens, R, Satwicz, T and McCarthy, L (2008), 'In-game, in-world: Reconnecting video game play to the rest of kids' lives', in K Salen (ed.), *The ecology of games: Connecting youth, games and learning*, Cambridge, MA: The MIT Press, pp. 41–66.

Teese, R, Lamb, S, Duru-Bellat, M and Helme, S (2007), *International studies in educational inequality, theory and policy*, Dordrecht, The Netherlands: Springer.

Wikipedia (2016), *Experience point*. Available from: https://en.wikipedia.org/wiki/Experience_point (Accessed 20 July 2016).

POST SCRIPT

This book reports on a study that took place and coincided with a wider upsurge of interest in the possibilities offered by digital games and games-based learning for schools. Consistent with calls for more nuanced and wide-ranging long-term studies of games in schools (see, for example, Young *et al.* 2012), the project provided the opportunity to look in detail at the experiences and explorations of teachers and students over an extended period of time, across diverse curriculum areas, diverse age groups, diverse levels of experience amongst teachers and diverse school systems and schools. By exploring these diverse situations, the project moved beyond 'best practice' accounts of learning with games to identify the complex ways in which they may be used by teachers and students.

The Serious Play project took place from 2011 to 2014 in Victoria and Queensland, Australia. In Australia, school systems are the responsibility of individual states, and until recently, curriculum was set at state level, reflective of the different histories and culture of each state. From 2010, however, a national curriculum body – ACARA (the Australian Curriculum, Assessment and Reporting Authority) – has gradually taken responsibility for setting national curriculum and assessment guidelines, with common curricula across each state. At the same time, individual states have their own guidelines and traditions, and interpret the national curriculum in their own way. Teachers and students in the Serious Play schools were therefore working within both state and national contexts, with curriculum and assessment requirements configured and coming together in ways that shaped practice and imposed external frameworks over teachers' work. These guidelines and expectations, in turn, articulated with these teachers' understandings of students and their needs, of how students learn, their classroom practice and their own principles and philosophies of teaching; together with their school's culture and history with respect to curriculum, pedagogy and assessment. The games and game-making software mentioned here were those in currency at the time of the research. Games that students played at home along with interrelated platforms, social media services and on- and offline media forms reflected not only the time and place of the study, but also their network of friendships, practices and interactions out of school. Students' use of games and/ or game-making software, and their comments, evaluations and responses, reflect the particularities of these games, these classrooms, these teachers and these schools. It is this specificity that makes their contribution to the study so valuable – nuanced accounts of real-world classrooms, what the use of games made possible, what was difficult and what students and teachers achieved.

As indicated in detail throughout the book's chapters, a range of nuanced learnings emerged from the project across the three years, about the role of the teacher, about students' perspectives and games expertise, and about the importance of learning context. The teachers were central in finding ways to work with games that engaged and extended students' understandings, deepened curriculum knowledge, and provided opportunities for creativity, conceptualisation and critique. It was not the games themselves, but what teachers did with them that made deep learning possible. Contrary to rhetoric which presents digital games, effectively, as teacher-proof learning machines where the game itself provides all that is needed, and all that is required is that students play, the teacher's role was crucial in creating pedagogical contexts that would make the best use of games. The teachers provided opportunities for reflection, connection and critique in games-based learning. They exercised professional judgment in selecting games and in designing games-based work in class that would allow students to develop deep understandings, skills and capabilities, in alignment with curriculum and assessment requirements mandated externally. The teachers provided opportunities for students to interact, explore and create; and to bring in out-of-school knowledge and expertise, to capitalise on the affordances of the games and game-making software with which they were engaged. They maintained an open and exploratory frame of mind to what might be possible, an openness to what students could achieve and a preparedness to recognise and value the insights, qualities and capabilities which students developed through making and playing with games. Drawing on deep disciplinary knowledge and professional judgments, they selected and combined games and activities from their suites of available resources in what we have termed curriculum curatorship – their expert coordination of various classroom resources to provide curriculum-aligned learning experiences, as discussed in Chapter 5.

The students' input, perspectives and expertise were also central to successful uses of games in the classroom. They played an important role in opening our eyes to what games might achieve, and how they saw and valued the use of games. Just as teachers brought their own professional judgments to bear, the students were astute judges and critics of the ways games were used in and out of the classroom, and of what they enabled and made possible. Listening to the student voice, respecting their views and learning from what they make of games contributed greatly to our understandings about best practice and games-based learning. Students valued games and games-based learning that provided opportunities to engage and socialise with each other; they liked the challenge and enjoyed options for accumulation, but also became frustrated and impatient with games which they saw as boring or overly 'educational', or when technological issues got in the way. They valued connections between fun and learning, recognised when games were good at developing skills such as problem solving, but were also astute critics with respect to what games can and cannot achieve. The best use of games in the classroom, from students' point of view, was when they were integral to the subject area or context, respectful of their age and abilities, and worked effectively as games.

Understanding context was also very important for gaining insight into how learning with games occurs, and the nature and purposes of play in formal and informal learning situations. The use of games in the classroom is significantly different from gameplay out of school, at the same time as calling on students' knowledge and experience of games in their leisure-time play. Leisure-time games and gameplay change when they are introduced into the formal context of the school and harnessed to more formal 'education' purposes. Sometimes, expertise and pleasures move across relatively smoothly, as in some of the *Minecraft* activities described here; elsewhere, students were required to juggle their out-of-school expectations, pleasures and behaviours to meet in-school requirements, as for example, in the case of *Statecraft X*. The classroom context also has implications for the kinds of games used, and the structure and organisation of games and play. Games used in the classroom, particularly 'serious' or educational games, may be purpose-built to fit school time frames and curriculum requirements more directly, in contrast to more open-ended longer-form leisure-time games. Where commercial and popular games are used, they may be adapted or changed from their original forms; differently scaffolded and designed, to fit in with the timetable, and with the disciplinary and other constraints and purposes of the school.

These three points – the role of the teacher, the role of the student, and the recognition of the effect of context on gameplay – were at the core of the skilful use of games by teachers and students in the project, and the opening up of a sense of possibility. For us, these insights enable a consideration that goes beyond the affordances of specific games and their relevance to learning. Games will come and go because digital culture evolves at a rapid pace. Understanding teachers' expertise as curriculum curators, students' insightful perspectives and the importance of context provides a way to think about learning with games that is less reliant on the specifics of a particular game or technological change. This book, we hope, is testimony to the Serious Play teachers, students and schools and what was achieved. As such, we hope, too, that it makes an important contribution to contemporary understandings about the robust and skilful use of games, and in deepening understandings of core issues at the heart of educational work with games.

Reference

Young, M, Slota, S, Cutter, A, Jalette, G, Mullin, G, Lai, B, Simeoni, Z, Tran, M and Yukhymenko, M (2012), 'Our princess is in another castle: A review of trends in serious gaming', *Review of Educational Research*, vol. 82, no. 1, pp. 61–89. Available from: doi: 10.3102/0034654312436980 (Accessed 5 August 2016).

INDEX